AF886766

MICROSOFT® WORD 5.5 MADE EASY

MICROSOFT® WORD 5.5

Made Easy

Paul Hoffman

Osborne **McGraw-Hill**

Berkeley New York St. Louis San Francisco
Auckland Bogotá Hamburg London Madrid
Mexico City Milan Montreal New Delhi Panama City
Paris São Paulo Singapore Sydney
Tokyo Toronto

Osborne **McGraw-Hill**
2600 Tenth Street
Berkeley, California 94710
U.S.A.

Osborne **McGraw-Hill** offers software for sale. For information on software, translations, or book distributors outside of the U.S.A., please write to Osborne **McGraw-Hill** at the above address.

This book is printed on recycled paper.

Microsoft® Word 5.5 Made Easy

Copyright © 1991 by McGraw-Hill, Inc. All rights reserved. Printed in the United States of America. Except as permitted under the Copyright Act of 1976, no part of this publication may be reproduced or distributed in any form or by any means, or stored in a database or retrieval system, without the prior written permission of the publisher, with the exception that the program listings may be entered, stored, and executed in a computer system, but they may not be reproduced for publication.

1234567890 DOC 9987654321

ISBN 0-07-881714-5

Information has been obtained by Osborne **McGraw-Hill** from sources believed to be reliable. However, because of the possibility of human or mechanical error by our sources, Osborne **McGraw-Hill**, or others, Osborne **McGraw-Hill** does not guarantee the accuracy, adequacy, or completeness of any information and is not responsible for any errors or omissions or the results obtained from use of such information.

CONTENTS AT A GLANCE

Introducing Microsoft Word xv

Getting Started 1

PART I

1 Basic Editing with Word 21

2 Moving and Copying Text 37

3 Searching and Replacing 45

4 Using Word's Windows 53

5 Merging Text Files 67

6 Using Glossaries 71

PART II

7 Basic Formatting with Word 81

8 Formatting Paragraphs and Tables 97

9 Formatting Pages and Footnotes 125

10 Formatting with Style Sheets 147

PART III

11 Printing Your Text 165

12 Using Merge for Form Letters 175

13 Choosing Word's Custom Options 189

PART IV

14 Outlining 197

15 Generating Tables of Contents and Indexes 215

16 Annotations, Bookmarks, and Cross-References 231

17 Spelling Correction, Hyphenation, and Thesaurus 237

18 Sorting 247

19 Retrieving Documents 253

20 Macros 263

21 Linking Documents 271

22 Revision Marks 277

23 Desktop Publishing with Word 283

PART V

A Editing Command Summary 291

B Formatting Keystrokes Summary 295

C Mouse Keyclicks Summary 297

D Word Menus 299

E Preparing the Word Program 317

F Using Other Programs That Work with Word 321

G Altering Printer Drivers 323

H Answers to the Review Questions 331

Index 341

CONTENTS

Introducing Microsoft Word xv

Getting Started 1

WORD PROCESSING TERMS 1
PREPARING FOR WORD 3
STARTING THE WORD PROGRAM 4
GIVING WORD COMMANDS 6
  Giving Commands with the Mouse 6
  Giving Commands from the Keyboard 11
  Command Dialogs 12
ENTERING NORMAL TEXT 14
  Making Paragraphs in Word 15
GETTING HELP 15
LEAVING WORD 16
REVIEW 17

PART I

1 **Basic Editing with Word** 21

LESSON 1: TYPING IN THE FIRST FILE 21
LESSON 2: SAVING TEXT IN A FILE 22
LESSON 3: MOVING AROUND AND INSERTING TEXT 23
  Moving Around with the Mouse 25
  Moving Around with the Keyboard 27
LESSON 4: MAKING A SELECTION WITH THE MOUSE 27
LESSON 5: MAKING A SELECTION WITH THE KEYBOARD 30

LESSON 6: GIVING THE EDIT UNDO COMMAND 31
LESSON 7: PRINTING TEXT 32
REVIEW 34

2 **Moving and Copying Text** 37

LESSON 8: MOVING TEXT WITHIN A DOCUMENT 38
LESSON 9: COPYING TEXT WITHIN A DOCUMENT 40
LESSON 10: SPEED COPYING AND MOVING 42
REVIEW 42

3 **Searching and Replacing** 45

LESSON 11: SEARCHING FOR TEXT 46
LESSON 12: REPLACING TEXT 48
LESSON 13: USING SPECIAL CHARACTERS IN SEARCH AND REPLACE 49
REVIEW 52

4 **Using Word's Windows** 53

LESSON 14: USING TWO PANES IN ONE WINDOW 54
Splitting Windows with the Mouse 54
Splitting Windows with the Keyboard 55
Editing with Two Panes 56
LESSON 15: USING TWO WINDOWS IN TWO FILES 58
LESSON 16: MOVING AND RESIZING WINDOWS 61
Moving and Resizing Windows with the Mouse 62
Moving and Resizing Windows with the Keyboard 62
LESSON 17: MAXIMIZING WINDOWS 63
Maximizing Windows with the Mouse 63
Maximizing Windows with the Keyboard 64
LESSON 18: USING VERTICAL WINDOWS 64
REVIEW 66

5 **Merging Text Files** 67

LESSON 19: MERGING TWO WORD FILES 68
LESSON 20: MERGING NON-WORD FILES 68
REVIEW 69

6 **Using Glossaries** 71

LESSON 21: CREATING A GLOSSARY 72
LESSON 22: STORING AND RETRIEVING GLOSSARIES 75
LESSON 23: SPECIAL GLOSSARY ENTRIES 76
LESSON 24: FINDING OTHER USES FOR GLOSSARIES 77
REVIEW 78

PART II

7 **Basic Formatting with Word** **81**

LESSON 25: AN INTRODUCTION TO FORMATTING 82
Direct Formatting Versus Style Sheets 83
LESSON 26: ENTERING FORMAT DIRECTIVES 84
LESSON 27: USING COMMON CHARACTER STYLES 85
LESSON 28: USING OTHER CHARACTER FORMATS 87
LESSON 29: GIVING CHARACTER STYLES WITH THE CTRL KEY 89
LESSON 30: USING GRAPHICS CHARACTERS FROM THE KEYBOARD 90
LESSON 31: COPYING CHARACTER FORMATS WITH THE MOUSE 93
LESSON 32: SEARCHING FOR CHARACTER FORMATS 95
REVIEW 96

8 **Formatting Paragraphs and Tables** **97**

LESSON 33: BASIC FORMATTING FOR PARAGRAPHS 98
LESSON 34: INDENTING PARAGRAPHS 99
LESSON 35: LINE SPACING FOR PARAGRAPHS 102
LESSON 36: SELECTING PARAGRAPH FORMATS WITH THE CTRL KEY 104
LESSON 37: ALIGNING PARAGRAPHS AND USING KEEPS 105
LESSON 38: COPYING PARAGRAPH FORMATS WITH THE MOUSE 107
LESSON 39: USING TABS 108
LESSON 40: SETTING TABS 110
Setting Tabs with the Mouse 110
Setting Tabs with the Keyboard 110
LESSON 41: USING LEADER CHARACTERS AND MAKING TABLES 111
LESSON 42: WORKING WITH COLUMNS 112
LESSON 43: CREATING SIDE BY SIDE PARAGRAPHS 114
LESSON 44: VERTICAL TABS 117
LESSON 45: BOXES AND BORDERS 118
LESSON 46: ABSOLUTELY POSITIONED PARAGRAPHS 119
LESSON 47: SEARCHING FOR PARAGRAPH FORMATS 121
REVIEW 121

9 **Formatting Pages and Footnotes** **125**

LESSON 48: SETTING PAGE MARGINS 127
LESSON 49: USING PRINT PREVIEW 131
LESSON 50: CREATING MULTI-COLUMN TEXT 133

LESSON 51: USING HEADERS, FOOTERS, AND PAGE NUMBERING 134
Insert Page Numbers Command 136
Headers and Footers 137
LESSON 52: PAGE BREAKS AND REPAGINATING 141
LESSON 53: USING FOOTNOTES 143
LESSON 54: NUMBERING PLEADINGS 144
REVIEW 145

10 **Formatting with Style Sheets** 147

LESSON 55: CREATING A STYLE SHEET 149
LESSON 56: SAVING, LOADING, AND PRINTING STYLE SHEETS 155
LESSON 57: USING STYLES IN YOUR DOCUMENTS 156
LESSON 58: GETTING THE MOST OUT OF STYLE SHEETS 161
REVIEW 161

PART III

11 **Printing Your Text** 165

LESSON 59: SELECTING A PRINTER DRIVER 167
LESSON 60: SETTING UP YOUR PRINTER FOR WORD 168
LESSON 61: SETTING THE PRINTER OPTIONS 168
LESSON 62: USING THE PRINT QUEUE 171
LESSON 63: SAVING PRINTED OUTPUT IN A FILE 172
REVIEW 173

12 **Using Merge for Form Letters** 175

LESSON 64: USING MERGE FIELDS 176
LESSON 65: USING THE DATAFILE FORMAT 177
LESSON 66: PRINTING YOUR DOCUMENT 179
LESSON 67: USING MERGE INSTRUCTIONS 179
REVIEW 187

13 **Choosing Word's Custom Options** 189

LESSON 68: USING THE VIEW PREFERENCES COMMAND 190
LESSON 69: USING THE UTILITIES CUSTOMIZE COMMAND 191
REVIEW 194

PART IV

14 **Outlining** 197

LESSON 70: INTRODUCTION TO WORD'S OUTLINING FEATURES 198
LESSON 71: CREATING AN OUTLINE 200
LESSON 72: TEXT EDIT AND OUTLINE EDIT MODES 203
LESSON 73: COLLAPSING AND EXPANDING 204
LESSON 74: REARRANGING YOUR OUTLINE 208
LESSON 75: NUMBERING YOUR OUTLINE 210
REVIEW 213

15 Generating Tables of Contents and Indexes 215

LESSON 76: HIDDEN TEXT 216
LESSON 77: INTRODUCTION TO TABLES OF CONTENTS 217
LESSON 78: SPECIFYING ENTRIES 219
Using the Heading Styles for Entries 219
Using Hidden Text for Entries 220
LESSON 79: CREATING THE TABLE OF CONTENTS 222
LESSON 80: ADVANCED USE OF TABLES OF CONTENTS 225
LESSON 81: CREATING AN INDEX 226
REVIEW 228

16 Annotations, Bookmarks, and Cross-References 231

LESSON 82: CREATING ANNOTATIONS 232
LESSON 83: USING BOOKMARKS 233
LESSON 84: CROSS-REFERENCES IN YOUR DOCUMENTS 234
REVIEW 236

17 Spelling Correction, Hyphenation, and Thesaurus 237

LESSON 85: INTRODUCTION TO SPELLING CORRECTION 238
LESSON 86: SPELLING 239
LESSON 87: HYPHENATION 241
LESSON 88: USING THE THESAURUS 244
REVIEW 245

18 Sorting 247

LESSON 89: SORTING TEXT 249
LESSON 90: SORTING NUMBERS 251
LESSON 91: SORTING IN TABLES 251
REVIEW 252

19 Retrieving Documents 253

LESSON 92: FILLING SUMMARY SHEETS 254
LESSON 93: SEARCHING FOR DOCUMENTS 257
REVIEW 261

20 **Macros** 263

LESSON 94: INTRODUCTION TO MACROS 263
LESSON 95: CREATING MACROS 265
LESSON 96: TESTING AND EDITING MACROS 268
LESSON 97: MACRO INSTRUCTIONS 269
REVIEW 270

21 **Linking Documents** 271

LESSON 98: LINKING SPREADSHEETS 272
LESSON 99: LINKING PICTURES 274
REVIEW 276

22 **Revision Marks** 277

LESSON 100: USING REDLINING FOR REVISIONS 277
LESSON 101: SAVING REVISED DOCUMENTS 280
REVIEW 281

23 **Desktop Publishing with Word** 283

LESSON 102: THE BEGINNING OF DESKTOP PUBLISHING 284
LESSON 103: DESKTOP PUBLISHING SOFTWARE 285
LESSON 104: SOME DESKTOP PUBLISHING TECHNIQUES 286
REVIEW 288

PART V

A **Editing Command Summary** 291

B **Formatting Keystrokes Summary** 295

C **Mouse Keyclicks Summary** 297

POINTING WITH THE MOUSE 298
USING THE BUTTONS 298

D **Word Menus** 299

E **Preparing the Word Program** 317

SETTING UP YOUR COMPUTER 318
INSTALLING A MOUSE 318
USING OTHER MICE 318
PREPARING WORD'S DISTRIBUTION DISKS 319
ARRANGING YOUR WORKSPACE 319

F **Using Other Programs That Work with Word** 321

USING OTHER TEXT PROGRAMS 322

G **Altering Printer Drivers** 323

RUNNING MAKEPRD 324
USING CHARACTER TRANSLATIONS 325
USING THE PRINTER CONTROL SEQUENCE 327

H **Answers to the Review Questions** 331

Index 341

INTRODUCING MICROSOFT WORD

Microsoft Word 5.5 Made Easy introduces you to this powerful word processing program and guides you step by step while you learn how to use it. The book is organized so that you first gain a general understanding of Word's features and then practice editing and formatting text. By the end of this book you will be ready to use Word for a variety of business and word processing purposes. This book covers the latest release of Microsoft Word, version 5.5.

The introduction explains the many advantages that Word offers. "Getting Started" tells you how to begin using Word. It includes information on how to start the program, how to give commands, and how to enter text.

Part I, Chapters 1 through 6, explains how to enter, edit, and print your text. These chapters give you a complete overview of Word's editing features. You will begin creating documents in the first chapter.

Part II, Chapters 7 through 10, describes Word's formatting commands. You will use these commands to make your document appear exactly as you wish when it is printed.

Part III, Chapters 11 through 13, discusses general Word topics, including additional printing topics, Word's merge capability, and various options that make Word easier to use.

Part IV, Chapters 14 through 23, shows how to use Word's advanced features to prepare business documents. These features include outlines, tables of contents, indexes, spelling correction, and sorting.

Part V, the appendixes, contains reference material on Word, detailed instructions on preparing Word for use, and answers to the review questions that end each chapter. In addition, this section discusses other programs that work with Word.

ABOUT THIS BOOK

This book will help you learn the advanced word processing features of Microsoft Word. It covers the many different aspects of using Word, and gives hints and practical suggestions for putting Word to work for you. This book supplements Word's documentation, the Microsoft Word reference manual, by showing you in a step-by-step fashion how to use Word.

Even though Word's features are advanced, they are relatively easy to master once you understand the concepts behind them. This book is arranged to teach you these concepts in a natural order, and it reinforces the concepts by giving you many examples to work on. The examples in the book relate to the many types of word processing that are performed in a typical business office, although Word is useful for anyone who needs advanced word processing.

Each chapter is broken into lessons, which are heavily illustrated with screens, so that you will know exactly what to expect when you begin to use the program. Many sections explain how to use the mouse with Word. There are also review exercises at the end of each chapter.

Although this book supplements your reference manual, it also contains information that is not covered there. For example, Appendix E, "Preparing the Word Program," gives you more complete information on how to set up your computer to use Word; Appendix F, "Using Other Programs That Work with Word," covers how other applications programs work with Word.

This book will be useful to anyone who has Microsoft Word, or to anyone thinking of buying it. Beginning users will find that the lessons are easy to follow and that they build on concepts learned earlier in the book. Intermediate users will find topics that were mentioned briefly in different parts of the Microsoft Word reference manual described fully in one source in this book, and advanced users will appreciate the reference material throughout the book, especially in the appendixes.

For those who have never used a word processing program before, this book explains beginning concepts when they first appear. Users who are familiar with other word processing programs will find that some of Word's features are new to them. These, too, are explained in full so that you can get a complete understanding of Word's capabilities.

The information in this book pertains to version 5.5 of Word running on the IBM PC or compatible system. If you have version 5.0, the great majority of the information here will apply. However, the way your screen looks and the way you give commands is much different in version 5.5 than it was in earlier versions.

If you are using an earlier version of Word than 5.5, you should upgrade your copy. Version 5.5 has an improved user interface and runs faster. Like every program, Word had bugs in its earlier version, and most of these have been fixed in version 5.5. Contact Microsoft to determine how you can upgrade to version 5.5.

WHAT IS MICROSOFT WORD?

A *word processor* is a computer program that lets you type and save text (such as memos, letters, reports, and books). Word processors such as Microsoft Word let you easily enter text for a document, revise the text once it has been entered (called *editing*), and print the text out on your printer in a professional form (called *formatting*).

There is a wide variety of word processing software available for many different computers. Some software gives you the bare minimum of capabilities, while other programs, such as Word, give you many more useful features to make word processing easier.

Microsoft also markets a version of Word for the Apple Macintosh. The Macintosh version has features similar to those of the PC version, although it has a different user interface. For more information on the Macintosh version of Word, see *Microsoft Word Made Easy for the Macintosh* by Paul Hoffman (Osborne/McGraw-Hill, 1989).

Word is useful for all types of word processing, such as writing short memos, business letters, financial statements, articles, books, and long reports. It is generally easy to use and has many advanced features that you can use or ignore, depending on the type of document you are writing. The more you use Word, the less you need to worry about what your text will look like, which means you can spend more time concentrating on what you want to say.

ADVANTAGES OF USING WORD

If you have compared Word to other word processing packages, you know that it has many features that others don't. Of course, having a plethora of features does not make a word processor good; you have to be able to use these features easily. Since most people need a fair amount of explanation to understand the usefulness of Word's features, they are mentioned briefly here and described fully in the rest of the book.

Word is one of the first word processing programs to use a *mouse,* which is a piece of hardware that you slide along your desk in order to point to portions of the screen. Many people think the mouse makes editing more natural than it is in most other programs. Many other word processors require you to move a *cursor* (a block or underline on the screen) until it is over some text you want to manipulate, then press a sequence of keys to give a command. Word's mouse, however, allows you simply to move a pointer around on the screen to point at what you want.

Using the mouse with Word can make editing much easier. For instance, if you want to delete a word, you simply move the mouse on your desk until the arrow on the screen is pointing at the word you want; then you press a button on the mouse, move the mouse to point at the word Delete near the bottom of the screen, press a button, and the word is deleted. This shows one of the mouse's big advantages: you do not have to remember which sequence of keys is required to delete a word.

You can, if you want, use Word without the mouse by giving all commands from the keyboard. You can use the PC's function keys and cursor control keys to give Word commands. In fact, since giving some commands with the keyboard is faster than with the mouse, some people use both.

Since it is common for you to make mistakes when you edit text, Word has an Undo feature that lets you take out your last change. This means that if you do something that you don't want, you can tell Word to undo it. This feature can save you a great deal of typing and frustration.

Microsoft has written Word so that you always use similar features of Word in similar fashion. For instance, if you have many choices to make after giving a command, pressing the TAB key moves between the choices. Similarly, if you are using the mouse, the meaning of pressing either of the two buttons (or of pressing both buttons) is consistent throughout Word.

If you are ever unsure of what you are doing in Word, the program can always offer help. This prevents you from having to look up information in the reference manual (or in this book) when you just want to know a small bit of information. The help that Word gives you is often more useful than the help you get from other programs, since it first gives you help on what you are currently doing and then makes it easy to ask for more information if you need it. You can leave the help window on the screen as you edit a document so that it is easy to get back to at any time.

One problem with many word processing programs is that you can only see a small portion of your document at a time. With Word, you can see many parts of the text at the same time in different parts of the screen by *opening windows.* This is very useful when you are writing a long document, since you can look at what you wrote earlier while you write new text. You can even use Word to look at different files on the screen at the same time and to move text between files.

When you write reports and memos, you usually have an idea of how you want them to be formatted. Many word processing programs make you spend a great deal of time putting your documents into the desired format. Word, on the other hand, makes formatting your document especially easy. Once you tell Word what format you want to use for a paragraph, for instance, it will use that for other paragraphs until you tell it differently. Word formats paragraphs for you as you write or change them; other word processors require you to reformat a paragraph each time you change it.

NEW FEATURES IN VERSION 5

Microsoft Word version 5 has many features that did not appear in previous versions. These make Word easier to use and more responsive to the way you work as you prepare business documents.

- You can repaginate your document as you work on other editing and formatting tasks.
- Word has *absolutely positioned* paragraphs that you can put anywhere on the page.
- You can edit in *page view* mode, which lets you see exactly how your text will print.
- There are more choices for paragraph borders.
- Graphics are better integrated into the program than before. You can also have graphics that are updated outside Word.
- You can leave bookmarks in your document and jump to those bookmarks quickly.

- Word now has a cross-referencing feature. When you encounter a specific topic in one part of your document, you can refer to other pages which mention that topic.
- It is much easier to add annotations to your documents.
- The macro language has many features for creating advanced macros.

Microsoft first released these features in Word version 5.0. Version 5.0 had the same *user interface* (that is, look of the screen and method for giving commands) as all previous versions of Word. In late 1990, Microsoft released version 5.5 which, although it has no new features, has a very different user interface. Most people prefer the new interface because it acts like other programs that they are familiar with. This book describes version 5.5.

USING WORD IN BUSINESS

You have probably heard of the many advantages that word processing offers for a business. Since Word has many more features than almost all word processors, it lets you do more work easily. For example:

- Once you set up a standard format for a particular document (such as a legal contract), you can use that format for similar documents. In the case of contracts, you then can simply type new information into the old format and not have to worry about appearance. The formats that you set up are kept in Word's style sheets.
- Most businesses have form letters (standard letters for which the computer fills in a different name and address), and many word processing packages let you write your own simple form letters. Word allows you to integrate other information into your form letters so that the letters look more personalized. Word can also read the names and addresses from data files stored by other programs, such as data base management systems. This feature is often called *mail merge.*
- Word's advanced formatting allows you to create reports that appear to have been professionally typeset. With Word, you can design the style of each page to your specifications and not worry about what it will look like if you change some of the text. You can also use printers that print with proportional spacing to make your printed output look like typesetting.

- Newsletters and other bulletins can be printed with many columns on one page, giving your writing a more professional look. You can also use many different type styles (such as boldface or italics) so that your headlines stand out from your text.
- You can use Word to make an outline and then use that outline to prepare a business document. You can have Word automatically number the headings in your outline and renumber them as you move or delete headings.

GETTING STARTED

Word Processing Terms
Preparing for Word
Starting the Word Program
Giving Word Commands
Entering Normal Text
Getting Help
Leaving Word

This chapter explains the few steps you need to follow before you can begin to use Word and shows you how to start up the program. After following the installation instructions, you can immediately start to edit and format documents; in fact, you will start using Word in Chapter 1 to enter a business letter that will be utilized throughout the next six chapters and in many other sections of the book as well.

If you have no word processing experience, the following section will give you a quick overview of many of the terms you will find in this book. If you are familiar with another word processor, you can probably skim the section very quickly.

WORD PROCESSING TERMS

Word processing programs give you two major capabilities: editing and formatting. *Editing* is the ability to enter text into the program, make corrections, save the text on disk, and later change the text. *Formatting* is the ability to specify how the text will look when you print it out. For example, formatting allows you to add special features to the printout, such as page numbers on each page, and to specify the width of the left and right margins.

In order to make a word processing program work, you give it *commands,* instructions that tell the program what you want to do. In Word, you can give commands by using the mouse or by pressing the function keys and the cursor control keys. *Function keys* are labeled F1, F2, and so on; you will find them along the top row or left two columns of your keyboard. *Cursor control keys* are both the arrow keys that are to the right of the main keyboard and the HOME, END, PGUP, and PGDN keys. Many keyboards have two sets of cursor control keys that have the same uses.

When you write a document, you *insert* text into a file. This is done simply by typing the text as you would on a typewriter. Once this has been done, you can use editing commands to correct mistakes or to rearrange the text. While you are editing, you can move around in the text so you can edit different parts. When you want to see text that is not on the screen, the word processing program will *scroll,* or move, the screen to the desired location. When you are done with a file, you can *save* it on disk; when you want to use the file later, you tell the word processing program to *load* it from disk.

If you have entered text that you no longer want in the file, you can *delete* it. Word allows you to delete groups of words or lines easily; for instance, if you want to delete a paragraph, you *select* the paragraph (with a selection command) and then delete it all at once. If, instead, you want to move the paragraph to some other location in the document, you can *cut and paste* the text as if you were using scissors and tape, inserting the paragraph in a new location.

When you write longer documents, you may want to find a specific part of the text so you can edit it. The easiest way to do this is to *search* for a particular word that is in the area you want to edit. Word, like most word processing programs, can also search your entire document and automatically change one set of words to another; this is called *global search and replace.* For instance, if you use one person's name throughout a file and want to change it to another name, you only have to give one search-and-replace command. When you are editing in Word, you normally edit just one file. However, you can edit more than one file at a time by opening a *window*; this is like splitting your screen into two smaller screens, each working on something different.

A word processing program with many formatting features can give you finished copy that looks professionally produced. When you use a typewriter, you often do a great deal of formatting, such as *indenting* the first lines of paragraphs (usually five spaces from the left margin) and putting the page number on each page. Word processing programs can do many formatting tasks for you automatically. For instance, if you want to insert a standard line of text at the top or bottom of each page (called a *header* or *footer*), you can tell the program to do that for you. (Notice the header at the top of this page.)

Like some other word processors, Word lets you use many different styles of characters (or *fonts*) in your text. For example, you can print in *italics*, the font used for introducing terms in this book. Other fonts that you can use in Word are **boldface** and SMALL CAPS. In fact, Word lets you use more fonts than most other word processors.

The way you format paragraphs can make a big difference in the appearance of the text. Word allows you to choose ragged-right or justified margins. *Ragged-right* text does not line up exactly; *justified* text lines up at the right margin, like the text in this book. In addition, some lines, such as titles and headings, can be *centered* between the margins.

When you reach the bottom of a page, you may not want the remainder of a paragraph to appear on the next page; you might prefer to leave extra white space at the bottom and put the full paragraph on the next page. Word allows you to *keep* a paragraph together to make the text more readable, although the pages may have uneven lengths. For aesthetics, it is usually necessary to prevent widows and orphans, and Word automatically does this for you. When the last line of a paragraph is typed at the top of a new page, it is called a *widow;* an *orphan* is the first line of a paragraph typed at the bottom of a page with the rest of the paragraph typed on the next page.

PREPARING FOR WORD

The Word program comes on many disks containing the programs and special files needed to run Word. Several other disks contain files that you will find useful. The Spell and Hyphenation Disk contains the spelling check program in Word. The Thesaurus Disk contains Word's thesaurus. The Printer Disks contain files needed to use various brands of printers (some of these files also appear on the Utilities/Setup Disk). Word also comes with Learning Word Disks, which contain an interactive teaching program.

You should make a copy of each disk using the PC-DOS COPY or DISKCOPY command. Use the copies instead of the originals when you use Word. Keep the originals in a safe place, away from the computer. You may even want to store them outside of the office. In case the copies are damaged or destroyed, you can make new copies from the originals.

To install Word on your disks, insert the Utilities Disk 1 in the A: drive. At the PC-DOS prompt, type **A:**, press ENTER, and then give the following command:

A>**SETUP**

Throughout this book, the part of an instruction printed in **boldface** is what you type in; here, you type **SETUP** and then you press the ENTER key.

note The screen examples used in this book were produced with a graphics adapter and monitor. If you have a nongraphics adapter, your screen may differ from those represented here.

You should have a few formatted diskettes for storing the text that you enter. If you have a hard disk, you do not need these diskettes, since you can keep everything on the hard disk.

If you have a mouse, you should install the mouse in your computer and have the mouse initialization program (sometimes called the *mouse driver*) loaded into memory before you run Word. The procedure for this is covered in Appendix E.

STARTING THE WORD PROGRAM

The method that you use to run Word depends on the type of disk you are using. For example, to run Word from a hard drive, give the **WORD** command at the PC-DOS prompt like this:

C>**WORD**

The Word program loads in the same fashion whether loading from floppy, hard, or RAM disks. First you see a startup screen, and then Word performs some initial setup operations. When all of the initial files are read, you should see the following screen:

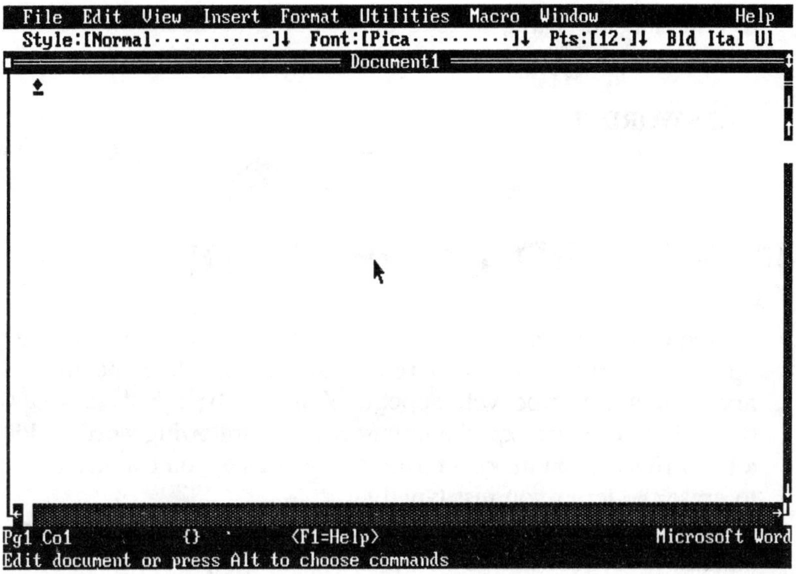

If you are using a mouse and a graphics monitor, you should see an arrow (called the *mouse pointer*) pointing up and to the left, near the middle of the screen:

If you are using a mouse and a nongraphics monitor, you will see a solid rectangular block for the mouse pointer. You are now ready to start entering Word commands and text.

If you wish, you can start Word with the name of the file that you want to edit. For example, if you want to edit the file called SAMPLE1, you can give PC-DOS the command

C>**WORD SAMPLE1**

Word also remembers the name of the last file that you edited. If you want to edit that file again, instead of including its name on the command line, you can use the /L option:

C>**WORD /L**

GIVING WORD COMMANDS

As soon as Word is loaded, it is ready for you to start entering text. In the upper-left corner, the bright rectangle with the diamond in it is where the first letters you type will appear. You can type just as you would on a typewriter. To start experimenting, type the following words: **This is just like a typewriter.** If you make a mistake as you type, you can use the BACKSPACE key to erase the letter you just typed.

Now press the ← key a few times and then the → key. Notice that the blinking underline moves to the left and right, leaving the diamond at the end of the line. The blinking underline is the *insertion mark,* which is described in detail later in this chapter. The diamond is a marker that shows you the end of the text and is sometimes called the *end-of-file marker.* Figure GS-1 shows the different areas of the screen.

So far you have only entered text, not edited it. To edit the text, you have to give Word commands. There are two ways to give commands: with the mouse and with the keyboard. You should read both of the following sections regardless of whether or not you have a mouse. Most concepts in this book are first explained in the sections for mouse users, since it is easier to show illustrations with the mouse. However, even if you have a mouse you should read the sections for keyboard users, since you will probably find that you will give Word commands with both the mouse and the keyboard.

To give a Word command, you choose a menu from the top of the screen and then choose a command from the menu. The menus correspond to the names at the top of the screen (File, Edit, View, and so on). Thus, every command comes under a menu. In this book, the command names tell you first the menu name, and then the command name. For instance, the Cut command in the Edit menu is called the Edit Cut command.

Giving Commands with the Mouse

The mouse is a simple tool used for pointing at parts of the screen. Word works with a wide variety of mice. Most mice have two buttons. If your mouse has three, refer to the mouse's instruction manual to determine which button to use when this book refers to the "right" button.

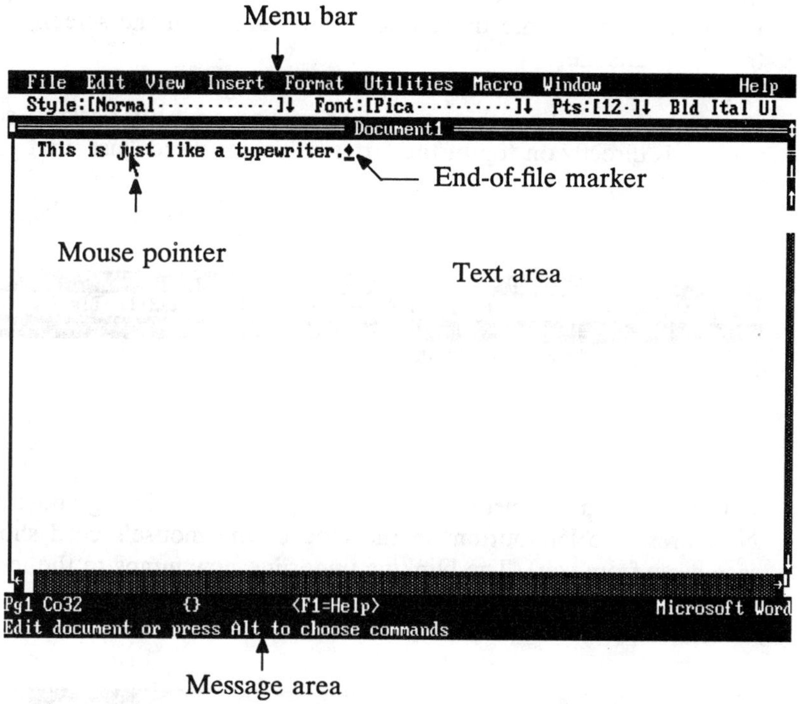

FIGURE GS-1. The Word screen

When you move the mouse on your desk, the pointer on the screen moves in the same direction. When you press one or both of the buttons on the mouse, the mouse sends a signal to Word. The pointer on the screen can take many shapes, depending on where it is on the screen. When it is in the text area (the large area where your typed-in text will appear), it is the arrow pointing up and to the left.

Moving the mouse around on your desk moves the pointer; however, this never executes a command. To tell Word that you want to do something with a piece of information, you must point the mouse at the information and press one of the two buttons on the mouse (sometimes you will press both together).

It may take some practice to get used to pointing with the mouse; a common mistake is to press the buttons so hard that you move the mouse, with the result that the pointer is no longer where you want it on the screen. When you point at information on the screen, it is the tip of the arrow, not the whole arrow itself, that Word uses to determine what you are pointing at. If you slowly move the tip to one of the borders of the screen, you will see the shape change.

As you use the mouse, you will find that your coordination will quickly improve. As practice, first move the mouse on your desktop so that the pointer is directly on top of the letter "u" in the word "just" that you typed.

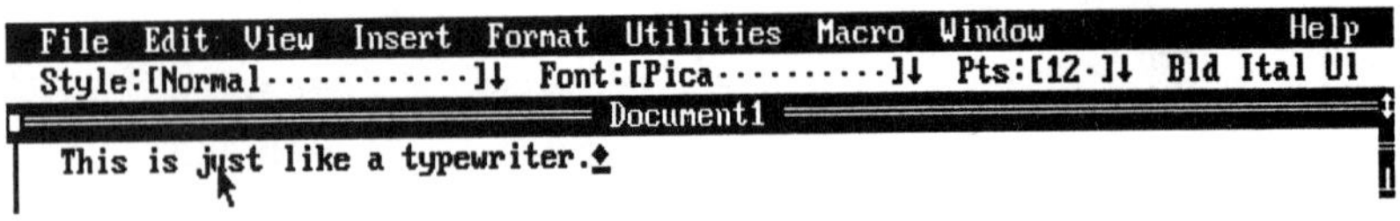

If you see a square instead of an arrow, you are pointing above the letters. Now press the left button on the mouse (the mouse's cord should always face away from you). The blinking underline now jumps to the letter "u."

The blinking underline is the insertion mark. This indicates that the next character you type will appear just before the letter that is underlined. To see this, type the letter **x**. Notice that the letter appears before the "u," which had the insertion mark under it. Press the BACKSPACE key to remove the "x" you just added.

When you want to add text to your document, move the insertion mark to where you want the new text to appear. Remember that what you type will appear just before the insertion mark. To add text to the end of a document, move the insertion mark under the end-of-file mark (the diamond).

Next, without moving the mouse, press the right button. The word "just" and the space after it are now selected.

You have now given a selection command; that is, you have "selected" a portion of text. Whenever you give Word commands that have an effect on text in your file, the effect is only on the selected text. You can have the whole document or any portion of it selected at any time. The text that is highlighted is the text that is currently selected (in this case, the word "just").

Now, again without moving the mouse, press both buttons at once and the whole sentence is highlighted, indicating that it has been selected.

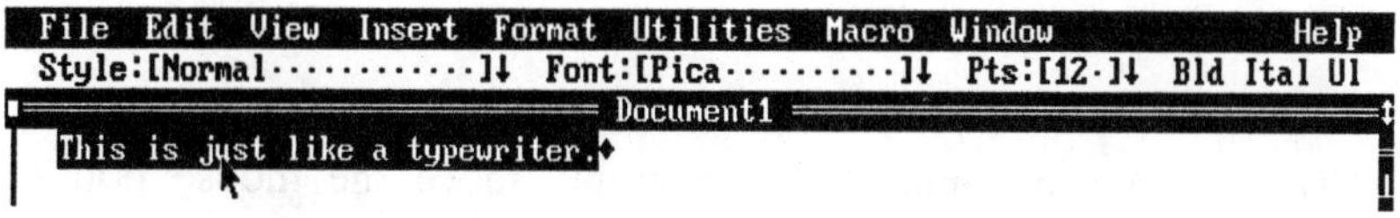

Notice that pressing the left and right buttons causes different effects; pressing either button or both together sends a different signal depending on what you are pointing at.

You cannot move the mouse pointer completely off the screen. A bit of the pointer will always show on the screen, even if it is near the edge. You can move the pointer to the middle of the screen again simply by moving the mouse around your desktop.

Remember that Word never executes a mouse command until you press one or both of the buttons. In different parts of the screen, the buttons have different meanings (summarized in Appendix C).

Once you have selected some text, you can move the pointer and the text will remain selected. Word will not change anything until you press a button on the mouse. You change the selection by moving to new text and pressing a button; this makes a new selection. You can have only one selection at a time.

To choose a menu, move the mouse pointer over the menu name and click the left mouse button. The commands in the menu appear over your document. You can try this out now. First point at the word "just" again and click the right mouse button so that only that word is selected. Move the mouse to the menu Edit and click the left mouse button:

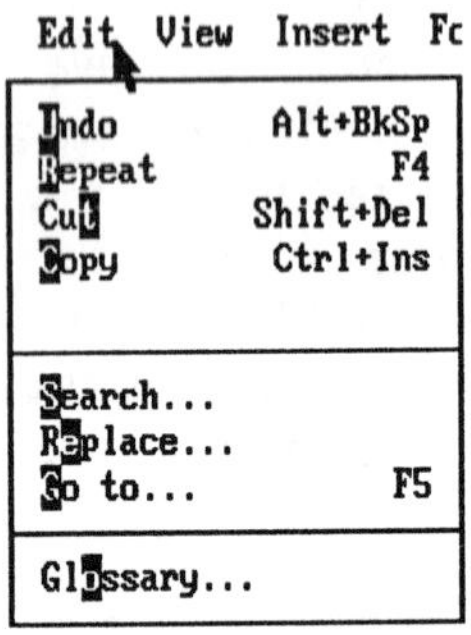

To choose a command from a menu, move the mouse pointer down the menu until it is pointing at the desired command, then click the left button. To see this, point at the word "Cut" in the Edit menu and click the left mouse button. Word executes the command, which in this case cuts the word "just" from the sentence.

You have now executed the Edit Cut command on the selected text.

You can see all of Word's commands by browsing through the menus. To do this, point at any menu and hold down the left mouse button. If you keep holding it down while moving the cursor left and right to other menus, the commands in each menu appear.

If you let go of the left mouse button when a menu is visible, the menu stays open. You may decide that you didn't really want to choose a command and want to get rid of the menu. Simply move the mouse pointer anywhere on the screen away from the menu itself, and click the left mouse button.

To see how Word inserts text, type **not** followed by a space. Word moves all the text to the right of your new characters, so that you always insert text at the selection.

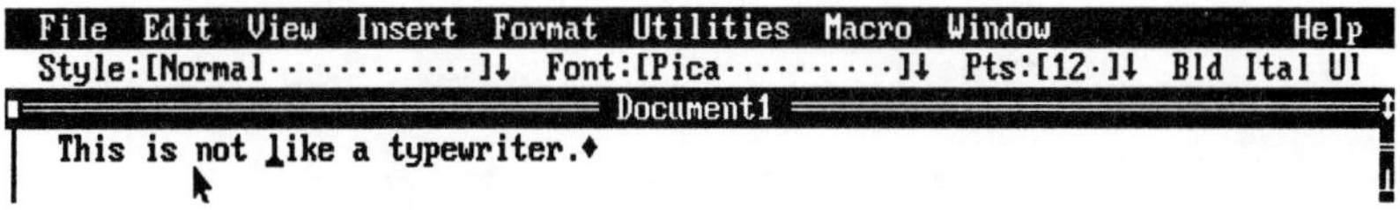

Giving Commands from the Keyboard

You can give Word commands from the keyboard almost as easily as you can with a mouse. Many people prefer using the keyboard for commands so that they do not need to move their hands as much. All commands in the menus are available with just two keystrokes.

The ALT key and the CTRL key are sometimes used in conjunction with other keys. You use the ALT key or the CTRL key somewhat as you would use the SHIFT key when you type capital letters: you hold the ALT or CTRL key down first; then, while still holding it down, press the other key. You will often use other special keys, including the ESC key, the TAB key (marked with two arrows pointing at vertical lines), the ENTER key (marked with the arrow pointing down and then to the left), the BACKSPACE key (marked with the arrow pointing left), the SCROLL LOCK key, the DEL key, and the INS key.

You can use the arrow and function keys to give selection commands as you did with the mouse in the last section. (If you followed the directions there, you may want to restore the sentence to its original state. Point the mouse at the word "Undo" in the Edit command menu and press the left button.) You can move the insertion mark (the blinking underline) around with the four arrow keys on the right side of the keyboard. Move the insertion mark to the letter "j" in "just." Now press ALT and while holding it down press F6, or press F8 twice; this selects the word "just."

There are three ways to give a Word command with the keyboard. The method used most often is to select menus and commands by typing the highlighted letters in the names. Another method is to move between the menus and commands with the arrow keys and press ENTER when you reach the desired menu or command. The third method is to use one of the shortcuts available for many Word commands.

The most common method is to type the highlighted letters in the menu and command names while holding down the ALT key. When no menu is selected, holding down the ALT key highlights a letter in each menu name, usually the first letter, as shown in the following illustration:

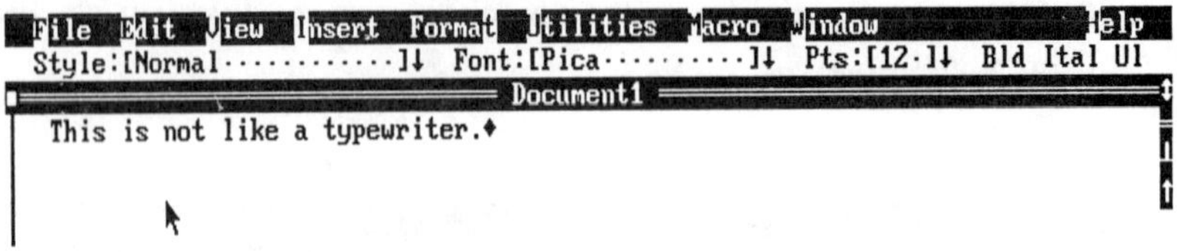

When you type the letter, the commands appear just as they did when you used the mouse. For instance, press ALT, then type **E** to see the Edit menu.

In each command in the menu, another letter is highlighted. Press that letter to execute the command. For example, the Cut command in the Edit menu has the "t" highlighted, so typing **T** executes the command. You can type **T** or press ALT-T: both give you the same effect.

If you want to use the arrow method, first press the ALT key and release it to highlight the menu bar. Notice that the File menu name is selected. Press the ← and → keys to select the desired menu, then press ENTER. When the menu appears, use the ↑ and ↓ keys to select the desired command, then press ENTER again to execute the command.

Many commands have keyboard equivalents, some of which are listed in the menus. For instance, notice the "Alt+BkSp" to the right of the Edit Undo command's name. This means that, without choosing the menu, you can press ALT and BACKSPACE at any time to execute the Edit Undo command (remember that you must press the ALT key first and while holding it down press BACKSPACE). All of the keyboard equivalents of Word commands are listed in Appendixes A and B.

Command Dialogs

Some commands need more information before they can execute. These commands have *command dialogs,* which are screens that let you specify information. Usually, any command that has a dialog has an ellipsis (three dots, or ...) after its name. You can enter information in a command dialog using actions similar to what you have just learned about the mouse and keyboard.

For example, give the File Printer Setup command. You will see the following:

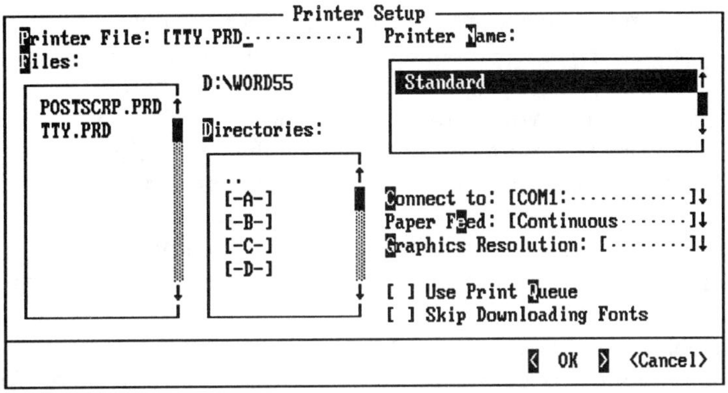

There are five types of information that you can fill in in a dialog:

- *Check boxes* let you turn an option off or on. These are enclosed in square brackets. An "X" between the brackets indicates that the option is turned on, while an empty space indicates that the option is turned off. In the File Printer Setup dialog, "Use Print Queue" and "Skip Downloading Fonts" are check boxes.
- *Option boxes* let you select only one option from a list of many. The options are marked with parentheses, and a period between one of the sets of parentheses indicates which option is selected.
- *List boxes* let you choose items from a list. If the list is longer than the box will hold, you can move the list up and down in the box to find the desired items. There are three list boxes in the File Printer Setup dialog: "Files," "Directories," and "Printer Name."
- *Drop-down lists* let you choose one item from a long list. You can move through the list and choose an item. Display lists are indicated by a choice in square brackets with a downward-pointing arrow to the right, such as the "Connect to," "Paper Feed," and "Graphics Resolution" lists in the File Printer Setup dialog.
- *Text boxes* let you type text into the dialog. For example, the "Printer File" entry at the top of the File Printer Setup dialog is a text box.
- *Command buttons* appear at the bottom of all dialogs. After you have made selections in the other parts of the dialog, you click or select one of these buttons to make the options take effect. Command buttons appear between "<" and ">" symbols. Almost every dialog has both "OK" and "Cancel" command buttons, like the File Printer Setup dialog.

When you make selections in a dialog, those selections do not take effect until you select the OK command button in the dialog. If you make some selections and change your mind, select the Cancel button; Word ignores any of the changes that you made in the dialog.

The actions you use to select items in a dialog depend on whether you are using a mouse or keyboard, but they are similar to the actions you used to select commands from menus. Of course, you can use either mouse or keyboard, depending on which you are most comfortable with. Most people prefer to use the mouse in dialogs, even if they use the keyboard for most other actions.

To select a check box or an option with the mouse, simply point between the square brackets or parentheses and click the left button. To move to a text box, click anywhere in the box. To select a command button, click on it.

To select an item in a list box with the mouse, point at the item and click the left mouse button. If the item you want isn't visible, click on the upward- or downward-pointing arrows at the right of the list box to move more items into the box. To see a drop-down list, click on the downward-pointing arrow and select the item as you do in a list box.

Using the keyboard, you can move to an item and select it by pressing the ALT key and the highlighted letter in the item's name. You can also use the arrow keys and the TAB key to move between the items (use the TAB key to move to the next item and the SHIFT-TAB key combination to move to the previous item). To turn a check box or option item on or off, press the SPACEBAR. To quickly execute the OK command button, simply press ENTER; to cancel the dialog, press ESC.

ENTERING NORMAL TEXT

As you have seen, Word lets you enter text in a fairly normal fashion. When you type in text, you can correct typing mistakes by pressing the BACKSPACE key to erase the character to the left of the selection. If you later move the selection indicator to an error in the text you did not catch immediately, you can also use the DEL key to delete the selected characters.

Word treats all characters in your document (whether they are letters, numbers, or symbols) the same way. The following sections discuss special symbols (for paragraphs, hyphens, and spaces) that Word treats as characters. You can insert them as you would normal text when you enter new text or when you edit.

Making Paragraphs in Word

In your text, each set of lines that is grouped as a unit is called a *paragraph.* Unfortunately, this is easy to confuse with the definition of paragraph that you learned in grammar school, which is a group of sentences developing an idea. In Word, a paragraph is really just a line or several lines that appear visually to be an independent unit. For instance, in a business letter, the line with the date, the lines that show the recipient's address, and the line with the salutation are all paragraphs, as is each group of sentences in the letter. When you see the word "paragraph" in this book and in the Microsoft Word reference manual, it will refer to Word's definition.

Word identifies the end of a paragraph by a special mark that it puts in your text when you press the ENTER key. For this reason, do not use the ENTER key at the end of each line inside a paragraph. One of Word's features that makes typing much easier is automatic *wordwrap,* which prevents you from having to decide where to end each line. As you type in a paragraph, Word automatically figures out where to start a new line. You only press ENTER at the end of the paragraph.

If you want to force Word to start a new line within a paragraph (but not start a new paragraph), hold down the SHIFT key while you press the ENTER key. This key combination is called NEWLINE, and it lets you make lines of different lengths within a paragraph that are unlike the lines of a paragraph made with wordwrap. The reason that you would use NEWLINE instead of starting a new paragraph is that many of Word's formatting commands pertain to the whole paragraph. If you signal a paragraph with ENTER, you have to format it; if you use NEWLINE, you only need to format the whole paragraph once.

A good example of using NEWLINE is in typing the recipient's address in a letter. You will learn in Chapter 13 how to see the difference between the end of a paragraph and NEWLINE; for now, it is not important.

GETTING HELP

Word's help system is a quick way to get information about a command or to figure out what is happening in the program. The Help menu lists choices that you can use to get information about any command and its options.

Word's help screens appear in a window over your document. You can treat the window like other Word windows, which you will learn about in Chapter 4. The Help menu has six commands: Index, Keyboard, Word 5.0 to 5.5, Learning Word, Using Help, and Help About.

The index is a list of all of the help topics available. You can select items in the index by moving the selection up and down, or by pressing the keys described in the index window itself. Other commands in the Help menu take you directly to information about the keyboard, differences between Word version 5.0 and version 5.5, the Learning Word tutorial that comes with Word, and information on how to use Help.

The Help About command tells you the version of Word that you are using and shows who it is registered to.

Microsoft Word includes a full-featured tutorial on the Learning Word Disk. You can run the tutorial by itself or with the Help Learning Word command.

You can open the help window at any time by pressing the F1 key. For instance, if you need help with a particular command, select the command in its menu, and then press F1. Word shows you help on that specific command. You can also press F1 when you are in a dialog to get help about the choices there.

LEAVING WORD

Since you have only entered practice text, it is unlikely that you want to save it in a file (don't worry; the real text comes at the beginning of the next chapter). When you leave Word, the program checks to see if you have saved your text in a file before it returns you to PC-DOS. It is easy, however, to tell Word not to bother.

When you want to exit from Word and return to PC-DOS, give the File Exit command. If there is text that you have not saved on disk (you will learn how to do this in the next chapter), Word will ask the following:

```
Microsoft Word

Do you want to save changes to Document1?

        < Yes > < No > <Cancel>
```

If you want to save your text, type **Y** or use the mouse to click on the word "Yes." In this case, however, you can type **N** or click on "No," since the material is just for practice. If you realize that you want to do more editing, press the ESC key or click on "Cancel."

REVIEW

1. *Running Word from PC-DOS*
   You can include different options when giving the WORD command. How do you tell Word to start editing a file called TIMECLCK.DOC on the B: disk? How do you tell Word to open the same file you used the last time you ran Word?

2. *Using the selection*
   Enter the following paragraph:

```
The inventory tracking program will also tell you when to re-
order stock. When the level of stock drops below a critical
limit, the program automatically alerts you to re-order, and
tells you approximately when you will be out of that item. This
feature alone makes the program a necessary part of your
inventory management.
◆
```

   What is the easiest way to select the words "below a critical limit" (with either the mouse or with the keyboard)?

3. *Deleting text*
   What is the easiest way to delete the last sentence from the text in question 2?

4. *Paragraphs*
   What keystrokes do you use to enter a NEWLINE character? Give an example in a business letter of using NEWLINE.

part I

USING WORD TO EDIT

Basic Editing with Word
Moving and Copying Text
Searching and Replacing
Using Word's Windows
Merging Text Files
Using Glossaries

chapter 1

BASIC EDITING WITH WORD

Lesson 1: Typing in the First File
Lesson 2: Saving Text in a File
Lesson 3: Moving Around and Inserting Text
Lesson 4: Making a Selection with the Mouse
Lesson 5: Making a Selection with the Keyboard
Lesson 6: Giving the Edit Undo Command
Lesson 7: Printing Text

This and the next five chapters show you how to enter and edit a variety of documents, from short memos to long reports. The lessons in this chapter use the sample business letter that you will type in the next section.

LESSON 1: TYPING IN THE FIRST FILE

Now that you know how to start Word, how to enter text, and a bit about giving Word commands, you are ready to type your first exercise, a business letter. Type it in using the rules you have learned so far. If you make mistakes, correct them with the BACKSPACE key or the DEL key. If you move the insertion mark around with the mouse or cursor keys, you will notice that when you type new text into Word, it always appears just to the left of the mark. Thus, if you want to add text to the middle of text that you have already entered, simply move the insertion mark to the desired location and type. (By the way, you should erase your practice sentence before you type in the letter.)

As you type the letter into Word, remember to press the ENTER key only at the end of each paragraph. Use the NEWLINE key (the SHIFT-ENTER combination) in the two addresses, and let Word form the other paragraphs with word-wrap. Don't be surprised if this feels a bit strange at first; you will find it more natural as you continue to use Word. Press ENTER twice to leave a blank line between the paragraphs (you will learn a better way in Chapter 8).

```
January 11, 1990

Chris Richford, Vice President
Manufacturer's Bank of the Northeast
1000 First Avenue
Millerton, CT  06492

Dear Ms. Richford:

I am pleased to send you the latest update on the results of our
expanded product line. The enclosed summary documents our
increased profit margin (7%) for the fourth quarter of 1989,
which is largely due to the successful introduction of our new
model, the DC50. In 1990 we expect to continue increasing our
profitable inroads into this new area.

As you can see, we are well within the projections we outlined to
you when you helped us obtain short-term financing. Thank you
again for all your assistance. If you have any questions
regarding this information, please feel free to call me.

Sincerely,


Thomas Mead, Controller
National Generators
1275 Oak Glen Industrial Park
Oak Glen,  CT  06410
```

LESSON 2: SAVING TEXT IN A FILE

Now that you have text that you want to keep, you need to know how to tell Word to save it in a file. To do this, you use the File Save As command. The Save As dialog lets you give a name to the file as well as specify the format that it should be saved in.

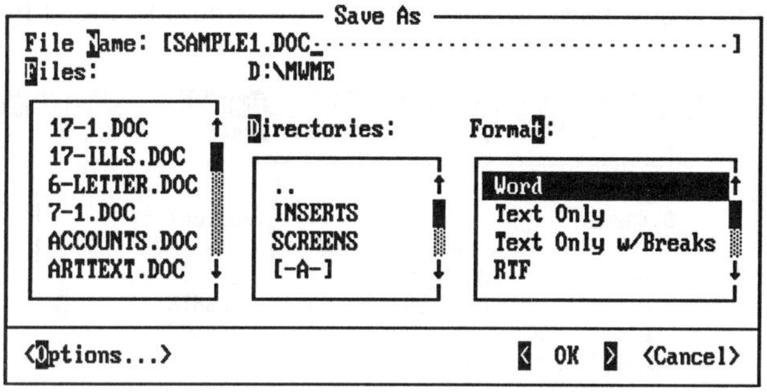

In the File Name text box, type **SAMPLE1** and press ENTER or click OK. Word saves the file on disk with the name SAMPLE1.DOC. Word prompts you for summary information. (You will learn more about this information in Chapter 19.) Press ESC or click Cancel. You can continue to edit the file if you wish, or you can leave Word with the File Exit command.

If you want to edit this file again later (which you will, since it is used in examples throughout the book), you will load it into memory with the File Open command. If you make editing changes in a file and you do not want to save those changes (for example, if you are experimenting with some of Word's commands and do not want to change the file on disk), use the File Exit command; when the command prompt asks if you want to save your changes, type N or click No.

LESSON 3: MOVING AROUND AND INSERTING TEXT

Word gives you many ways to move around in a file when you are editing. You can select any part of a file by using the mouse or cursor control keys. You can always tell where you are in a file by noting where the selection or insertion mark is.

You may recall that when you add letters to text, Word inserts them in front of the insertion mark. This means that everything to the right of what you type is moved ahead. If you want to type over text, that is, type characters over existing text (this is rare), press the INS key. The INS key is a *toggle,* which means that you press it once to turn on the overtyping feature and press it again to turn off the feature and resume inserting text. When you are in overtype mode, you see the letters "OT" near the lower-right side of the screen.

To start this lesson, move to the beginning of the SAMPLE1 file. If you have closed the file or quit Word since saving the file, open it with the File

Open command. The dialog for the File Open command looks like this:

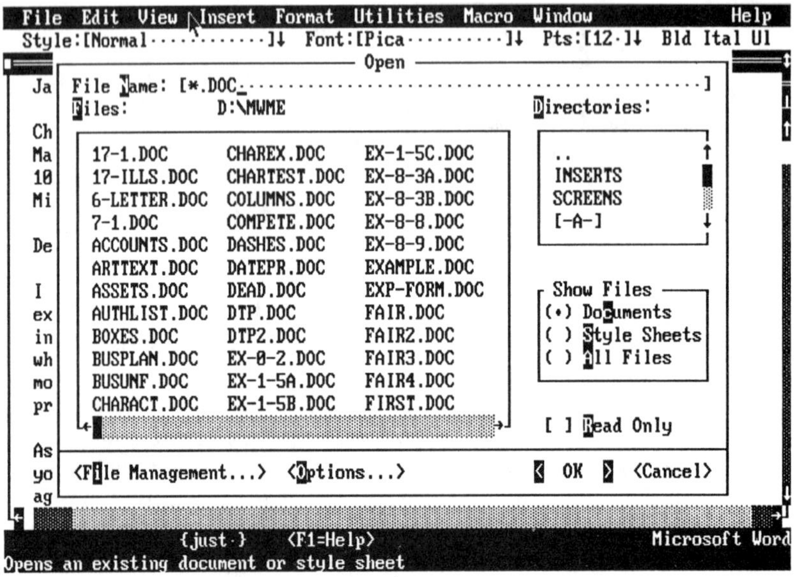

You can type in a file name or select the file from the list, then choose OK.

To get to the beginning of an open file, hold down the CTRL key and press HOME. Your screen should now look like this:

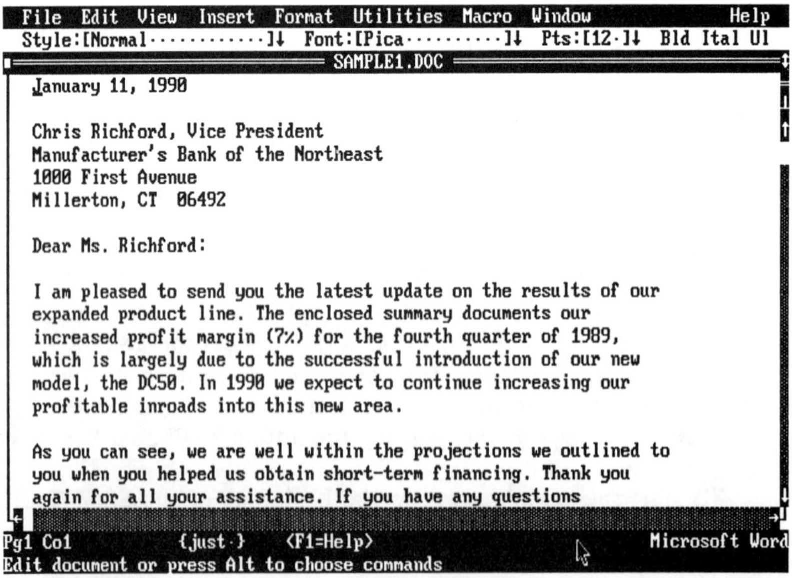

(Incidentally, to get to the end of the file, you use CTRL-END.)

As you saw in the last chapter, it is easy to change the selection by using the mouse and the arrow keys. Using the mouse, you simply move the pointer to the character you want and press the left button; using the keyboard, you simply press the ↑, ↓, ←, and → keys.

Moving Around with the Mouse

The right border of the screen is called the *scroll bar,* because you use it to move through your text with the mouse (scrolling is just a fancy word for moving). You use the scroll bar to move text up and down in the window. This is why the part of the screen that has your text is called a *window:* it is like a window over your long scroll of text, and you can only see what is in the window. The scroll bar has arrows at the top and bottom, a gray area between the arrows, and a black rectangle called a *thumb* (which appears as a white rectangle on the reversed screens in this book):

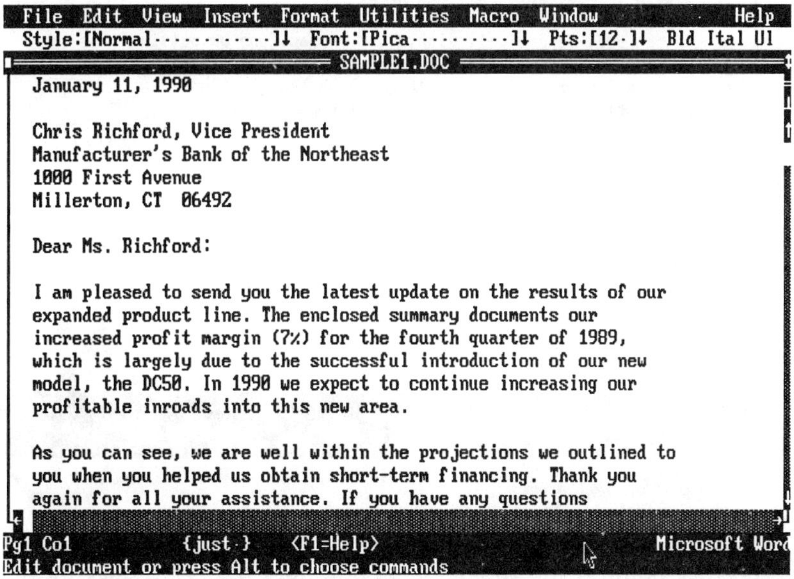
File Edit View Insert Format Utilities Macro Window Help
Style:[Normal············]↓ Font:[Pica··········]↓ Pts:[12·]↓ Bld Ital Ul
SAMPLE1.DOC
January 11, 1990

Chris Richford, Vice President
Manufacturer's Bank of the Northeast
1000 First Avenue
Millerton, CT 06492

Dear Ms. Richford:

I am pleased to send you the latest update on the results of our expanded product line. The enclosed summary documents our increased profit margin (7%) for the fourth quarter of 1989, which is largely due to the successful introduction of our new model, the DC50. In 1990 we expect to continue increasing our profitable inroads into this new area.

As you can see, we are well within the projections we outlined to you when you helped us obtain short-term financing. Thank you again for all your assistance. If you have any questions

Pg1 Co1 {just·} <F1=Help> Microsoft Word
Edit document or press Alt to choose commands

To see text that is off the bottom of the window, you click on the downward-pointing arrow at the bottom of the scroll bar. When you do this, the text scrolls up in the window. The longer you click on the downward-pointing arrow, the more text will scroll up. If you click and release quickly, only a few lines will scroll.

Word lets you scroll by more than just a single line at a time. To scroll down by a full page, click once in the gray area between the thumb and the downward-pointing arrow.

Notice that the thumb moves as you scroll using either method. The thumb indicates how far you are from the beginning of your document. When what you are viewing is close to the beginning of the file, the thumb is at the top of the scroll bar; when you are viewing the middle section of your document, the thumb is in the middle of the scroll bar; and so on. When you scroll page by page, you must point between the thumb and the arrow that is in the direction you want to go. Thus, if the thumb is in the middle of the scroll bar (the window you see is in the middle of your document) and you want to go up by a page, you click between the thumb and the upward-pointing arrow:

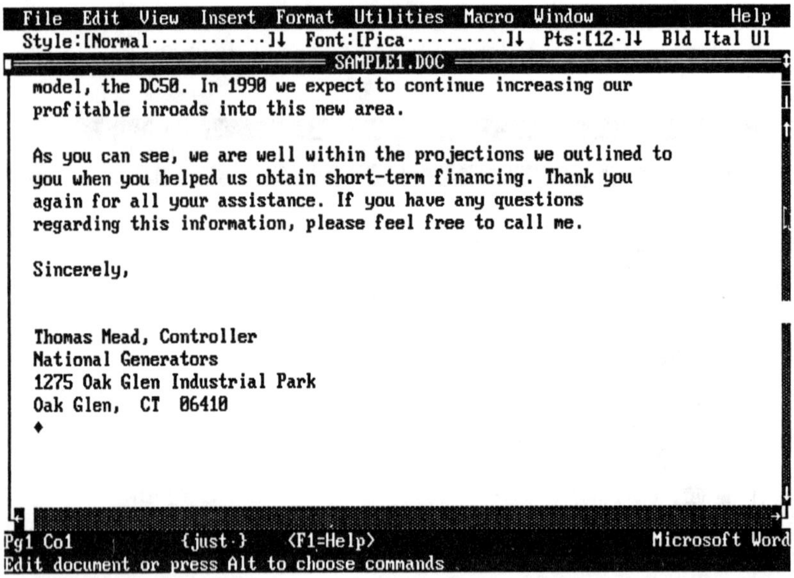

You can also use the thumb to go to a particular place in your document. To do this, point at the thumb, click and hold the left mouse button, and drag the thumb to the desired place. Thus, to get to the end of the document, click and drag the thumb to the bottom of the scroll bar. In long documents, you will find this to be especially useful if you know approximately where you want to look for text.

As you scroll through the text with the mouse, the insertion mark does not move; thus, you might not always see the selection on the screen when you move the text around. If you want to move the insertion mark to the screen that you are viewing, you do so in the normal way: point at the character and press the left button.

Moving Around with the Keyboard

Moving around your text with the keyboard is fairly easy, since the IBM PC's keys are already labeled for cursor movement. You have already seen how to move the insertion mark with the four arrow keys and how to use CTRL-HOME and CTRL-END. The HOME and END keys are used for moving to the beginning and end of the line that the insertion mark is currently on. CTRL-PGUP and CTRL-PGDN move the insertion mark to the beginning of the first or last line of the current screen but do not scroll the text.

You cannot move part of a page at a time or thumb through the text with the keyboard as you can with the mouse. However, you can move a full screen up and down with the PGUP and PGDN keys. You can also use the SCROLL LOCK key to cause Word to scroll line by line through your text with the ↑ and ↓ keys. Like the INS key, the SCROLL LOCK key is a toggle. When you first press SCROLL LOCK, Word displays the letters "SL" in the bottom line of the screen:

With the scroll lock on, each time you press the ↑ or ↓ key, the screen shifts one line. You use PGUP and PGDN to shift one page.

Table 1-1 shows the keys you use for moving the insertion mark.

LESSON 4: MAKING A SELECTION WITH THE MOUSE

As you saw in the last chapter, the Edit Cut command always deletes the entire selection. There are other commands that edit and format the selec-

Key	Where Moved
←	Previous letter
→	Next letter
↑	Previous line
↓	Next line
CTRL-←	Beginning of previous word
CTRL-→	Beginning of next word
CTRL-↑	Beginning of previous paragraph
CTRL-↓	Beginning of next paragraph
HOME	Beginning of current line
END	End of current line
CTRL-PGUP	Beginning of current screen
CTRL-PGDN	End of current screen
PGUP	Previous screen
PGDN	Next screen
CTRL-HOME	Beginning of file
CTRL-END	End of file
SCROLL LOCK	Line-by-line scrolling (toggle)

TABLE 1-1. Cursor Control Keys Used to Move the Selection

tion; these commands are covered throughout the book. Word lets you make six different kinds of selections with the mouse so you can edit or format the text: no selection (just the insertion mark), a word, a sentence, a line, a paragraph, and the entire document. If you want to select a variable amount of text, a portion of text not included in the six choices (several words but not a sentence, several sentences but not a paragraph, several paragraphs but not an entire document), you can make selections of varying lengths depending on your purpose.

You already saw in the last chapter how to select a word and a sentence using the right button and both buttons. To review the steps, point at any letter in the word "update" in the first sentence of the letter. Press the left button to set the insertion mark, press the right button to select the entire word, and press both buttons together to select the entire sentence.

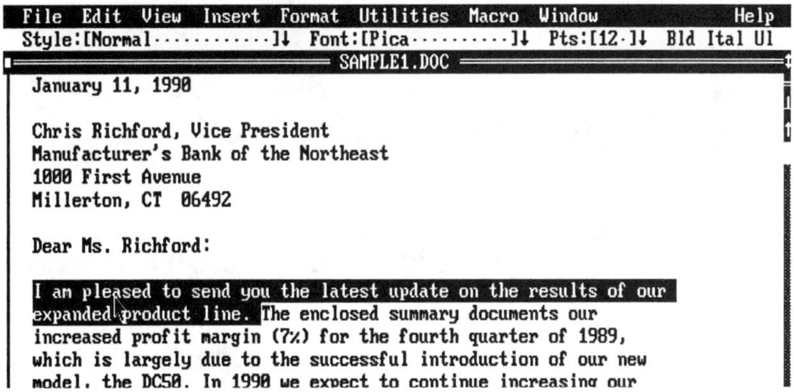

To select larger areas of text, move the mouse pointer into the *selection bar,* the blank column between the left edge of the window and the text. When you point to the selection bar, the arrow changes and points up and to the right. For example, point to the selection bar on the line beginning with "which."

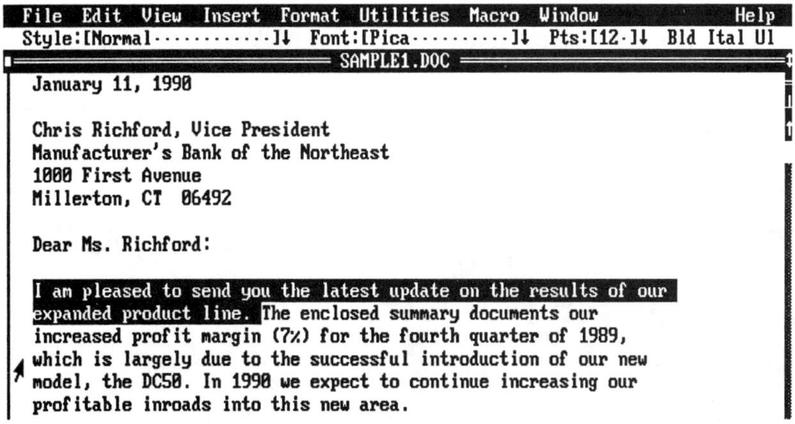

The mouse buttons now have different functions. Pressing the left button selects the entire line, pressing the right button selects the entire paragraph, and pressing both buttons together selects the entire document. Experiment with each of these choices.

None of these choices may be exactly what you want, however. For example, assume that you want to delete the phrase "regarding this information" in the second text paragraph. To do this, you hold down the left button while pointing at the first character you want to select, and while holding the button down, move the mouse to the end of the desired selection. Notice that as you move the pointer, the selection indicator stretches.

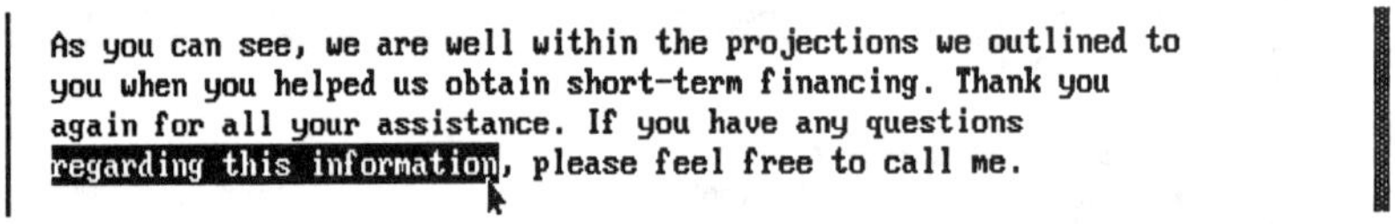

You can stretch the selection indicator in either direction. Thus, you can start either at the beginning (the "r" in "regarding") or at the end (the "n" in "information") of the selection you want.

You can select any text on the screen with this method; however, the text must be a connected group of words. To select text on the line that precedes or follows the line you started on, simply move the mouse up or down, always holding down the left button. Again, this may take a bit of practice; at first you will sometimes move the mouse farther than you want. This is fine, however, since you can simply move back to your intended position.

If the text that you want to select is not completely on the screen, you can extend the selection by scrolling the screen. To do this, start your selection and briefly bring the pointer into the upper or lower screen border. Word then scrolls the screen by a few lines, and you can continue to modify your selection. Sometimes Word scrolls more than you expect, especially on fast PCs, so using this method may be a bit tricky.

Spend some time experimenting with different methods of selecting varying amounts of text. Remember that you can always select a portion of text by starting at either end and moving the mouse to cover the whole portion.

LESSON 5: MAKING A SELECTION WITH THE KEYBOARD

You can use ALT-F6, ALT-F8, and ALT-F10 to select a portion of text. These keys allow you almost as much flexibility as the mouse.

ALT-F6 selects the word to the right of the current selection. Pressing the key many times moves the word-long selection indicator throughout the text. ALT-F8 selects the sentence that the selection indicator is currently in; pressing repeatedly moves the sentence-long selection indicator to the right.

ALT-F10 selects the current paragraph, and pressing it again moves the selection indicator up to the next paragraph.

You can make selections with the movement keys you saw earlier in this chapter by holding down the SHIFT key. For example, if the insertion mark is under a letter, to select that letter and the next two letters, hold down the SHIFT key and press the → key three times. To extend the selection down one line, press SHIFT-↓.

If you want to select a variable amount of text, you must be able to extend a selection to include it. To do this with the keyboard, you use the F8 key, which toggles the selection extension. When you press F8, notice that the letters "EX" appear in the bottom line of the screen. The letters "EX" tell you that if you move the selection indicator, it will stretch as you move until you press ESC to turn the toggle off.

For example, assume that you want to select the phrase "regarding this information" in the second text paragraph. Move the selection to the "r" in "regarding," and then press F8. Now use either the → or CTRL-→ to stretch the selection indicator. Experiment with this, moving with both the cursor control keys and the function keys just described.

You can also use the F8 key to select units of text by pressing it repeatedly. The second time you press it, Word selects the current word. The third time Word selects the sentence, then the paragraph, then the entire document.

LESSON 6: GIVING THE EDIT UNDO COMMAND

Now that you know how to select any text you want, you can experiment with the File Cut command and the DEL key by selecting different amounts of text. With some word processors, when you delete information it is gone forever. With Word, however, you can use the Edit Undo command to restore text that has been deleted with the BACKSPACE key, the DEL key, or the File Cut command.

The Edit Undo command restores your text to the way it was before your last edit. For example, if you select a paragraph of text and then delete it with the DEL key, you can use the Edit Undo command to bring the paragraph back, even if you have moved to a new selection.

note The Edit Undo command only works to restore the last editing command that you have given (such as giving the Edit Cut or Edit Copy command or pressing BACKSPACE a few times) and cannot restore earlier edits.

The Edit Undo command can also undo your last Edit Undo command. This may seem strange, but it is useful if you are not sure that you want to restore an edit you have made. For example, if you delete a sentence but are not sure that you deleted the correct sentence, you can undo the deletion, and if it turns out that you did delete the correct sentence, simply give the Edit Undo command again.

To experiment with the Edit Undo command, delete the date from the letter:

```
 File  Edit  View  Insert  Format  Utilities  Macro  Window              Help
 Style:[Normal············]↓  Font:[Pica··········]↓  Pts:[12·]↓  Bld Ital Ul
=========================== SAMPLE1.DOC ======================================

  Chris Richford, Vice President
  Manufacturer's Bank of the Northeast
  1000 First Avenue
  Millerton, CT  06492
```

Now give the Edit Undo command or press ALT-BACKSPACE, and the date is restored:

```
 File  Edit  View  Insert  Format  Utilities  Macro  Window              Help
 Style:[Normal············]↓  Font:[Pica··········]↓  Pts:[12·]↓  Bld Ital Ul
=========================== SAMPLE1.DOC ======================================
  January 11, 1990

  Chris Richford, Vice President
  Manufacturer's Bank of the Northeast
  1000 First Avenue
  Millerton, CT  06492
```

As you will see in later chapters, you can use the Edit Undo command to reverse a number of different editing commands. You may find it to be a safety net at a critical moment. Remember, however, that Edit Undo can only restore your last edit; anything done before that cannot be undone.

LESSON 7: PRINTING TEXT

Normally, the primary purpose of word processing is to obtain a finished printed document. At this point you have learned the basics of using Word to input and edit a document. Now that you have edited your text, you may want to see it on a printed page.

To print the file that you are editing, use the File Printer Setup and File Print commands. The File Printer Setup command lets you tell Word what type of printer you are using and how that printer is attached to your PC. The File Print command actually sends the file to the printer.

When you give the File Printer Setup command, you see a dialog similar to this:

```
┌────────────────────────── Printer Setup ──────────────────────────────┐
│Printer File: [POSTSCRP.PRD_·····]  Printer Name:                      │
│Files:                                                                 │
│ ┌──────────────────┐  D:\WORD55        ┌─────────────────────────┐    │
│ │POSTSCRP.PRD     ↑│                   │Standard                ↑│    │
│ │TTY.PRD          █│  Directories:     │                        █│    │
│ │                  │  ┌────────────┐   │                        ↓│    │
│ │                  │  │..         ↑│   └─────────────────────────┘    │
│ │                  │  │[-A-]      █│  Connect to: [COM1:···········]↓ │
│ │                  │  │[-B-]       │  Paper Feed: [Continuous·······]↓│
│ │                  │  │[-C-]       │  Graphics Resolution: [········]↓│
│ │                  │  │[-D-]       │                                  │
│ │                 ↓│  │           ↓│  [ ] Use Print Queue             │
│ └──────────────────┘  └────────────┘  [ ] Skip Downloading Fonts      │
├───────────────────────────────────────────────────────────────────────┤
│                                            < OK >   <Cancel>          │
└───────────────────────────────────────────────────────────────────────┘
```

These choices are covered in detail in Chapter 11; you are only concerned with the first one "Printer File," which selects the type of printer you are using.

The printers that Word knows how to use are listed in the *Word Printer Information* manual. If you have one of the printers listed, Word can use some of the special features that the printer offers (such as proportional spacing and subscripts). If you have a printer that is not listed, you can still use many of Word's formatting features; in fact, if you try to use a formatting feature that is not available on your printer, Word will make its best effort to do what you want, instead of giving you an error message.

The "Printer File" choice tells Word which *printer driver* to use. A printer driver is a special subprogram that tells Word how to talk with your printer. If you have looked at the directory of your Printer Disks, you may have noticed many files with the extension " .PRD." These are the printer drivers. You can tell which printer each file is for by the file name.

Word's default choice for a printer driver is TTY.PRD. TTY is an acronym for a technical term (teletypewriter) meaning "any old printer." If you do not have a printer that Word knows about, you should use this driver. If you have a printer that is listed in the manual, you should copy the corresponding .PRD file to the disk where you run Word and type in its name here (you don't need to do that for this lesson, since every printer can be used with TTY).

If you have the correct .PRD file somewhere on your disk, you can type in its name now. Choose the desired driver name from the list. Click on OK or press ENTER to finish the File Printer Setup command.

Give the File Print command or press SHIFT-F9. The File Print dialog looks like:

```
                          Print
Standard PostScript on COM1:                  (POSTSCRP.PRD)
============================================================
Print:  [Document·······]↓   To
Copies: [1_·············]    (•) Printer
Paper Feed: [Continuous·]↓   ( ) File: [·············]

Page Range: [All········]↓  Pages: [··················]

<Printer Setup...>  <Options...>        < OK >  <Cancel>
```

All of the default choices listed are probably fine, so click on OK or press ENTER to print your document.

Be sure that your printer is turned on and that it is properly connected to your computer. To print your text, execute the Printer choice in the main Printer menu, and the file is printed. If you want to stop the printer, press the ESC key. It may take awhile for the printer to stop printing.

REVIEW

1. *Saving and loading your text in a file*
   If you forget the name of the file you want to load, how can you request a list of files on disk? Name the steps (for both mouse and keyboard) for opening a file called ORDER.DOC.
2. *Moving and making selections*
   What are the six types of selections you can make with the mouse, and how do you make them? How do you extend a selection with the keyboard?

REVIEW (*continued*)

3. *Thumbing with the mouse*
   How do you use the mouse to go directly to the beginning of a file? To the end? To the middle?

4. *Recovering text*
   Which of the following actions can be reversed with the Edit Undo command?

   a. Going to the end of the file

   b. Deleting a phrase

   c. Changing a letter from lower- to uppercase

   d. Selecting a sentence

5. *Simple printing*
   What should you do before giving the File Print command?

chapter 2

MOVING AND COPYING TEXT

Lesson 8: Moving Text Within a Document
Lesson 9: Copying Text Within a Document
Lesson 10: Speed Copying and Moving

So far you have learned how to enter text, how to move the selection, and how to use the Edit Cut command and the DEL key to remove text from a document. This chapter explains how to use the Edit Cut and Edit Paste commands to move text from one part of a file to another and to make many copies of a piece of text in your file.

The ability to move sections of text is one of the most useful features of word processing. For instance, you may decide after writing a report that you want to change the order of paragraphs or sentences. Since you can rearrange your ideas after seeing them on paper or on the screen, your finished writing will be much better organized. In the next lesson, you will see that moving text is easy to do with Word.

LESSON 8: MOVING TEXT WITHIN A DOCUMENT

To temporarily delete selected text so that it can be moved, you use the Edit Cut command or press the SHIFT-DEL key on the keyboard. When you use the Edit Cut command, a pair of curly braces appears at the bottom of the screen. The braces contain what you deleted, or at least the beginning and end of what you deleted.

For example, select the word "well" in the second paragraph of the SAMPLE1 letter and delete it with the Edit Cut command. Notice that the bottom line of the screen now shows the following:

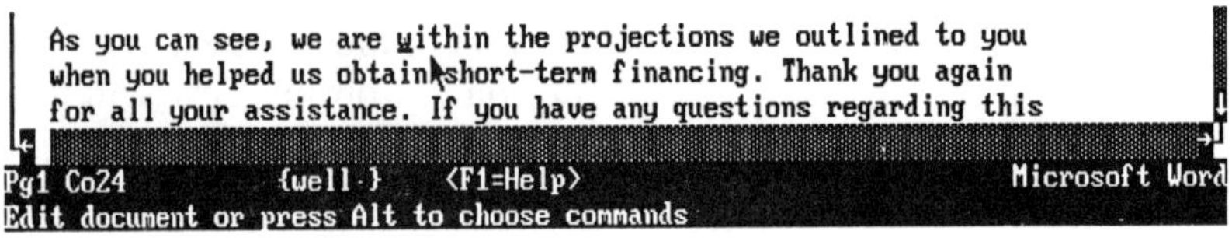

The curly braces indicate the contents of the *scrap,* which is a place where Word holds the last text you deleted. You can imagine the scrap as a holder for the chunk of text that you deleted last; every time you use the Edit Cut or Edit Copy command, the contents of the scrap are wiped out and replaced with the new text. Thus, if you now select another word in the SAMPLE1 file and delete it, afterward you will see that the scrap no longer contains the word "well." When the text no longer appears in the scrap, you cannot use the Edit Undo command to restore it.

If you delete more than eight characters at once, a few of the first and last characters will be shown in the scrap with ellipses (...) between them. For instance, give the Edit Undo command to restore the word "well" in the second paragraph; then select the entire first sentence of the paragraph. Delete the sentence, and the scrap will show something like the following:

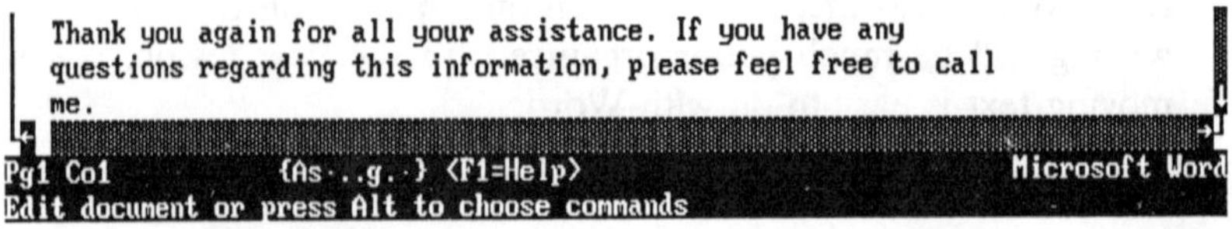

Use the Edit Undo command to restore the sentence.

Note that deleting characters with the BACKSPACE key does not put the characters in the scrap; only the Edit Cut command and the Edit Copy command (described later) put text there. However, you can still use the Edit Undo command to restore text erased with the BACKSPACE key.

The Edit Paste command copies the contents of the scrap to the current position of the insertion mark. The quickest way to give the Edit Paste command is from the keyboard: you simply press SHIFT-INS. If you give the Edit Paste command when text has been selected, the new text will go before the first letter in the selection.

You may be able to guess how you can move text from one part of a file to another: first select and cut the text you want to move, move to the position where you want the text, and use the Edit Paste command. For instance, try switching the second and third sentences of the second paragraph. To do this, select the third sentence by pointing at a character in the sentence and pressing both buttons, or by pressing the F8 key three times. Now delete the sentence with the Edit Cut command.

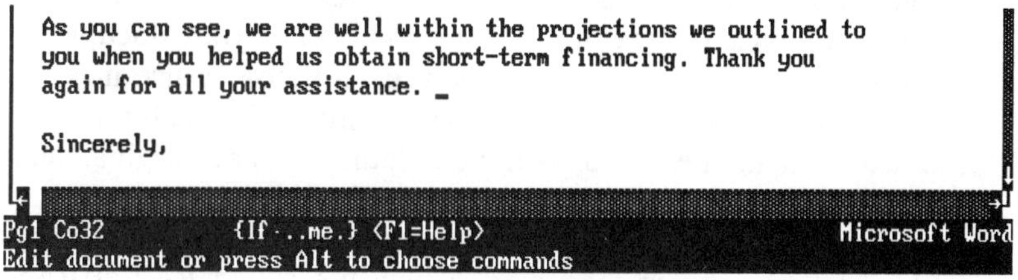

Now move the insertion mark to the beginning of the second sentence and give the Edit Paste command. Add a space between the sentences.

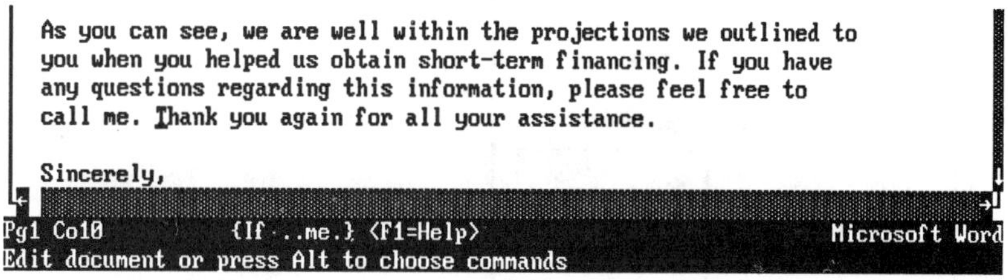

Notice that Word automatically reformats the paragraph for you.

This is the way that you most often use the scrap. Since it can hold any amount of information, you can use it to move large portions of your text.

This is also a convenient method for moving phrases around in a sentence to see different effects on sound and meaning. Practice moving text around in your file using the scrap.

Note the important difference between the Edit Cut command and the DEL key. The Edit Cut command (SHIFT-DEL) deletes to the scrap; the DEL key deletes text but doesn't move it to the scrap. Thus, you should only use the DEL key when you are sure you don't want to reinsert the text.

LESSON 9: COPYING TEXT WITHIN A DOCUMENT

The scrap is also useful for making copies of parts of your text. Although copying text is not as common as moving text, you may find that you need to use one sentence or line of text over and over in your document. If you copy the text, you will not have to retype it each time you use it.

To copy text, you use the Edit Copy command, which puts the contents of the selection in the scrap without deleting it. The original text remains in your document, and a copy of it appears in the scrap.

Before beginning the following example, you should stop editing the SAMPLE1 file and instead start a new file called PATTERNS. To do so, give the File New command. Word displays this:

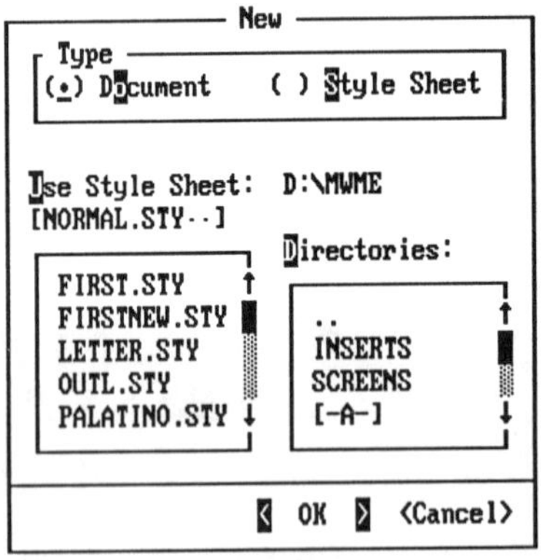

The defaults in this dialog are what you want, so click on OK or press ENTER. The screen now shows the two files open in two overlapping windows:

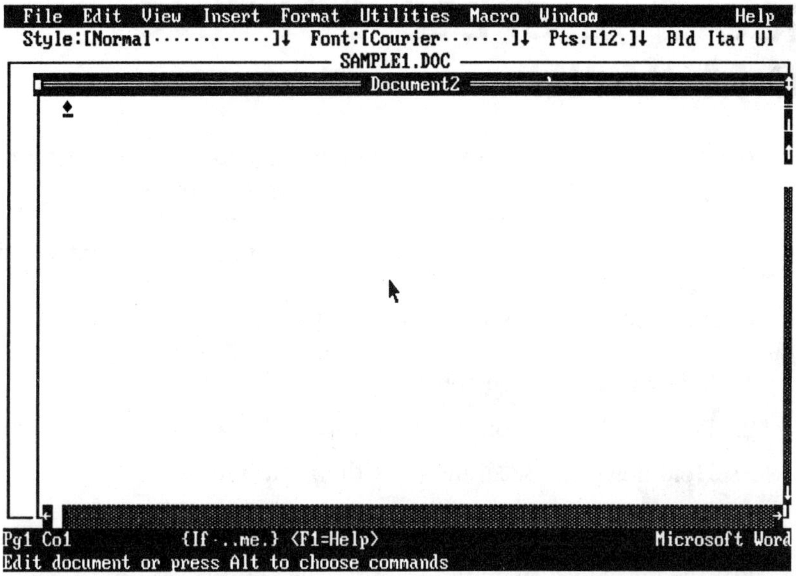

The new window is on top of the first one, leaving only a small portion of the first window visible at the top and left of the screen. Chapter 4 explains more about how to use two windows. For now, you can ignore the SAMPLE1 window in the back.

Now you can begin the copy operation. First type in five asterisks (*****), press ENTER, and then select the asterisks (excluding the paragraph marker):

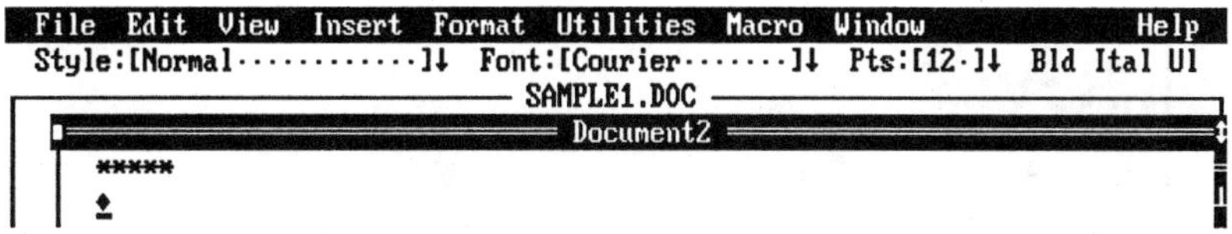

Use the Edit Copy command to copy these to the scrap; then press SHIFT-INS five times or give the Edit Paste command five times. You have quickly made a line of 30 asterisks. Now select the whole line, copy it to the scrap, and press SHIFT-INS five times again. As you can see, this is much easier than typing 180 asterisks.

You won't often need to copy text from one part of a document to another. You might find the ability to do so useful, however, in transcribing a song with repeated lyrics in a chorus, and in similar instances. You will also see its use in Chapter 4, where you will copy text from one file to another.

LESSON 10: SPEED COPYING AND MOVING

If you are using a mouse, you can move and copy text without using the scrap. Word calls this *speed copying* and *speed moving.* You may want to use speed copying and moving instead of the methods shown earlier in this chapter for greater speed or if there is text in the scrap that you do not want to change.

Speed copying consists of three steps:

1. Select the text to be copied.
2. Point to the position where you want the copied text to be inserted.
3. Hold down CTRL-SHIFT and click the right button.

Speed moving is similar to speed copying; the only difference is that you use just the CTRL key instead of both the CTRL and the SHIFT key.

1. Select the text to be moved.
2. Point to the position where you want the selected text to appear.
3. Hold down the CTRL key and click the right button.

REVIEW

1. The scrap

Where are the contents of the scrap shown on the screen? What commands put text into the scrap?

2. Moving text

State the steps needed to move the first three words from the beginning to the end of the following sentence:

Over the years, she became less tolerant of noisy neighbors.

REVIEW *(continued)*

3. *Copying text*
   Describe a fast way to make the following picture:

chapter 3

SEARCHING AND REPLACING

Lesson 11: Searching for Text
Lesson 12: Replacing Text
Lesson 13: Using Special Characters in Search and Replace

You can use the mouse or keyboard to move the selection indicator up, down, left, or right. If you know where you want to go (for example, "about 20 lines down" or "to the end of the file"), there are ways of quickly moving around your text. However, you will often want to move the selection indicator to a specific word or phrase. Instead of searching visually for the phrase, you can move exactly where you want with one command, the Edit Search command.

Searching has many uses other than simply moving to a certain word or phrase. For instance, you can find the first occurrence of a particular word by moving to the beginning of a document and then searching for the word. You can review your text to see whether you defined new terms when they first appeared. Since you can also search for groups of words, you can easily check for phrases that you may have overused.

LESSON 11: SEARCHING FOR TEXT

The Edit Search command quickly moves the selection indicator to the first instance of a word or phrase. The movement is always relative to your current position in a file; for example, if you are in the middle of a file and search for the word "invoice," Word will find the next occurrence of "invoice" that appears in the text.

Open the SAMPLE1 file again, move to the beginning of the file, and give the Edit Search command. The dialog is:

```
                         Search
Text to Search for:
[_..............................................]
                                        Direction
[ ] Whole Word                          ( ) Up
[ ] Match Upper/Lowercase               (•) Down

<Search for Formatting Only...>  < OK >  <Cancel>
```

Enter the word **please** and press the ENTER key or click OK (as before, you can first correct errors in the text to be searched with the BACKSPACE key). The selection indicator will jump to the first instance of the word "please" in the letter, which in this case is in the word "pleased."

If you want to search for the same word or phrase again, you do not need to retype it. Give the Edit Search command again, and notice that the text line is already filled in with your last choice.

```
                         Search
Text to Search for:
[please_........................................]
                                        Direction
[ ] Whole Word                          ( ) Up
[ ] Match Upper/Lowercase               (•) Down

<Search for Formatting Only...>  < OK >  <Cancel>
```

To find the next instance of the word "please," simply execute the command again.

The Edit Search command's three choices are very easy to understand.

- The "Whole Word" choice indicates whether you want Word to restrict your search to isolated words. If you select this, and the text you are searching for is "the," Word will not stop if it finds "they." Thus, not selecting this tells Word to stop even if the text you are searching for is part of another word.

- For "Match Uppercase/Lowercase," you must decide if Word should pay attention to whether the letters in the text line are upper- or lowercase. Not selecting this, the default, causes Word to ignore case, meaning that Word will not notice the difference between upper- and lowercase letters as it searches the text. Selecting this is more restrictive: the text must be an exact match of the word or phrase on the text line, including capital letters. Thus, if you select the case choice and you are searching for "the," Word will not stop when it finds "The."

- The "Direction" choice indicates whether you want to search forward (Down) or backward (Up) in the text.

Word remembers the last setting for each of these choices whenever you use the Edit Search command. For example, if you select the case choice, the next time you give the Edit Search command it will still be selected.

To see how to use the three choices, move to the beginning of the second paragraph and give the Edit Search command. Enter the word **you** as the word to search for, and change the direction from Down to Up.

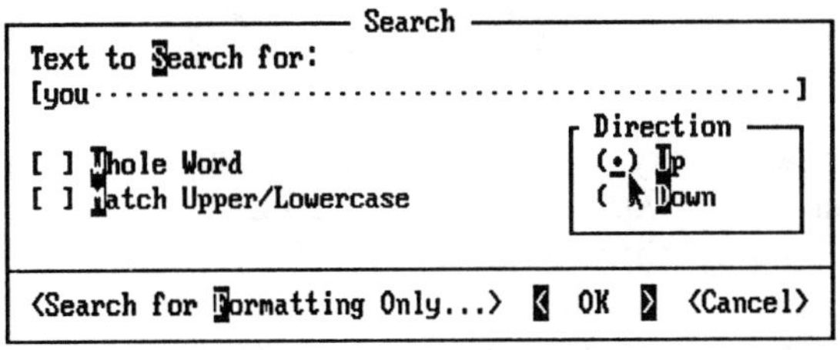

When you execute the command, the word "you" in the first paragraph is selected.

Move the selection to the beginning of the file again. Give the Edit Search command again and change the text line to **As** (with a capital "A"), the direction to "Down," and select the case option.

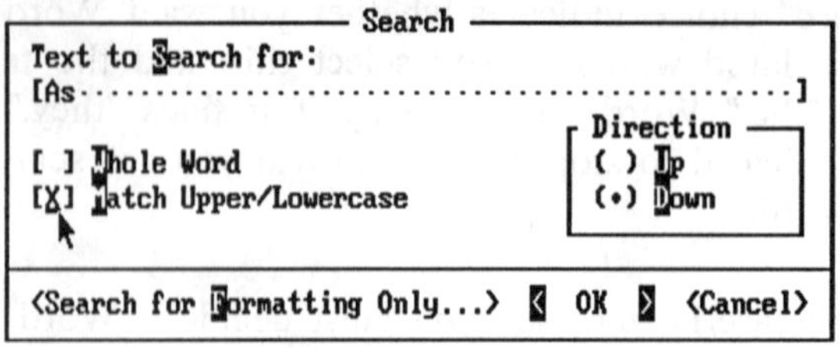

When you execute the command, the word "As" at the beginning of the second paragraph is selected; if you had not changed the case to "Yes," the "as" in the word "increased" in the first paragraph would have been found first.

To see the effect of the whole word option, move to the beginning of the file, give the Edit Search command again, and change the text line to **as**. Select the whole word option, and unselect the case option. When you execute the command, Word will skip over the "as" in "pleased" and go directly to "As" in the second paragraph.

The text that you search for can have up to 40 characters. It can also include special characters, which are discussed at the end of this chapter. If Word finds the text, it is selected. If the text does not appear in the file, Word displays a message and does not move the selection indicator.

LESSON 12: REPLACING TEXT

It is common to replace every instance of a particular word or phrase in a document with some other word or phrase. For example, you may want to change "pleased" to "happy" throughout a letter. Or you may need to change many (but not all) instances of a person's name to another name. You may also want to replace a wordy phrase with a more concise one throughout a document.

Word's Edit Replace command lets you change all instances of one word or phrase to another. You can also have Word show you each instance of the phrase you want to change and then choose whether or not to change it, based on its context.

The Edit Replace command gives you choices similar to those of the Edit Search command. For instance, go back to the top of the file, give the Edit Replace command, and enter **pleased** for "Text to Search for" and **happy** for "Replace with."

```
------------------ Replace ------------------
Text to Search for:
[pleased·····································]

Replace with:
[happy·······································]

[ ] Whole Word                  [X] Confirm Changes
[ ] Match Upper/Lowercase

<Replace Formatting Only...>      < OK >  <Cancel>
```

Note that the direction choice from the Edit Search dialog is gone; the Edit Replace command always moves forward (Down).

The menu also includes a "Confirm Changes" choice. If you unselect this choice, Word simply replaces each occurrence of the specified word or phrase without asking for confirmation. If you select the confirm choice, Word stops at each word to be replaced and gives you three choices. Click "Yes" to indicate that you want to make the replacement for the current selection, or "No" to indicate that you do not. If you want to stop replacing, press the ESC key or click "Cancel."

As you might guess, the Edit Replace command can ease the job of changing many items in a long file. For instance, if one person is mentioned repeatedly throughout a long memo and that person has changed jobs within the company, you may have to change many instances of the person's name. The Edit Replace command allows you to do this with just one command. If the person's name needs to be changed in many, but not all, instances, the confirm choice lets you look through the file easily.

If you do not select the case choice when replacing text, Word will intelligently choose how to replace the letters. For instance, if you choose to change "airplane" to "boat" with no case requirement and Word finds the word "Airplane," it will replace it with "Boat," since this is most likely what you would want. Word's rule is that words with initial- or all-capital letters (Airplane or AIRPLANE) are replaced with corresponding capital letters (Boat or BOAT).

LESSON 13: USING SPECIAL CHARACTERS IN SEARCH AND REPLACE

Word searches for the exact text you specify in the Edit Search and Edit Replace commands. However, there are times when you will want Word to search for less specific text. The Edit Search and Edit Replace commands allow you to include special characters in order to make your search more broad. There are two classes of special characters: the *question mark* and *caret characters.*

If Word sees a question mark in the text you tell it to search for, it will assume that any character can match it. (If you are familiar with "wildcard" characters in MS-DOS file names, this is identical to the question mark used there.) For example, if you search for "f?r," Word will stop when it finds "far," "for," "fur," and so on. The question mark indicates that any character at all (even numbers and punctuation marks) can be in the position you indicate.

You may also want to search for characters that are special to Word but that you cannot normally enter in the Edit Search or Edit Replace command. For instance, you may want to find the word "The" preceded by a TAB character. Since you can't normally enter a TAB character as text to search for (Word will think you want to move to the next choice of the Edit Search command), you need a way to indicate that you want to search for the TAB character. This is done with a caret character.

Caret characters are special characters that you precede with a caret mark (^). The caret characters are shown in Table 3-1.

Character	Meaning
^s	A nonbreaking space
^t	A TAB character
^p	A paragraph marker
^n	A NEWLINE character (SHIFT-ENTER)
^d	A section or page marker (described in Chapter 7)
^w	White space; this is any number of spaces, tabs, paragraph marks, NEWLINE characters, section markers, and page-break characters
^-	A nonrequired hyphen
^^	A caret character (^)

TABLE 3-1. The Caret Characters

note Notice that you use two characters, the caret and the character indicated. A caret character is not a control character.

To search for the word "me," followed by a paragraph marker and the word "Now," the search text would be as follows:

```
─────────────────── Search ──────────────────────
Text to Search for:
[me^pNow_·····································]
                                      ┌ Direction ─┐
[ ] Whole Word                        │ ( ) Up      │
[ ] Match Upper/Lowercase             │ (•) Down    │
                                      └─────────────┘
─────────────────────────────────────────────────
<Search for Formatting Only...> < OK > <Cancel>
```

In the Edit Replace command, you can enter any of the listed special characters in the blank for "with text" except the question mark and "^w." If you use a question mark, it is actually inserted there; if you use a "^w," it is replaced with a "w."

For instance, if your text contains the words "Mr. Chen" with a nonbreaking space and you want to replace it with a normal space, you would give the command this way:

```
─────────────────── Replace ─────────────────────
Text to Search for:
[Mr.^sChen·····································]

Replace with:
[Mr. Chen_·····································]

[ ] Whole Word                  [X] Confirm Changes
[ ] Match Upper/Lowercase
─────────────────────────────────────────────────
<Replace Formatting Only...>     < OK > <Cancel>
```

REVIEW

1. *Finding text*
   Assume that you are in the middle of a long report. How would you find the second occurrence of the phrase "not profitable" before your current position? How would you find the next occurrence of the phrase "From the preceding" at the beginning of a sentence?

2. *Changing phrases throughout a file*
   You have decided to change all instances of the word "buy out" to "takeover" in a memo. What should you consider before using the Edit Replace command?

3. *Searching with special characters*
   You are sure that you used the word "fundamentally" somewhere in a long memo, but the Edit Search command does not find it. What should you try next?

chapter 4

USING WORD'S WINDOWS

Lesson 14: Using Two Panes in One Window
Lesson 15: Using Two Windows in Two Files
Lesson 16: Moving and Resizing Windows
Lesson 17: Maximizing Windows
Lesson 18: Using Vertical Windows

Word's use of windows will probably save you more time than any of its other editing features. As discussed in "Getting Started," a window is a view of a file that you are editing. Many word processors have only one window, the full screen, so you can view only one part of a document at a time. Word, however, can give you simultaneous views of different parts of one file or simultaneous views of different files.

Up to now you have used only one window in Word. You can easily split the large window into smaller, independent panes. A *pane* is part of a window. Panes always show parts of the same document.

You can edit text in any pane or window you choose. You can also open many independent windows to different files and easily move from window to window. At first this may seem like a feature that only advanced users would want; however, it is likely that you can now start using panes and windows in your everyday editing and find a number of different uses that meet your particular needs.

For instance, if you are editing the top of a letter and want to look at some information near the bottom, you do not need to take your attention away from either part if you split your window into two panes. If you are writing a memo and need to look at a report you wrote earlier, you can use one window for the memo and another window for the report.

LESSON 14: USING TWO PANES IN ONE WINDOW

To see how two panes can greatly help editing one document, start Word normally with one window on the SAMPLE1 file. You can now split the window horizontally to get two views of the file. When you are looking at two parts of one file, it is common to make a horizontal split about halfway down the screen.

Splitting Windows with the Mouse

Notice the double horizontal line near the top of the vertical scroll bar. To split the window into two panes, point at this double horizontal line, click and hold down the left mouse button, and drag it down to the place where you want the border between the two parts of the window to be. For example, to make a horizontal split, drag the double line down to near the middle of the document.

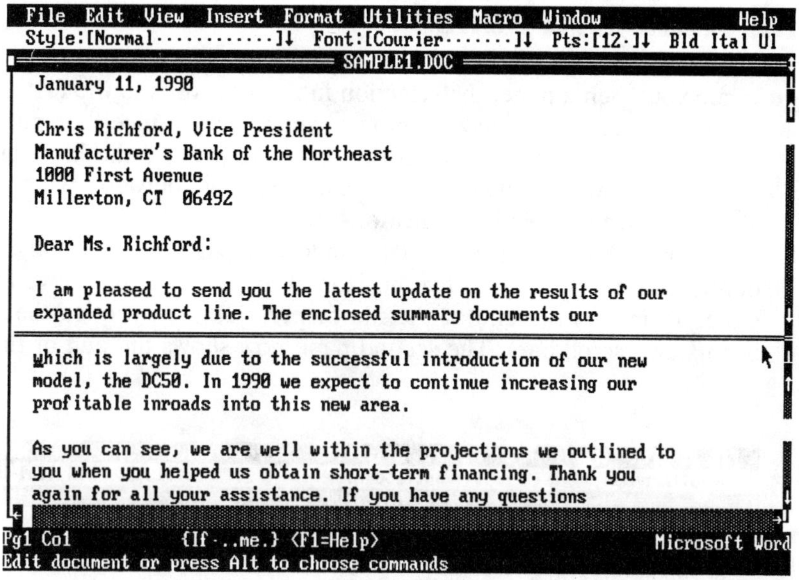

To close a pane (that is, "unsplit" the window), point at the double horizontal line, click and hold down the left mouse button, and drag it up to the top row of the window. When you release the mouse button, only the bottom pane remains. If you want only the top pane to remain, drag the line to the bottom of the window instead. You can also double-click on the arrow icon at the right edge of the double horizontal line to unsplit the window.

Splitting Windows with the Keyboard

Use the Window Split command to make two panes out of the window containing the selection indicator. You then use the ↑ and ↓ cursor control keys to drag the split line to the place you want. When you have selected the location you want for the split, press the ENTER key.

To close a pane (that is, "unsplit" the window), give the Window Split command again, and move the split line up to the top row of the window. When you press ENTER, only the bottom pane remains. If you want only the top pane to remain, move the line to the bottom of the window instead.

Editing with Two Panes

When you open a pane, the selection indicator moves to the first character of the new pane. If you have a mouse, simply point to either pane, and the selection indicator will move to that pane. If you use the keyboard, press F6 or SHIFT-F6 to switch between panes. As you move between panes, Word will always move the selection indicator.

The text that you view in each window or pane can be changed independently. For example, open two horizontal panes again and move to the lower pane. Thumb to the end of the file or press CTRL-END (notice that each pane has its own scroll bar). The second pane now shows the end of the file.

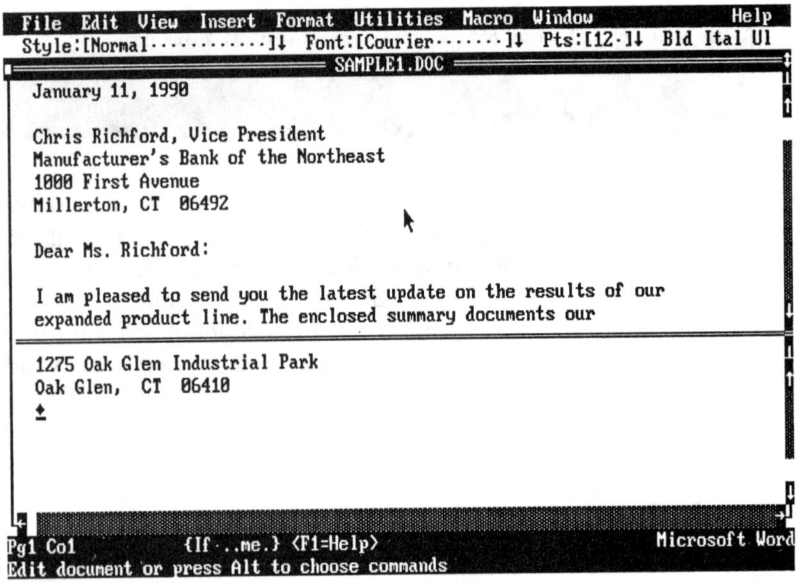

Now move to the beginning of the file in the lower pane so both panes show the same text. Jump back to the top pane and after the line "1000 First Avenue," add the line **Suite 120** and notice that the second pane is updated almost simultaneously.

Windows and panes can be used independently. You can also use the Edit Search command to find specific information in one window without losing your place in the other.

The Edit Copy, Edit Cut, and Edit Paste commands become even more powerful when they are used with multiple windows, since you can use the scrap to move text from one window to another without losing your place in either part of the file. This lets you instantly see the results of moving text as you perform the commands.

For instance, you might want to see the effect of adding "From" and the sender's name to the top of the letter. You can do this easily by viewing the beginning of the letter in one window and the end of the letter in the other window.

With the window split into two panes, position the text as follows:

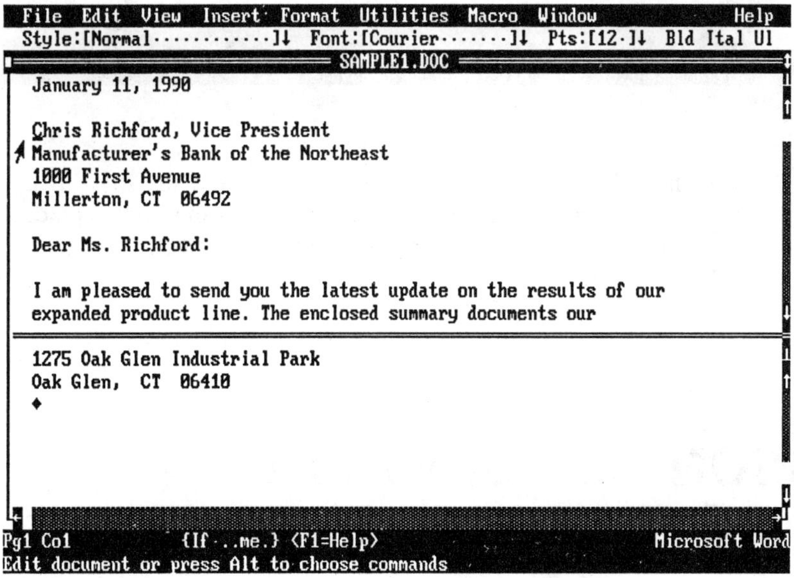

Type **From:**, press the ENTER key, and move to the second pane. Select the line with Thomas Mead's name.

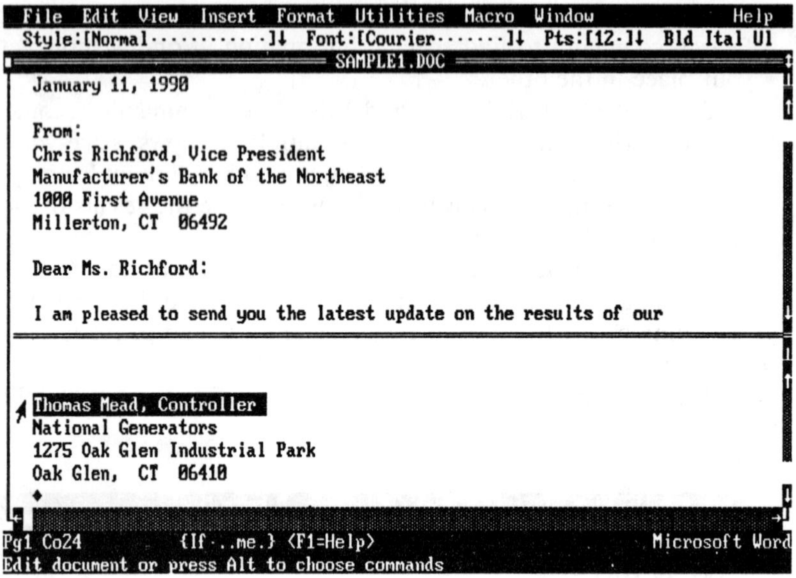

Give the Edit Copy command: you can now see the line in the scrap. Now move to the top pane and use the Edit Paste command to place the name on the "From:" line. Add another line by pressing ENTER.

LESSON 15: USING TWO WINDOWS IN TWO FILES

You may have already guessed that the next step in using windows is to use one window to look at one file and a second window to look at a different file. To look at two different files, you simply use the File Open command in one of the windows to load in a new file.

First, clear the changes that you just made. Give the File Close command. When Word prompts you whether you want to save your changes, choose "No." Give the File New command to open a new, empty file. Now enter in the following short report:

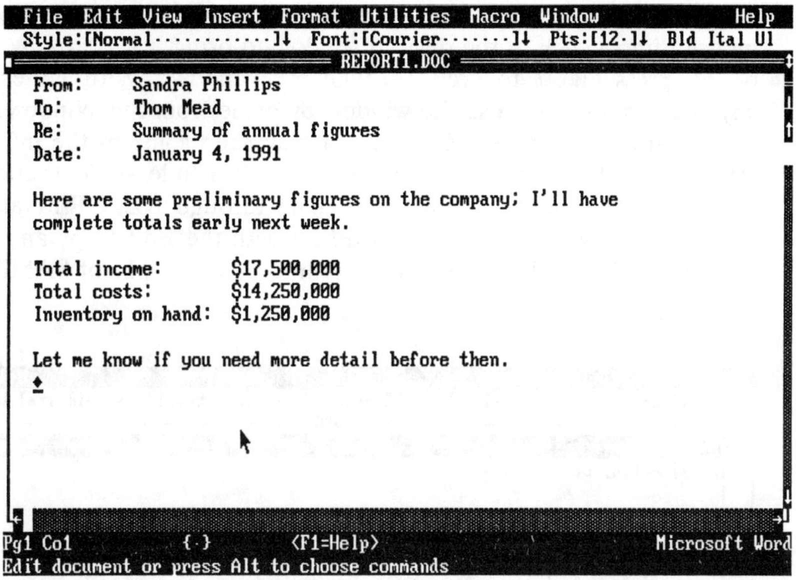

Save this on disk with the name REPORT1.

Now open the SAMPLE1 file with the File Open command. This window opens on top of the REPORT1 file:

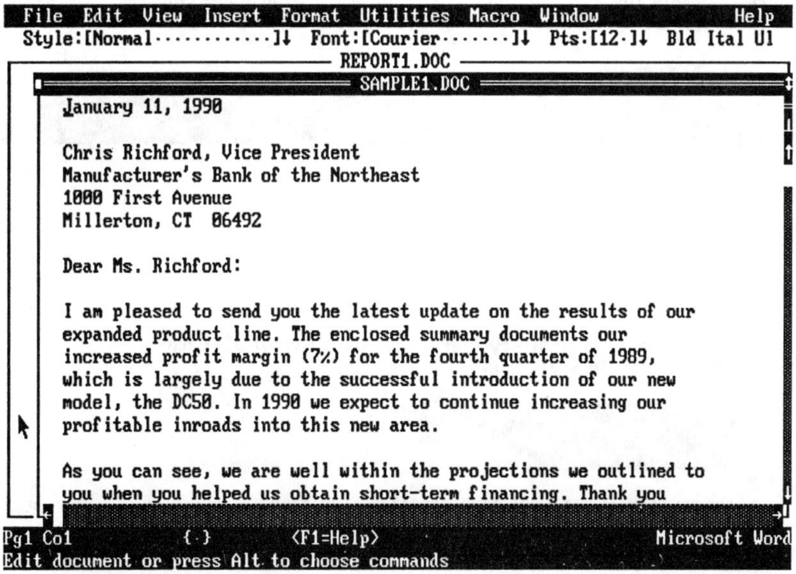

You can move back and forth between these two windows easily. With the mouse, simply click in the desired window to bring it forward. With the keyboard, press CTRL-F6 to cycle through the windows. With either mouse or keyboard, you can choose the window by name from the Window menu.

As you are editing SAMPLE1, you may need some of the information in REPORT1—for instance, if you wanted to include some round numbers. You could see those numbers by paging through REPORT1 and you can even copy the whole table to SAMPLE1 with the Edit Copy and Edit Paste commands. To do this, add text between the paragraphs of SAMPLE1:

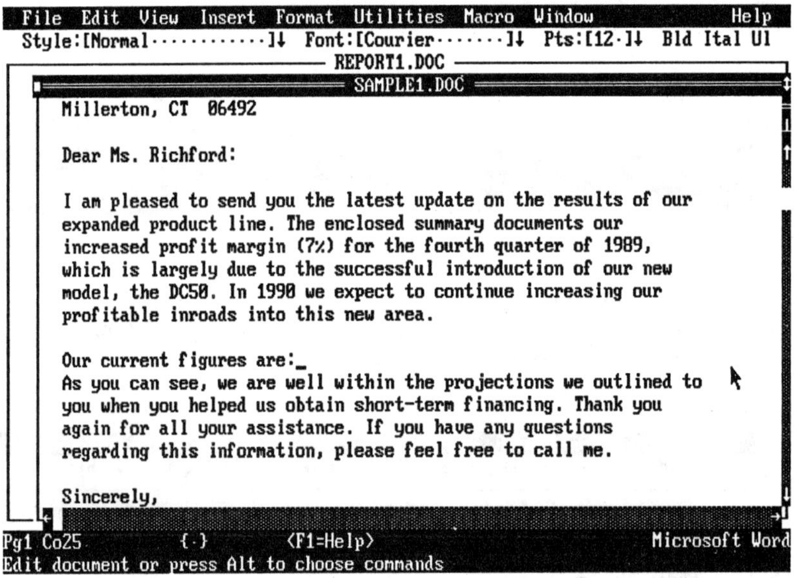

Now move to the REPORT1 window and select the figures:

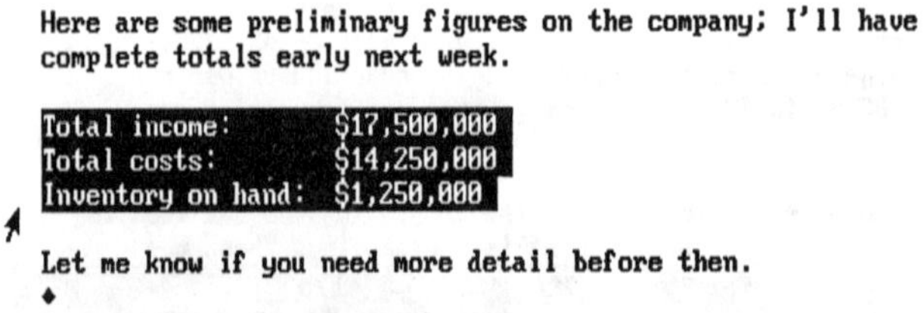

Use the Edit Copy command to copy these to the scrap; switch to the other window, and use the Edit Paste command to copy the text from the scrap to the line below the new text.

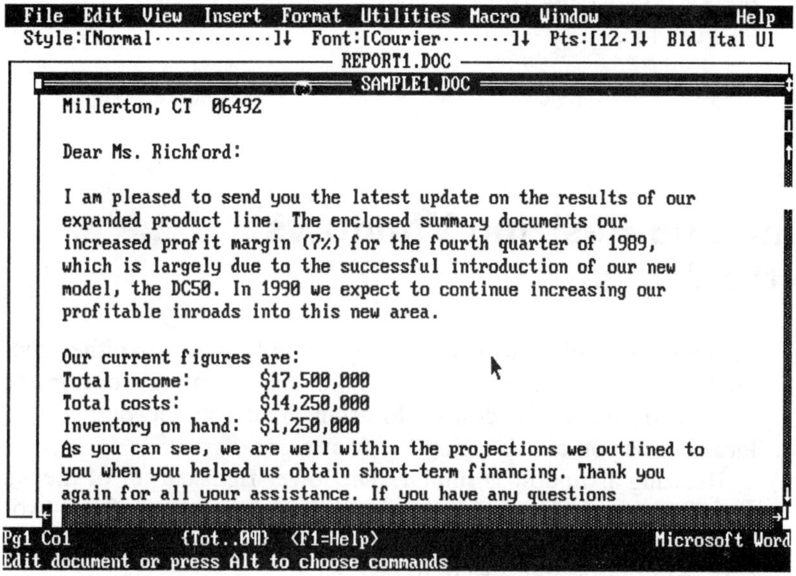

Of course, if you have more than two windows active, you can have that many files open at the same time. If you have edited the text in a window, remember to save it with File Save before closing the window. If you don't, Word will remind you that the window has been edited and ask whether you want to save the edits.

LESSON 16: MOVING AND RESIZING WINDOWS

As you saw in the previous lesson, you can have two or more windows (or panes) open at the same time. If they overlap, you can only see the contents of one window at a time. This may be what you want, since you can see a great deal more text in each window when they are almost full-screen size.

You might, however, want to move and shrink the windows so that you can see all the text in both of them, as you could when you split one window into two panes. For instance, you may want to enlarge the second window of the previous example so that you will have more area on the screen for editing the SAMPLE1 file (this, of course, reduces the amount of text you see in REPORT1).

Moving and Resizing Windows with the Mouse

To move a window with the mouse, simply point at either the top or left border of the window, click and hold the left mouse button, and drag the window frame to the desired location. You can see both the old and new locations as you are dragging the frame.

Resizing a window is similar. The lower-right corner of the window is the *grow box*, the L-shaped character at the intersection of the two scroll bars. Point at the grow box, click and hold the left mouse button, and drag the corner to the desired location.

Moving and Resizing Windows with the Keyboard

The Window Move and Window Size commands let you adjust the windows using the arrow keys on your keyboard. After you give the Window Move command, you press the arrow keys until the window is in the desired position, then press the ENTER key. The Window Size command lets you move the lower-right corner of the window to make the window larger or smaller.

LESSON 17: MAXIMIZING WINDOWS

If you have more than one window on your screen, you may want a full-size view of an individual window. Rather than close the other windows, you can instead *maximize* the window you want to see. When you maximize a window, you enter *maximize mode,* where any window you view occupies the full screen.

Maximizing Windows with the Mouse

To maximize a window with the mouse, point at the two-headed arrow in the upper-right corner of the window and press the left mouse button. For example, to maximize the top of two windows, you would point as shown here:

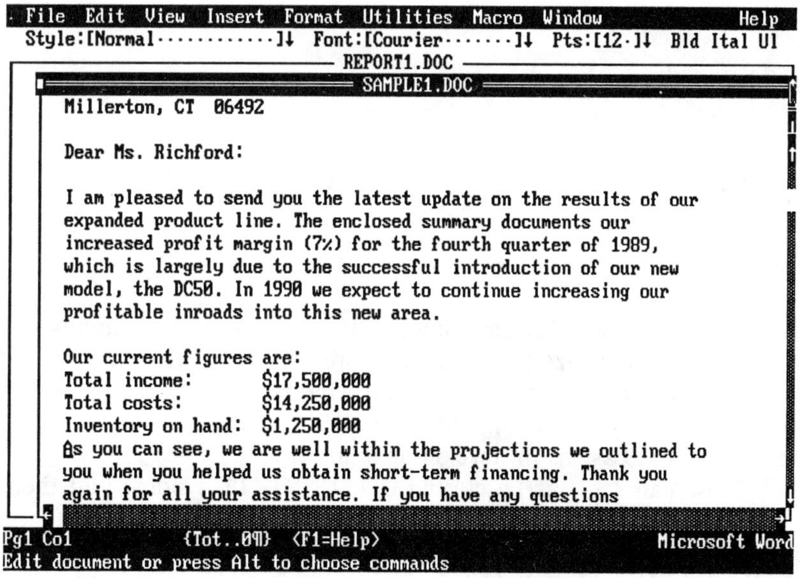

When you click the left button, the window fills the screen. Word displays "MX" at the bottom of the screen to remind you that you are in maximize mode.

To switch to another window, you must now select from the Window menu or click in the desired window with the mouse.

When you are finished with the maximized windows and want to go back to overlapping windows, simply point at the two-headed arrow in the current window and press the left button.

Maximizing Windows with the Keyboard

To maximize a window with the keyboard, use the Window Maximize command. To switch to the next window, press CTRL-F6. To go back to overlapping windows, give the Window Restore command.

LESSON 18: USING VERTICAL WINDOWS

Since most text files have lines that are at least 60 columns long, you will probably use horizontal windows more often than vertical windows. The only time you are likely to use vertical windows is if you have very narrow text (less than 40 columns). However, Word makes moving around in vertical windows as easy as in horizontal windows.

You can see this by closing the REPORT1 window and then opening a second copy of the SAMPLE1 file. To do this, give the File Open command and pick the SAMPLE1 file. This opens a second window into the same file. Note that the two windows have ":1" and ":2" after the file names.

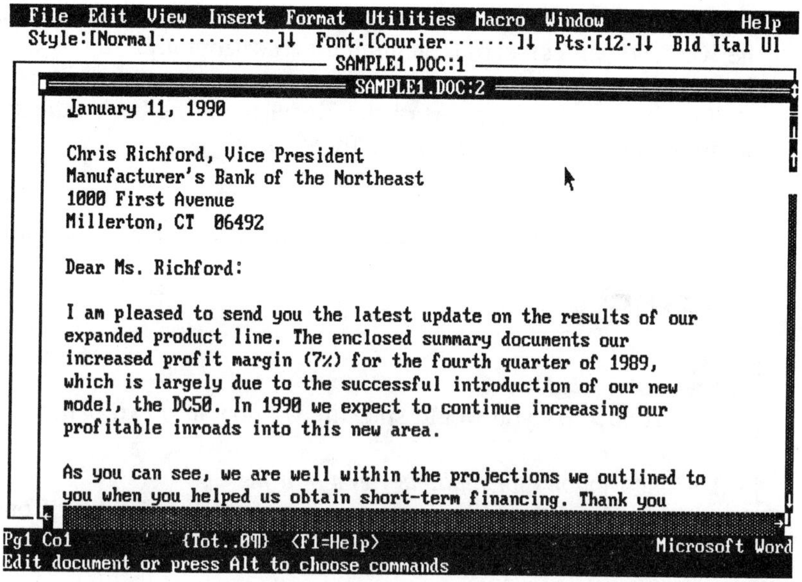

Now use the commands you learned earlier in this chapter to resize and move the windows. You want both windows to be the same size: full height and half width. Your screen should look like this:

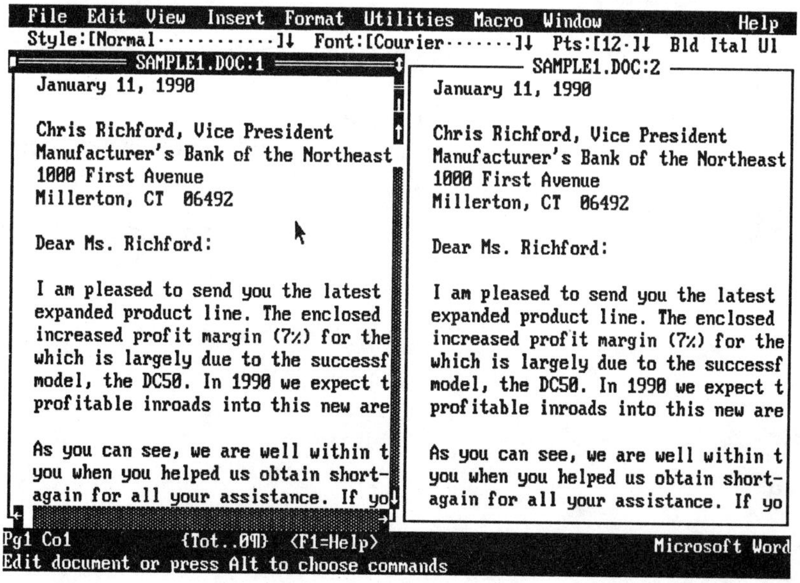

If your text is wider than the window and you want to see the text outside the window, you can scroll each window horizontally. This is done in much the same way as vertical scrolling. For instance, to move the text in the right window to show the right part of the file, click on the horizontal scroll bars at the bottom of the windows, or use the → key.

REVIEW

1. *Creating windows*
   Describe how you would split the window into two panes.

2. *Using windows for multiple views of a file*
   In which of the following situations would two views of one file be useful?

   a. Moving a sentence from the beginning of a memo to the end

   b. Moving a sentence from the beginning of a paragraph to the end

   c. Changing all instances of one word to another

   d. Comparing two tables in a long report

3. *Using windows with multiple files*
   Describe a situation in which you would want to have three windows open, each looking at a different file.

chapter 5

MERGING TEXT FILES

Lesson 19: Merging Two Word Files
Lesson 20: Merging Non-Word Files

In Chapter 2, you learned how to use the scrap to copy and move text in a file. Often, however, you will want to include a copy of an entire file in a file that you are editing. For instance, you may keep important charts in separate files so you can include them in a variety of memos without having to cut and paste them from other memos. Word allows you to do this easily with the Insert File command.

You can also merge two files by selecting an entire file, copying it to the scrap with the Edit Copy command, opening the second file, and adding the scrap to the second file with the Edit Paste command. However, there are a few situations where this is not desirable. For example, if you have text in the scrap, you may not want to lose it when you merge the files. The file you are merging may be very large so you could possibly run out of memory (however, Word will warn you before this happens). You may also want to merge a non-Word file. This chapter covers how to merge files without using the scrap. With Word you can access information from other software, such as paint programs and Excel. See Chapter 21 for more information.

LESSON 19: MERGING TWO WORD FILES

The Insert File command moves a Word document to the file you are editing at the selection indicator. The Insert File command is nearly identical to the File Open command except that it does not open a new file.

Since the File Insert command allows you to merge files easily, you can keep information that may be used in many documents in separate files and then transfer it as you need to. This is easier than having to remember which report has the information you want and then copying the information using the scrap. This procedure is useful for standard introductory paragraphs for letters, annual sales and inventory levels, lists of employees, standard product descriptions, price lists, and other documents.

For example, if you have a file called SALESTAB that you want to incorporate into a letter, you execute the Insert File command and select the name of the file you want to insert into the current file.

LESSON 20: MERGING NON-WORD FILES

Word can merge any text file whether or not you created it with Word. A file produced by an applications program (such as an accounting program or a report manager) can be copied into a Word file with the Insert File command or simply loaded with the File Open command. After you save the file, you can use Word commands to format the file.

You will probably want to edit the non-Word file that you transfer, because its format may not match your other Word documents. It is also likely that Word will treat each line in the non-Word file as a paragraph; you might be able to avoid this result by inserting NEWLINE characters where necessary.

You should be careful when transferring files from other word processing programs, since many of these use special formatting codes in text files. Word does not recognize the codes inserted by other programs, so you may have problems incorporating text from other word processing programs unless they allow you to save text without the codes.

note Many word processing programs can save files in a "nondocument" or "ASCII" format, which means that they save a file as plain text without special formatting codes. You should use this format whenever you know that you will later read a file with Word.

Remember that program files (ones whose file extensions are ".COM" or ".EXE") are not text and cannot be read with Word. Similarly, many data base management programs store data in nontext form, and Word can only use data that is in text form. Look in your program's manual for instructions for storing data as text.

REVIEW

1. *Merging Word files*
   Briefly state the difference between merging files with the Insert File command and with the Edit Copy command.

2. *Including non-Word files in Word*
   What types of files cannot be merged or loaded with Word?

chapter 6

USING GLOSSARIES

Lesson 21: Creating a Glossary
Lesson 22: Storing and Retrieving Glossaries
Lesson 23: Special Glossary Entries
Lesson 24: Finding Other Uses for Glossaries

As you work more with a word processor, you will probably find that particular phrases or blocks of text are used over and over, such as the name of a company or a long product name. Typing this text many times in a report or memo is tedious, and copying it from another file each time it is used can take almost as long as typing it.

Word eliminates this problem with *glossaries.* A glossary is a set of abbreviations that correspond to longer phrases. Instead of repeatedly typing in the longer phrase, the user simply types in the abbreviation. Any phrase or block of text may be abbreviated. An abbreviation can consist of as many as 31 letters or numbers—for example, "gemco1." One active glossary is available when you run Word, although you can store many separate glossaries on disk. For instance, in the SAMPLE1 file, Thomas Mead's name and address could be saved as an abbreviation in the glossary, since he often types his address at the bottom of a letter. Chris Richford's name and address and the

Abbreviation	Contents
ng	National Generators
thomaddr	Thomas Mead, Controller National Generators 1275 Oak Glen Industrial Park Oak Glen, CT 06410
richford	Chris Richford, Vice President Manufacturer's Bank of the Northeast 1000 First Avenue Millerton, CT 06492

TABLE 6-1. Possible Glossary Entries for SAMPLE1

name "National Generators" could also be saved. Table 6-1 shows the suggested entries for this glossary.

Glossaries can be great timesavers since they prevent you from having to retype sections of text that you often use. They also prevent typing mistakes in commonly used terms and names (it could be very embarrassing to misspell a client's company name in a letter). The rest of this chapter explains how to set up glossaries and how to use the entries in them. Although glossaries are an advanced feature available in only a few word processing programs, it is likely that you will find many uses for them after reading this chapter.

LESSON 21: CREATING A GLOSSARY

Glossary entries (an abbreviation and its associated text) are created with the Edit Glossary command. You also use the Edit Glossary command to store all of the glossary entries that are in memory to disk.

You can use the SAMPLE1 letter to see how to save entries. To save Chris Richford's name and address as the abbreviation "richford," select the text, execute the Edit Glossary command, and enter **richford** for the glossary name. The Edit Glossary dialog now looks like this:

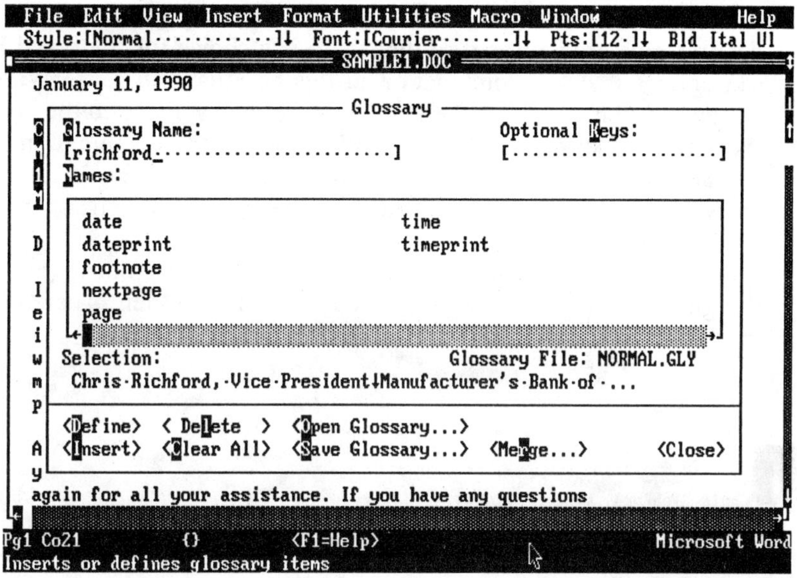

Click the Define button or press ALT-D to save this glossary entry to memory.

Now that you have saved the first entry in glossary memory, you can use it as you enter text instead of typing the whole name and address (you will do this shortly). There are three ways to expand an abbreviation to its full text: with the Edit Glossary command, with the F3 key, or with a special key combination you specify.

To use the F3 key, simply enter the abbreviation in your text and press the F3 key. Word looks to the left of the selection and expands the abbreviation. This is the method you will use most often when you use glossaries, since it is faster than using the Edit Glossary command. To insert Chris Richford's name and address as you are typing or editing text, enter **richford** and press the F3 key.

There is a second way to expand glossaries with the F3 key: type the abbreviation, select it, and then press the F3 key. This allows you to type a document without expanding the abbreviations; you can then go back, select an abbreviation, and press the F3 key. However, the most common way to use Word's glossaries is to expand the abbreviations as you type them.

The second method for inserting glossary text is to use the Edit Glossary command and pick the glossary name from the list. Put the insertion mark at the point in your document where you want the inserted text, give the Edit Glossary command, choose the item from the list by highlighting it, and click the Insert button or press ALT-I.

There is a third, even faster way of inserting glossary text. When you define a glossary item, notice that there is a choice for "Optional Keys." You can enter a CTRL-key combination in this box that will cause Word to insert the entry when you press the key. To assign a key, move to the box and press the desired CTRL-key combination; Word fills in the combination in readable characters. For example, if you want CTRL-R to enter the "richford" glossary entry, move to the Optional Keys choice and press CTRL-R (Word fills in "<ctrl R>").

To practice expanding abbreviations, save the three entries in Table 6-1 to the glossary (you have already saved "richford"). Open a new window with the File New command to start a new letter:

```
January 22, 1990

Chris Richford, Vice President
Manufacturer's Bank of the Northeast
1000 First Avenue
Millerton, CT  06492

Dear Ms. Richford:

This confirms our conversation earlier today that National
Generators will install a new payroll program at the end of this
month, and that all of National Generators' payroll checks will
be drawn on the new account we set up.

Sincerely,

Thomas Mead, Controller
National Generators
1275 Oak Glen Industrial Park
Oak Glen,  CT  06410
```

Instead of typing the names and addresses or the company name in the body of the text, use the abbreviations in the glossary. Start by entering the date and then type **richford**:

```
 File  Edit  View  Insert  Format  Utilities  Macro  Window              Help
 Style:[Normal............]↓  Font:[Courier.......]↓  Pts:[12·]↓  Bld Ital Ul
                                SAMPLE1.DOC
                                 Document2
   January 22, 1990

   richford
```

Now press the F3 key:

```
 File  Edit  View  Insert  Format  Utilities  Macro  Window              Help
 Style:[Normal············]↓  Font:[Courier·······]↓  Pts:[12·]↓  Bld Ital Ul
                              SAMPLE1.DOC
                               Document2
    January 22, 1990

    Chris Richford, Vice President
    Manufacturer's Bank of the Northeast
    1000 First Avenue
    Millerton, CT  06492
```

Continue the letter, using the abbreviations when you can. If you assigned CTRL-key combinations, use them for even faster text entry.

If you want to remove some of the entries in the glossary, use the Delete button in the Edit Glossary command. Use the Save Glossary button to save the current glossary on disk. If you add abbreviations to the glossary, you should save them with this command before you exit from Word.

LESSON 22: STORING AND RETRIEVING GLOSSARIES

Glossaries are stored in files with the extension .GLY. When you start up Word, it looks for a file called NORMAL.GLY; if it finds the file, it loads its abbreviations with your text file. In general, you will use only one glossary file, so if you name it NORMAL.GLY, it will always be loaded automatically for you. Glossaries are loaded and saved with the Open Glossary and Save Glossary buttons in the Edit Glossary command.

To load a new glossary, give the Edit Glossary command and click the Open Glossary button. This replaces the current glossary with one from disk. The Merge button reads a glossary from disk and merges it with any currently loaded abbreviations. If you already have abbreviations in memory when you use the Merge button, the new abbreviations are merged with the old ones. If the file that you are merging has some of the same abbreviations as those already in memory, the new text will replace the old text in those definitions.

note Remember to save the glossary before you exit from Word. Otherwise all your new entries will be lost.

To print your glossary, use the File Print command. In the "Print" field, select "Glossary." All entries for the current glossary will appear in a neatly formatted list.

LESSON 23: SPECIAL GLOSSARY ENTRIES

Word has some predefined glossary names that automatically update certain information in your documents. Two of these entries are replaced with the current time or date. They are useful for inserting time-dependent information in a document.

- **time** is replaced on the screen by the current time.
- **date** is replaced on the screen by the current date.

Other special entries do not display current data on the screen. Instead, they are displayed in parentheses. However, when you print your document, these entries are replaced with data that is current at the time of printing. These special glossary entries are

- **page** prints as the current page number. This is useful in running heads (described in Chapter 9).
- **footnote** prints the special character used by the Format Footnote command (see Chapter 9).
- **timeprint** prints the time that the printing occurred.
- **dateprint** prints the date that the printing occurred.
- **clipboard** inserts material from the Windows Clipboard. This entry appears only if you are running Word under Microsoft Windows version 2 or a later version.

- **nextpage** inserts the number of the next page. (This is used only in legal documents in countries other than the U.S.)

For example, in a document type **dateprint** and press F3.

```
 File  Edit  View  Insert  Format  Utilities  Macro  Window              Help
 Style:[Normal············]↓  Font:[Courier·······]↓  Pts:[12·]↓  Bld Ital Ul
                              SAMPLE1.DOC
                               Document2
   This information is current as of (dateprint)
```

When printed, it will look like this:

This information is current as of March 27, 1990

LESSON 24: FINDING OTHER USES FOR GLOSSARIES

Glossaries can reduce typing and increase accuracy in many different applications. The following list should give you some ideas for using glossaries in your daily word processing. Table 6-2 shows examples of some of these uses.

- Complex scientific phrases, such as the names of chemicals, long theory names, process names, and the names of reactions

- Standard legal citations, case names, and legal jargon

- Long, nearly identical names, such as model numbers

- Phrases that are heavily used in a document

Abbreviation	Contents
13cb	Anhydrous 1,3-dichlorobenzene, U.S.P.
rsae	Rivest-Shamir-Abel encryption
mcatcom	Methyl-selenium catalytic combustion
yrox	Youngblood-Roberts oxidation
fiduc	34 N.E. 2d 68, 70
rw	Roe v. Wade
eqpro	Equal protection of the laws
cll2	Colonial 12-422 Model S
cc	Press the CTRL-C key

TABLE 6-2. Suggested Uses for Glossaries

REVIEW

1. *Using glossaries to reduce typing and mistakes*
   Suggest how you can use different abbreviation names to distinguish the following pairs of abbreviations:

   a. Microsoft Word, *Microsoft Word*

   b. *The New York Times, New York Times*

   c. automatic error recovery, automated error recovery

2. *Recalling abbreviations*
   How can you get a list of all of the currently defined abbreviations?

3. *Saving and restoring glossaries*
   How do you cause a glossary to be automatically loaded when you start Word?

part II

USING WORD TO FORMAT

Basic Formatting with Word
Formatting Paragraphs and Tables
Formatting Pages and Footnotes
Formatting with Style Sheets

chapter 7

BASIC FORMATTING WITH WORD

Lesson 25: An Introduction to Formatting
Lesson 26: Entering Format Directives
Lesson 27: Using Common Character Styles
Lesson 28: Using Other Character Formats
Lesson 29: Giving Character Styles with the CTRL Key
Lesson 30: Using Graphics Characters from the Keyboard
Lesson 31: Copying Character Formats with the Mouse
Lesson 32: Searching for Character Formats

As part of the editing process, you will want to alter the way your text looks so your reader will more readily understand your meaning, and so the information is presented in an interesting form. Word's formatting capabilities let you choose exactly how your text will look on paper when it is printed out.

In order to make formatting easier, Word stores a great deal of information with your text. You do not see the special formatting codes that Word stores in your text; instead, the screen displays the result of those special codes, which is the properly formatted text.

Adding a formatting characteristic to text is called *direct formatting.* The concept of direct formatting is easy to grasp, since it is so similar to what you normally do when typing text. For instance, when you make changes on a first draft, you might decide to underline a phrase or indent paragraphs. In doing this you are adding characteristics directly to text.

LESSON 25: AN INTRODUCTION TO FORMATTING

The basic concept behind Word's formatting is that all text has certain characteristics associated with it. After you have specified the characteristics (such as underlining and indenting), Word automatically displays the text with those attributes.

If you move the text to some other place in your document, the characteristics move with it. You can thus enter an entire document without worrying about its formatting, and then move to the beginning of the text and format the document. Or, if you wish, you can format your text as you enter it. Each time you add a characteristic, you see it instantly. You can experiment with different formats, seeing which one best fits the meaning of the text.

Word gives you three "units" of formatting: characters, paragraphs, and sections. At the level of the smallest unit, Word lets you change the format of each character. For example, you can underline, boldface, or italicize characters with different formatting commands. Character formatting is most often used to make certain words stand out in your text. The following illustration shows some character formats.

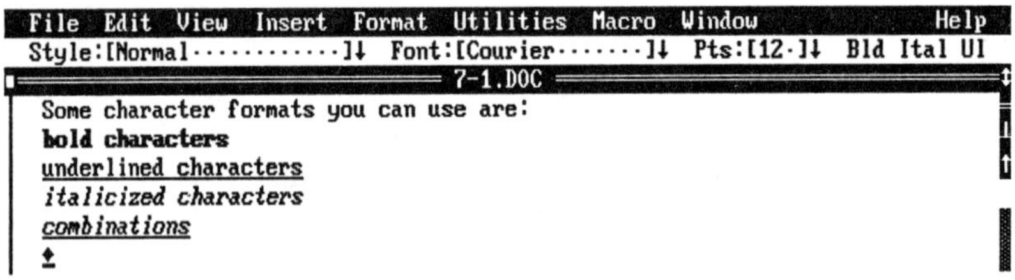

You have already learned to use the ENTER key to make paragraphs in Word; paragraphs are the second formatting unit. The paragraph is important to Word because Word stores formatting information for each paragraph when you press ENTER. In fact, all of the characteristics of a paragraph are stored in the character that is placed on the screen when you finish a paragraph.

For instance, many people like to indent every paragraph five spaces. Most word processors require you to press the TAB key (or to press the

SPACEBAR five times) at the beginning of each paragraph; Word, on the other hand, remembers this format once you have specified it and inserts the spaces for you in succeeding paragraphs unless you tell it otherwise. Other paragraph formats that you specify include the indentation of the entire paragraph and alignment with the margin.

You will often want to set different formatting characteristics for a particular paragraph. For example, when you include a long quotation in text, you usually indent the whole quotation a few spaces from the margin. Tables, which are treated as paragraphs in Word, are also formatted differently from normal text paragraphs.

Since Word stores paragraph formatting characteristics in the paragraph mark, you can use the Edit Copy and Edit Paste commands to use the special formatting characteristics of one paragraph again for another paragraph. Simply copy the paragraph mark that you want to the scrap, move to the character after the other paragraph mark that you want to replace, press BACKSPACE, and then paste in the new paragraph mark. All of the formatting characteristics are then applied to the new paragraph, for example, another long quotation.

Word lets you set up different characteristics for each section, which is the third formatting unit. These are usually characteristics that do not change from paragraph to paragraph (for example, page headings and margin size). Since sections correspond to chapters of a book, you can, for example, format the introductory material differently from the chapters. You do not see section formatting on the screen; instead, it appears when you print your text on the printer or use Print Review.

It is important to remember that each element of your text, whether it is a character, a paragraph, or a section, has a set of formatting instructions attached to it. The end result is that formatting your documents is much easier with Word, since you can copy the specifications for one element from one formatting unit to another.

Direct Formatting Versus Style Sheets

You may be wondering what all of these "characteristics" are. They will be discussed in this chapter and in Chapters 8 and 9, and are listed in Appendix B. For now, think of a direct formatting characteristic as a description of how the text looks or its position on the page.

In addition to direct formatting, Word allows you to use a *style sheet,* which is a list dictating how various elements in your document will be formatted; the style sheet lets you associate a particular element of text (such as headings, regular paragraphs, and quotations) with a format. Style sheets make it easier for you to format consistently, since you do not need to remember what format you apply to each text element. Also, if you decide to change the format for a text element throughout a document, change the style sheet and Word automatically changes the format for you.

The major difference between direct formatting and style sheets is that

- With direct formatting, you select some text and tell Word how you want it to look.
- With style sheets, you select some text and tell Word what kind of text it is; Word formats it according to your previous definitions for that element.

Most people find that direct formatting is much easier to learn than the style sheet method, since direct formatting is so similar to what they normally do when they type. For that reason, this book presents direct formatting before style sheet instructions. When you get to Chapter 10, you will understand enough about formatting to understand the power of using style sheets. You can then decide which you want to use as your primary formatting method.

LESSON 26: ENTERING FORMAT DIRECTIVES

You can enter formatting commands in Word with either the commands in the Format menu or special key combinations. In fact, you can give all of Word's formatting commands with either the mouse or the keyboard alone; however, most people use both, selecting the fastest method for each command. The Format menu commands are much like the editing commands that you have already learned. The Format menu shows you commands for all types of text formatting. These commands have dialogs listing the different types of formats available.

You do not need to use the Format menu to enter every formatting command. Some character and paragraph formatting commands can be entered by pressing the CTRL key and a letter at the same time, such as CTRL-B to boldface characters. These key sequences are described in this chapter and in Chapter 8.

The most common type of formatting used is character formatting. For instance, book and magazine publishers commonly use italics for emphasis, foreign words, and book titles; they use underlining and boldface in different kinds of headings. The rest of this chapter discusses character formatting, Chapter 8 discusses paragraph formatting, and Chapter 9 discusses section formatting.

LESSON 27: USING COMMON CHARACTER STYLES

The purpose of using character styles is to make the reader notice a group of characters or words. This is often useful for emphasis, but common publishing practices also require it; for instance, book titles should generally be shown in italics.

Type in the following text, which will be used to experiment with character formatting.

```
 File  Edit  View  Insert  Format  Utilities  Macro  Window            Help
 Style:[Normal·············]↓  Font:[Courier·······]↓  Pts:[12·]↓  Bld Ital Ul
═══════════════════════════ CHARACT.DOC ═══════════════════════════
  Books and magazines often contain a variety of character styles
  which you can now incorporate into your reports and memos. For
  example, it is common to italicize foreign words such as deja vu,
  or to use italics to indicate emphasis. Boldface characters are
  often used in headings to make them stand out on a page,
  sometimes in conjunction with underlining.

  Word gives you even more character styles to work with, however.
  Legislation often uses strikethrough characters to indicate
  wording in old laws that is being deleted. You may choose to put
  a phrase in all capital letters to highlight it, or you may put
  it in small caps to indicate that it stands by itself. If your
  printer supports other fonts, subscripts, superscripts, or double
  underlines, Word lets you use those, too.
  ♦
```

Save this on disk with the name CHARACT.

If you want to change the style of a group of characters, you will first select the group and then use the Format Character command. The following dialog appears:

```
┌──────────────────── Character ────────────────────┐
│Font: [Courier_·························]↓         │
│Point Size: [12····]↓  Color: [Black·····]↓        │
│                                                   │
│[ ] Bold                                           │
│[ ] Italic              ┌ Position ──────┐         │
│[ ] Underline           │(•) Normal      │         │
│[ ] Double Underline    │( ) Superscript │         │
│[ ] Small Caps          │( ) Subscript   │         │
│[ ] All Caps            └────────────────┘         │
│[ ] StrikeThru                                     │
│[ ] Hidden                                         │
├───────────────────────────────────────────────────┤
│                      < OK >  <Cancel>             │
└───────────────────────────────────────────────────┘
```

You can change any of the toggles to indicate the styles you want. In fact, you can choose more than one style for your text. For example, you might want a title on a report to be both underlined and boldface.

The styles that most people use in their writing are plain (no italics, boldface, and underlining). Now, as an experiment, first select the words "deja vu" in the text and give the Format Character command. Select the italic option and execute the command. When the dialog disappears, you'll see that the words "deja vu" have been made italic. If you are using a nongraphics display adapter or the color text option of Word (which is described in Chapter 13), note that the words appear on the screen in color, not in italics. Move the selection away from the words so you can see them better.

Books and magazines often contain a variety of character styles
which you can now incorporate into your reports and memos. For
example, it is common to italicize foreign words such as *deja vu*,
or to use italics to indicate emphasis. Boldface characters are
often used in headings to make them stand out on a page,
sometimes in conjunction with underlining.

Choosing boldface and underlining is similar to choosing italics. Select the words "stand out" and then boldface them by giving the Format Character command; select the word "underlining" and give the command to underline it. If you wish, you can also underline the period after it. Note that boldface characters sometimes do not look very different on the screen from normal characters, depending on the type of monitor you have.

Books and magazines often contain a variety of character styles
which you can now incorporate into your reports and memos. For
example, it is common to italicize foreign words such as *deja vu*,
or to use italics to indicate emphasis. Boldface characters are
often used in headings to make them **stand out** on a page,
sometimes in conjunction with underlining.

As mentioned before, you can apply more than one style to text. To see this, select "in conjunction" and give the Format Character command. Now select both the bold and underline options.

Books and magazines often contain a variety of character styles
which you can now incorporate into your reports and memos. For
example, it is common to italicize foreign words such as *deja vu*,
or to use italics to indicate emphasis. Boldface characters are
often used in headings to make them **stand out** on a page,
sometimes **in conjunction** with underlining.

When you use the Format Character command, Word first checks the current formatting. For example, if you select the word "underlining" again and give the Format Character command, you can see that the underline option is already selected:

```
──────────────────── Character ──────────────────────
Font: [Courier·························]↓
Point Size: [12····]↓  Color: [Black·····]↓

[ ] Bold
[ ] Italic                  ┌ Position ──────────┐
[X] Underline               │ (•) Normal         │
[ ] Double Underline        │ ( ) Superscript    │
[ ] Small Caps              │ ( ) Subscript      │
[ ] All Caps                └────────────────────┘
[ ] Strikethru
[ ] Hidden
─────────────────────────────────────────────────────
                          < OK >  <Cancel>
```

Even if your screen does not show bold, italics, or underline very well, Word can show you what characteristics text on it has. To do this, you want to see Word's *ribbon,* a line that appears directly under the menu line. If your ribbon is not visible on the screen, give the View Ribbon command. The ribbon looks like this:

```
 File  Edit  View  Insert  Format  Utilities  Macro  Window          Help
 Style:[Normal············]↓  Font:[Courier·······]↓  Pts:[12·]↓  Bld Ital Ul
```

This shows the style, font, character size, and whether the selected characters are bold, italic, or underlined.

The ribbon has another handy feature for mouse users. You can make the selected characters bold, italic, or underlined simply by clicking on the indicators at the right side of the ribbon. For instance, to make the selection bold, click on "Bld."

LESSON 28: USING OTHER CHARACTER FORMATS

Word also lets you specify strikethrough, uppercase, small caps, and double underline. You can experiment with these styles:

Books and magazines often contain a variety of character styles which you can now incorporate into your reports and memos. For example, it is common to italicize foreign words such as *deja vu*, or to use italics to indicate emphasis. Boldface characters are often used in headings to make them **stand out** on a page, sometimes **in conjunction** with underlining.

Word gives you even more character styles to work with, however. Legislation often uses ~~strikethrough~~ characters to indicate wording in old laws that is being deleted. You may choose to put a phrase in ALL CAPITAL letters to highlight it, or you may put it in SMALL CAPS to indicate that it stands by itself. If your printer supports other fonts, subscripts, superscripts, or double underlines, Word lets you use those, too.

As you can see from the example, it is easy to overuse character styles. Most book and magazine publishers avoid using too many styles so that the text doesn't end up looking like an old-time circus poster.

Some printers can handle superscripts, subscripts, and double underlines, while others can't. It is always safe to specify these character formats in your documents even if your printer can't print them, since Word knows what your printer can and can't do and will compensate for them. For instance, if you specify double underline and your printer can't make one, Word will simply print a single underline.

Superscripts and subscripts are chosen from the Position choice of the Format Character command. These are often useful in scientific or technical papers. You can also use superscripts for footnotes (discussed in Chapter 9).

Many dot-matrix, ink-jet, and laser printers allow you to use more than one text font. Some daisy-wheel printers do so as well, but you often have to change print wheels. If your printer supports more than one text font, you can choose the font and character size with the first two choices on the Format Character menu. The fonts that various printers support are listed in the *Microsoft Word Printer Information* manual. If you have a color printer, you can choose a color for the text as well.

You can also change the font and character size with the ribbon. With the mouse, simply choose the font or size from the drop-down list. With the keyboard, press CTRL-F to select the font list or CTRL-P to select the size list. (Repeating CTRL-F or CTRL-P brings up the appropriate dialog.)

Once you have experimented with all of the available character styles, print out the file on your printer to see how it looks. Some styles may look strange on some printers (this is especially true if you mix styles). Remember that Word does not mind if you request a style that your printer can't use; it will make its best guess about how the text should look based on your printer's capabilities.

You may have noticed the hidden character style on the menu and wondered why you would want to hide characters. Word uses hidden characters to make the table of contents and index for documents, as you will see in Chapter 15. You can also use hidden text for annotations, which are discussed in Chapter 16. After hiding text with the hidden character format, you can see it again with the View Preferences command discussed in Chapter 13.

LESSON 29: GIVING CHARACTER STYLES WITH THE CTRL KEY

Using the Format Character command to change character styles can be tedious and slow since you need to give the command over and over. Word allows you to select character styles with CTRL-key combinations.

Table 7-1 shows the CTRL-key combinations used to select character styles. As before, select the text you want to change; then use the appropriate

Format	**CTRL-Key Combination**
Normal	CTRL-SPACEBAR
Italic	CTRL-I
Bold	CTRL-B
Underline	CTRL-U
Small caps	CTRL-K
Double underline	CTRL-D
Subscript	CTRL-MINUS
Superscript	CTRL-PLUS or CTRL-EQUAL
Hidden	CTRL-H

TABLE 7-1. Character Formatting with CTRL-Key Combinations

CTRL-key combination. For example, select the words "Books and magazines" in the previous file; then press CTRL-I to put the words in italics. To add underlining, press CTRL-U:

```
Books and magazines often contain a variety of character styles
which you can now incorporate into your reports and memos. For
example, it is common to italicize foreign words such as deja vu,
or to use italics to indicate emphasis. Boldface characters are
often used in headings to make them stand out on a page,
sometimes in conjunction with underlining.
```

(To make the words normal again, you would press CTRL-SPACEBAR, but leave them alone for now.)

You saw in Chapter 6 how you can assign a CTRL key to a glossary entry. If you do this with one of the CTRL keys from Table 7-1 and press that CTRL-key combination, you will get the glossary entry, not the formatting action. You can still get the formatting action without having to use the Format Character command, however, by preceding the CTRL-key combination with CTRL-A. Thus, if you have assigned CTRL-I to a glossary entry but want to make the selected text italic, press CTRL-A, CTRL-I.

After you give a particular style with a CTRL-key combination, you may want to select other characters and format them with the same style. A quick way to do this is to select the characters and press F4, which repeats the last formatting command.

LESSON 30: USING GRAPHICS CHARACTERS FROM THE KEYBOARD

You may have noticed that the IBM PC screen can display a number of characters that are not on the keyboard. You can enter these characters into your text by using the ALT key and a number. Be warned, however, that there are only a few printers that can actually print these characters. If you add these characters to your Word document and use a printer that does not understand them, you can get unpredictable results (such as strange printing or large gaps in the printout).

The characters available are shown in Table 7-2. To enter these characters, press the NUMLOCK key to get into numlock mode, hold down the ALT key, and type the number on the numeric keypad (not the numbers on the top row of the keyboard). You must enter all three digits. When you release the ALT key, the character will be displayed on the screen. You must be in numlock mode (you will see "NL" at the bottom of the screen).

Number	Character	Number	Character
1	☺	140	î
2	☻	141	ì
3	♥	142	Ä
4	♦	143	Å
5	♣	144	É
6	♠	145	æ
14	♫	146	Æ
15	☼	147	ô
16	►	148	ö
17	◄	149	ò
18	↕	150	û
19	‼	151	ù
20	¶	152	ÿ
21	§	153	Ö
22	▬	154	Ü
23	↨	155	¢
24	↑	156	£
25	↓	157	¥
26	→	158	Pt
27	←	159	*f*
28	∟	160	á
29	↔	161	í
30	▲	162	ó
127	⌂	163	ú
128	Ç	164	ñ
129	ü	165	Ñ
130	é	166	ª
131	â	167	º
132	ä	168	¿
133	à	169	⌐
134	å	170	¬
135	ç	171	½
136	ê	172	¼
137	ë	173	i
138	è	174	≪
139	ï	175	≫

TABLE 7-2. Graphics Character Set

Number	Character	Number	Character
176	░	211	╙
177	▒	212	╘
178	▓	213	╒
179	│	214	╓
180	┤	215	╫
181	╡	216	╪
182	╢	217	┘
183	╖	218	┌
184	╕	219	█
185	╣	220	▄
186	║	221	▌
187	╗	222	▐
188	╝	223	▀
189	╜	224	α
190	╛	225	β
191	┐	226	Γ
192	└	227	π
193	┴	228	Σ
194	┬	229	σ
195	├	230	µ
196	─	231	τ
197	┼	232	φ
198	╞	233	θ
199	╟	234	Ω
200	╚	235	δ
201	╔	236	∞
202	╩	237	∅
203	╦	238	ϵ
204	╠	239	∩
205	═	240	≡
206	╬	241	±
207	╧	242	≥
208	╨	243	≤
209	╤	244	⌠
210	╥	245	⌡

TABLE 7-2. Graphics Character Set (*continued*)

Number	Character	Number	Character
246	÷	251	√
247	≈	252	^{n}
248	○	253	^{2}
249	•	254	■
250	·		

TABLE 7-2. Graphics Character Set (*continued*)

To see this, first remove the character formatting from "deja vu" by selecting it and pressing CTRL-SPACEBAR. Next, to change the "e" in "deja vu" to an "é," delete it and enter ALT-130. To change the "a" to an "à," delete it and enter ALT-133:

Books and magazines often contain a variety of character styles
which you can now incorporate into your reports and memos. For
example, it is common to italicize foreign words such as *déjà vu*,
or to use italics to indicate emphasis. Boldface characters are
often used in headings to make them **stand out** on a page,
sometimes **in conjunction** with underlining.

LESSON 31: COPYING CHARACTER FORMATS WITH THE MOUSE

Now that you know how to apply a format to a character, you may be inclined to go back and add character formats to other files that you have created with Word. Giving the Format Character command or entering CTRL-key sequences can get tedious, however, so Word allows you to copy the format of one set of characters to another without having to specify the actual format. Note, however, that this only applies if you use a mouse; there are no equivalent steps for keyboard users.

When you want to do this, you first format one set of characters. You next select the second set of characters, point at the characters that have the format you want to copy, hold down the CTRL-SHIFT key, and press the left button. You can then select another set of characters and repeat the process.

These steps are best explained by example. Suppose that you want to change the first word in each sentence in the CHARACT file to boldface (this is admittedly strange but it's a good exercise). First, change the word "Books" to only boldface, and then select the word "For" in the second sentence:

```
Books and magazines often contain a variety of character styles
which you can now incorporate into your reports and memos. For
example, it is common to italicize foreign words such as déjà vu,
or to use italics to indicate emphasis. Boldface characters are
often used in headings to make them stand out on a page,
sometimes in conjunction with underlining.
```

Now point at the word "Books":

```
Books and magazines often contain a variety of character styles
which you can now incorporate into your reports and memos. For
example, it is common to italicize foreign words such as déjà vu,
or to use italics to indicate emphasis. Boldface characters are
often used in headings to make them stand out on a page,
sometimes in conjunction with underlining.
```

Press the CTRL-SHIFT key and the left button, and the word "For" will be changed to bold:

```
Books and magazines often contain a variety of character styles
which you can now incorporate into your reports and memos. For
example, it is common to italicize foreign words such as déjà vu,
or to use italics to indicate emphasis. Boldface characters are
often used in headings to make them stand out on a page,
sometimes in conjunction with underlining.
```

Now move the selection to the word "Boldface" in the third sentence and, pointing at "Books," press the CTRL-SHIFT key and the left button again.

```
Books and magazines often contain a variety of character styles
which you can now incorporate into your reports and memos. For
example, it is common to italicize foreign words such as déjà vu,
or to use italics to indicate emphasis. Boldface characters are
often used in headings to make them stand out on a page,
sometimes in conjunction with underlining.
```

You can continue to do this for any number of words or phrases.

LESSON 32: SEARCHING FOR CHARACTER FORMATS

Once you have added character formatting to a file (as you have with the CHARACT file), you can search for words on the basis of their formatting. Assume, for instance, that you are editing a long report in which book titles are italicized. You can quickly locate the book titles by finding all instances of words in italics.

To search for a character format, issue the Edit Search command. In the dialog, click "Search For Formatting Only," select "Character" as the formatting level, specify the type of formatting you are searching for, and then execute the command. If the character format you have specified is located, Word selects the first instance of the format, and extends the selection until it comes to a character that lacks the format.

For example, go to the beginning of the CHARACT file and give the Edit Search command.

Select the options in the dialog as shown here:

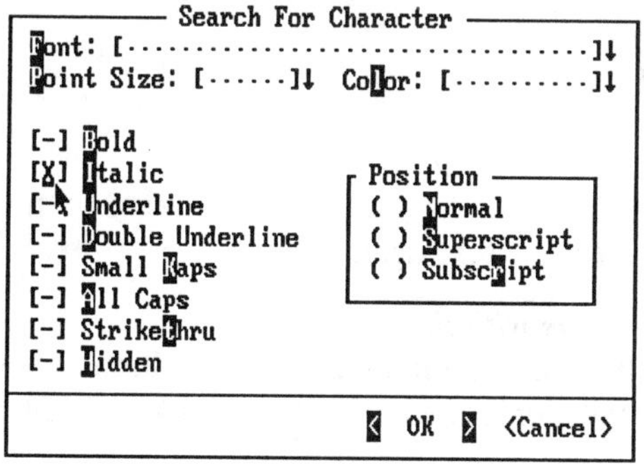

and click on the "OK" box. Word selects "and magazines":

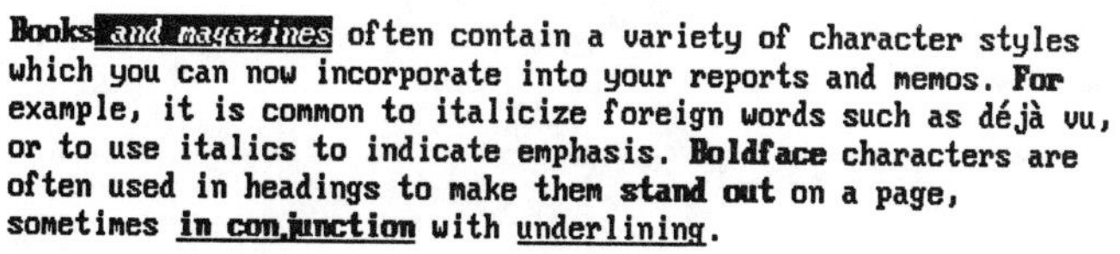

REVIEW

1. *Formatting characteristics*
   Which of the following are formatting characteristics of characters, paragraphs, or sections?

   a. Headings at the top of each page

   b. Indentation of the first line of a paragraph

   c. Superscripted numbers

2. *Changing text styles*
   Which character formats would be appropriate for

   a. Book titles

   b. Emphatic sentences in an emergency procedures manual

   c. Footnote numbers

3. *Using the CTRL key for Format Character commands*
   Give the procedure for first making a word boldface, then boldface and underlined, then regular text again.

4. *Entering graphics characters with the ALT key*
   What is the main restriction on entering graphics characters with the ALT key and a three-digit number?

5. *Copying character formats with the mouse*
   What is the procedure for copying character formats?

6. *Searching for character formats*
   How would you search for a word that was underlined and in italics?

chapter 8

FORMATTING PARAGRAPHS AND TABLES

Lesson 33: Basic Formatting for Paragraphs
Lesson 34: Indenting Paragraphs
Lesson 35: Line Spacing for Paragraphs
Lesson 36: Selecting Paragraph Formats with the CTRL key
Lesson 37: Aligning Paragraphs and Using Keeps
Lesson 38: Copying Paragraph Formats with the Mouse
Lesson 39: Using Tabs
Lesson 40: Setting Tabs
Lesson 41: Using Leader Characters and Making Tables
Lesson 42: Working with Columns
Lesson 43: Creating Side by Side Paragraphs
Lesson 44: Vertical Tabs
Lesson 45: Boxes and Borders
Lesson 46: Absolutely Positioned Paragraphs
Lesson 47: Searching for Paragraph Formats

One of the best ways to make letters and reports look professional is to use consistent formatting throughout the document. For example, if you indent your paragraphs, all paragraphs should be indented the same amount.

All headings should also be formatted consistently, so that the reader can quickly determine what you are saying. In a report, it is often important to see section headings and topics quickly. If your document is organized around an outline, your use of consistent formatting for each level of information will help the reader understand the meaning of the whole document.

Formatting paragraphs in Word is quite easy since Word associates a format with each paragraph. You can specify paragraph formatting when you enter the paragraph, and you can later change the formatting if you change your mind (just as you can with character formatting, described in Chapter 7). Word automatically uses the same format for each paragraph until you tell it otherwise. That way, all of your text paragraphs look the same until you give different formatting commands.

Tab stops are a format characteristic that you can set for a paragraph. Word's tab stops work just like those on a typewriter, but with one additional feature: if your writing includes figures and tables, you can easily use one set of tab stops for one table and a different set for another table.

LESSON 33: BASIC FORMATTING FOR PARAGRAPHS

Word stores a paragraph's format in the mark at the end of the paragraph. You may have noticed that an extra blank character is inserted at the end of each paragraph; this is the paragraph mark that is inserted when you press the ENTER key.

You can choose from a variety of paragraph formatting options. To see a list of them, select any text in the paragraph and give the Format Paragraph command.

If you are doing a lot of paragraph formatting, it is useful to show the *ruler* at the top of the window. To show the ruler if it is not already visible, give the View Ruler command. You can also show the ruler by clicking on the ruler icon at the right side of the window. The ruler icon is the inverted "T" below the "split" icon.

For example, load the SAMPLE1 file into Word and select the "I" in the first text paragraph. Now give the Format Paragraph command:

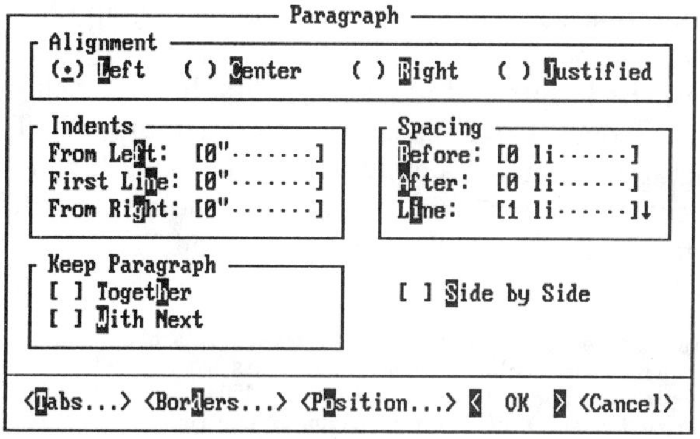

The ruler tells where your paragraph indentations are and where each tab stop is. The numbers on the ruler correspond to every inch; when you enter the settings for paragraph indentations, you give the position in inches. To set tab stops, you use the Format Tabs command, which is discussed later in this chapter.

As in other Word dialogs, you simply choose the characteristics that you want the selected paragraph to have. The choices are described in the following lessons. Many of the paragraph formatting commands can be executed with CTRL key sequences (like those used in character formatting) instead of with the menu.

Remember that you can change the formatting of a paragraph at any time. Word has default settings for all of the paragraph formatting choices (sometimes called the "normal" choices), but it is likely that these will not be the best choices in every instance. For example, you may enter some text in a memo with normal paragraph formatting and then decide later to indent the paragraph from both margins to make it stand out on the page. You can change the margins, see how the paragraph looks, and decide to keep the new format. You can, of course, always change it back at any time.

LESSON 34: INDENTING PARAGRAPHS

The most common paragraph format changes that you will make will be to indent the whole paragraph and the first line. These can be changed with the From Left, First Line, and From Right choices of the Format Paragraph dialog. Throughout this section, remember that paragraph indentation is always relative to page indentation, which you will learn about in Chapter 9.

In common business letters and memos, the first line of each paragraph is indented from the margin by five spaces, or about half an inch. To do this in the Format Paragraph command, simply change the value for the first line to .5 inch, and execute the command. Notice that the paragraph is now indented, and the text is automatically wrapped around.

```
    I am pleased to send you the latest update on the results of
our expanded product line. The enclosed summary documents our
increased profit margin (7%) for the fourth quarter of 1989,
which is largely due to the successful introduction of our new
model, the DC50. In 1990 we expect to continue increasing our
profitable inroads into this new area.
```

Sometimes you want to indent an entire paragraph from the left and right margins. This is common for direct quotations in reports. Indenting is also used a great deal in letters, especially for the date and closing (remember that these are considered paragraphs in Word). On a typewriter, you use the TAB key or SPACEBAR to move each line to the place you want; in Word, you simply indicate the indentation from the left margin once. To see how this is done, select the date at the beginning of the letter and use the Format Paragraph command to set the left indent to 3 inches.

```
                              January 11, 1990

Chris Richford, Vice President
Manufacturer's Bank of the Northeast
1000 First Avenue
Millerton, CT  06492
```

To specify inches, you can use either the double-quote mark (") or the abbreviation "in" after the number (3" or 3in). You would probably indent the closing and the name and address also.

The measurement indicated in the First Line choice is relative to that in the From Left choice. That is, if you want to indent the entire paragraph 1 inch and the first line half an inch beyond that, set the left indent to 1 inch and the first line to .5 inch. If you do not want to indent the first line but want to move the entire paragraph 1 inch from the margin, you would set the left indent to 1 inch and the first line to 0 inches.

This brings up an interesting situation: What if you want the first line to start to the left of the rest of the paragraph? This format is called a *hanging indent* or an *outdent.* To see how this is formatted, select the first full paragraph, give the Format Paragraph command, and set the From Left indent to 1 inch and the First Line indent to −.5 (negative one-half) inch. The result is shown here:

```
Dear Ms. Richford:

    I am pleased to send you the latest update on the results of
        our expanded product line. The enclosed summary
        documents our increased profit margin (7%) for the
        fourth quarter of 1989, which is largely due to the
        successful introduction of our new model, the DC50. In
        1990 we expect to continue increasing our profitable
        inroads into this new area.
```

Be sure not to set the From Left indent choice to a negative number. You can use negative numbers only with the First Line choice, not with the left and right indent choices.

It is unlikely that you will change a paragraph's right margin unless you are also changing the left margin. Experiment by changing the right indent choice on the first full paragraph to 2 inches:

```
Dear Ms. Richford:

    I am pleased to send you the latest
        update on the results of our
        expanded product line. The enclosed
        summary documents our increased
        profit margin (7%) for the fourth
        quarter of 1989, which is largely
        due to the successful introduction
        of our new model, the DC50. In 1990
        we expect to continue increasing
        our profitable inroads into this
```

The Edit Undo command will remove the effects of the most recent changes.

If you show the ruler, the current indentation is displayed. The left square bracket ([) shows the left indent, the right square bracket (]) shows the right indent, and the vertical bar (|) shows the first-line indent. For example, if the left margin is indented 1 inch and the first line is outdented .5 inch, the ruler bar would appear as follows:

```
 File  Edit  View  Insert  Format  Utilities  Macro  Window              Help
 Style:[Normal*···········]↓  Font:[Courier·······]↓  Pts:[12·]↓  Bld Ital Ul
═════════════════════════════ SAMPLE1.DOC ══════════════════════════════════
 L0····¦····[·········2·········3·········4····]····5·········6·········7·····
  January 11, 1990

  Chris Richford, Vice President
  Manufacturer's Bank of the Northeast
  1000 First Avenue
  Millerton, CT  06492

  Dear Ms. Richford:

       I am pleased to send you the latest
           update on the results of our
           expanded product line. The enclosed
```

These indentation choices illustrate the reason that you want to treat related text as one paragraph by using NEWLINE instead of ENTER. Remember that you use NEWLINE (SHIFT-ENTER) to go to a new line without starting a new paragraph. When you change the indentation with the Format Paragraph command, all the lines are formatted together since they are in one paragraph.

For example, assume that you want to move the lines with Thomas Mead's name, company, and address 3 inches from the left margin. If each line ends in a NEWLINE character, you can give just one Format Paragraph command for the set of four lines, instead of having to give it on each line. To see how this works, change the paragraph breaks to NEWLINE characters (if you did not use NEWLINE originally) by placing the selection at the end of each line, using the DEL key, and then typing in the NEWLINE character. Notice that the screen looks the same. Select this paragraph, give the Format Paragraph command, and set the left indent to 3 inches. The lines now move together:

```
Sincerely,


                              Thomas Mead, Controller
                              National Generators
                              1275 Oak Glen Industrial Park
                              Oak Glen,  CT  06410
```

LESSON 35: LINE SPACING FOR PARAGRAPHS

You can modify the number of lines above, below, and inside a paragraph. In the examples that you have typed up to this point, you have inserted blank lines between paragraphs as if you were doing so on a typewriter, by pressing the ENTER key an extra time. Now you will see how to have Word do this automatically with the Format Paragraph command.

Although using this method is no easier than pressing the ENTER key, it allows you to enter text more consistently. Remember that one of the goals of using Word's formatting features is to make your documents look as consistent as possible. Instead of having to remember how many lines you want after each paragraph and pressing the ENTER key that many times, Word remembers to do this for you in the paragraph format.

If you want to insert blank lines between paragraphs, it is usually easier to specify them as space before the paragraph, not after. Thus, you should change space before the paragraphs to 1 line in SAMPLE1.

You now need to eliminate the empty paragraphs that you created when you used the ENTER key; to do this, place the selection indicator at the end of the extra lines and press the DEL key. This makes the letter look as it did before.

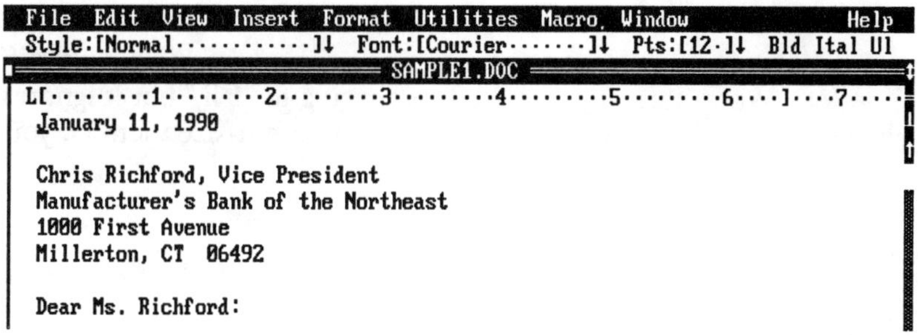

Remember to check that the lines between the closing and Thomas Mead's name are specified as 2 lines before the paragraph.

Line spacing allows you to specify that a particular paragraph is double- or triple-spaced. Direct paragraph formatting does not allow you to specify line spacing for an entire document. Thus, if you entered a document with single spacing, you must then change each paragraph to double or triple spacing. However, you can enter a document with double or triple spacing by formatting the first paragraph and then typing in the others.

For instance, to double-space the first paragraph in SAMPLE1, select any part of it and change the line spacing to 2 lines.

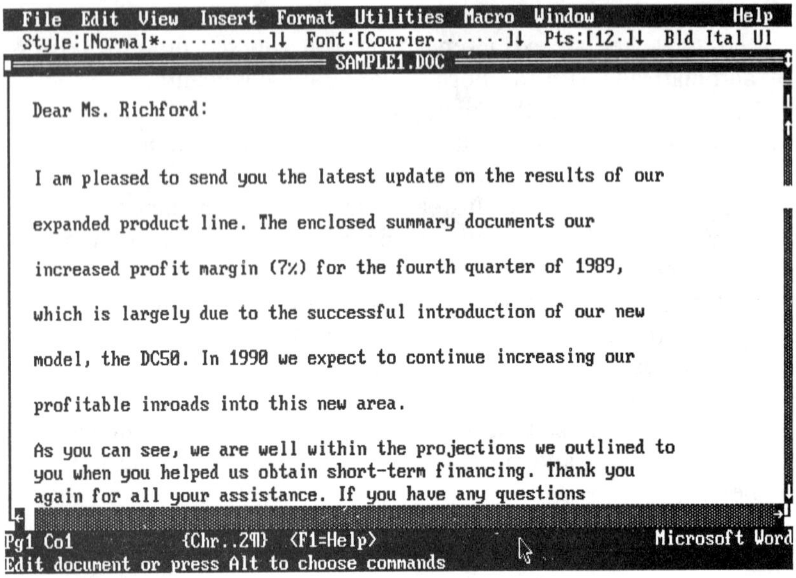

If you use different fonts on a single line, you may have different-sized letters. Word normally sets the line spacing to "1 li," but it ignores the size of the letters on the line. If you are using different-sized letters, you should use "Auto" instead of "1 li."

LESSON 36: SELECTING PARAGRAPH FORMATS WITH THE CTRL KEY

You can choose paragraph styles with CTRL-key combinations, just as you did in Chapter 7 with character styles. Table 8-1 shows the styles available.

As you can see, some of these key combinations, such as CTRL-M and CTRL-N, do not set an absolute format. Instead, they change the current settings of the paragraph by a small amount. You can use these key combinations repeatedly to move the margins.

For instance, select any part of the first paragraph of the letter; then press CTRL-N. Notice that the paragraph moves .5 inch:

```
Dear Ms. Richford:

     I am pleased to send you the latest update on the results of
     our expanded product line. The enclosed summary documents
     our increased profit margin (7%) for the fourth quarter of
     1989, which is largely due to the successful introduction of
     our new model, the DC50. In 1990 we expect to continue
     increasing our profitable inroads into this new area.
```

If you press CTRL-N again, the paragraph will move farther to the right. To move it back, use CTRL-M.

LESSON 37: ALIGNING PARAGRAPHS AND USING KEEPS

All of the paragraphs you have typed in so far have been *left-aligned.* This means that each line begins at the left margin and is formatted with word-wrap, but the right margin is ragged. As discussed in the Getting Started chapter, books and magazines often use justified margins, which means that, in addition to beginning at the left margin, the spaces between words on each line vary so that each line ends on the right margin (for instance, this book uses justified margins). Many people find justified text easier to read, and more professional looking in reports.

Format	CTRL-Key Combination
Normal	CTRL-X
Decrease left indent .5 in	CTRL-M
Increase left indent .5 in.	CTRL-N
Hanging indent	CTRL-T
Open 1 line before	CTRL-O
Double spacing	CTRL-2
Single spacing	CTRL-1
Left-aligned	CTRL-L
Justified	CTRL-J
Centered	CTRL-C
Right-aligned	CTRL-R
Indent left and right	CTRL-Q

TABLE 8-1. Paragraph Formatting with CTRL-Key Combinations

Almost all of your writing will be either left-aligned or justified; however, Word also lets you center each line of text in a paragraph, which is often useful for headings or for text that you want to stand out on a page, such as warnings. For a trendy look, you can even format right-aligned text, which makes the left margin ragged and aligns the right margin.

The four styles of paragraphs (left-aligned, justified, centered, and right-aligned) are shown here:

```
This is a normal paragraph that is left-aligned. This means that
the right margin will be ragged, but that each line begins on the
left margin.

This paragraph is justified. When you finish  typing  each  line,
Word puts extra spaces on the line to make it line  up  with  the
right margin.

A centered paragraph has white space on each line equal distance
 from the two margins. This is usually only used for headings or
                          special text.

    This paragraph is right-aligned. As you can see, each line is
lined up against the right margin, but the left margin is ragged.
                 This is an interesting, but rarely used, format.
±
```

Clear the SAMPLE1 file from your screen and enter the text for each paragraph; then use the Format Paragraph command to set the alignment. Experiment by adding text to the centered and right-aligned paragraphs to see how Word shuffles the characters as you type them.

Remember that you can use the NEWLINE character to start a new line without starting a new paragraph. You can use NEWLINE with the centered format to make text stand out on a page. For example, enter the following as a single paragraph using NEWLINE characters:

```
WARNING!
Do not use this product
without first consulting your physician.
±
```

Now use the Format Paragraph command or press CTRL-C to center the paragraph:

```
                         WARNING!
                  Do not use this product
            without first consulting your physician.

±
```

When you write memos and reports that are longer than one page, you may find that Word breaks the last paragraph on the page in an inappropriate place. Word automatically prevents widows (only the last line of a paragraph on the top of a page) and orphans (only the first line of a paragraph on the bottom of a page) by moving lines to or from a page as necessary. Word will never leave one line of a paragraph stranded on a page.

There are times when you will want to keep the whole paragraph together; for instance, in tables or figures blank space at the bottom of a page is preferable to splitting up the information. To keep a paragraph together, select the Together option in the Format Paragraph command.

Word prevents widows and orphans to make your documents look better. If you do not want Word to prevent widows and orphans, unselect the widow/orphan control in the Utilities Customize command.

LESSON 38: COPYING PARAGRAPH FORMATS WITH THE MOUSE

In Chapter 7 you learned how to copy character formats from one set of characters to other sets; here you will learn the similar process for copying paragraph formats. Copying paragraph formats is an excellent way to format tables, since you can make the table without worrying about the format, choose the format for one section, and then copy it throughout the table.

You may recall that character formats are copied by selecting the text you want to format, pointing at the format that you want to apply to the text, and pressing CTRL-SHIFT and the left button. Paragraph formats are copied in much the same way: select the part of the paragraph you want to format, move the pointer to the selection bar alongside the paragraph you want to copy from, and press CTRL-SHIFT and the left button.

In the next example, the first paragraph is left-aligned, while the second is right-aligned.

```
A paragraph that is left-aligned looks much more natural than one
that is right-aligned, since most people are used to seeing text
that comes from a typewriter.

      Of course, it is almost impossible to make a right-aligned
 paragraph on a typewriter. In fact, it is usually very hard just
              to make a center-aligned paragraph on a typewriter.
♦
```

To right align both paragraphs, select any part of the first paragraph and then point to the selection bar in the second paragraph:

```
A paragraph that is left-aligned looks much more natural than one
that is right-aligned, since most people are used to seeing text
that comes from a typewriter.

       Of course, it is almost impossible to make a right-aligned
 paragraph on a typewriter. In fact, it is usually very hard just
              to make a center-aligned paragraph on a typewriter.
```

Now press CTRL-SHIFT and the left button to copy the formatting to the first paragraph:

```
A paragraph that is left-aligned looks much more natural than one
 that is right-aligned, since most people are used to seeing text
                                    that comes from a typewriter.

       Of course, it is almost impossible to make a right-aligned
 paragraph on a typewriter. In fact, it is usually very hard just
              to make a center-aligned paragraph on a typewriter.
```

LESSON 39: USING TABS

Setting up tables in your text is often one of the hardest chores in word processing. Even if the tabs are set just right, your data often does not fit on the page. Adding a column of text can be nearly impossible. However, if you set the tabs correctly with Word, you will find that making tables is very easy.

You set and move tabs with the Format Tabs command. The Format Tabs command displays a dialog with any currently active tabs displayed in an inset box:

```
┌──────────────────────── Tabs ─────────────────────────┐
│Tab Position:  ┌ Alignment ──┐   ┌ Leader ───┐          │
│[0.5"_·······] │ (•) Left    │   │ (•) 1 None│          │
│ ┌──────────┐  │ ( ) Center  │   │ ( ) 2 ....│          │
│ │ 0.5"    ↑│  │ ( ) Right   │   │ ( ) 3 ----│          │
│ │          │  │ ( ) Decimal │   │ ( ) 4 ____│          │
│ │         ↓│  │ ( ) Vertical│   │           │          │
│ └──────────┘  └─────────────┘   └───────────┘          │
│To be Cleared:                                          │
├────────────────────────────────────────────────────────┤
│<Set>  <Clear>  <Clear All>  < OK >  <Cancel>           │
└────────────────────────────────────────────────────────┘
```

In your text, you skip to the tab stop the same way you do on a typewriter: by pressing the TAB key.

Word has four different types of tabs: *left, center, right,* and *decimal.* The type of tab indicates where the text will line up against it. A left tab is like a tab stop on a typewriter: the text begins at the tab stop and continues to the right. A right tab is the opposite of a left tab: the text starts to the left of the tab stop and ends at the tab stop.

The following example should clear up any confusion between these two types of tabs. The first tab (the column beginning "NE") is a left (normal) tab stop. The second (with the numbers) is a right tab stop. Notice that the numbers all end at the tab.

```
Northeast          NE       5530
South              S        4950
Midwest            MW      12150
Pacific            P        8810
                           -----
Total                      31440
```

In general, left tabs are used for text and right tabs are used for numbers. Right tabs are especially useful if you include a sum for the group of numbers, since numbers of different lengths then line up correctly.

A center tab causes the text to be centered around the tab stop, much like a centered paragraph; these are useful for headings of columns. A decimal tab causes numbers with decimal points to line up with the decimal point on the tab. In the next example, the first tab stop is a center tab and the second tab stop is a decimal tab:

```
  Manufacturing      35,772.19
    Marketing         8,339.71
     Support         27,100.00
Shipping and Tax        952.81
```

Center and decimal tabs are used much less frequently than left and right tabs. The following shows how different types of tabs align text and decimal numbers.

```
              The tab is set here --->|
                                      This is a left-aligned tab.
                          This is a center-aligned tab.
             This is a right-aligned tab.
The following are decimal tabs:
                                   $9327.44
                                      12.0
```

LESSON 40: SETTING TABS

Setting tabs is very easy. You can either use the Format Tabs dialog or set them directly on the ruler. The Format Tabs dialog lets you set tabs very precisely. Using the ruler to set tabs is faster, and you can see where your tabs are as you set them. Regardless of which method you use, you should always select one or more paragraphs that you want to apply the tab settings to before you change the tabs.

Using the Format Tabs dialog, enter a measurement in the "Tab Position" text field and click the "Set" button. All of the tabs you have entered are listed in the scrolling list below the text field. As you set a tab position, you also specify the type of tab and the leader (described later in this chapter). To remove a tab setting, highlight it in the scrolling list and click the "Clear" button. As you might guess, the "Clear All" button removes all tab stops at once.

Setting tabs with the ruler gives you more direct feedback as you set tabs, since the paragraph changes each time you add or remove a tab. This makes it easy to see if the tabs you specify are the ones you want.

Setting Tabs with the Mouse

You must first specify the type of alignment you want the added tab to have. The letter at the left of the ruler indicates the type of tab you are adding (L, R, C, and D for left, right, center, and decimal). To change the letter, point at it and click. When you have the correct tab type, simply point to the position you want on the ruler and click. You can add as many tabs this way as you want. (There is also a sixth option, a vertical bar, which is described later in this chapter.)

To move a tab, point to the tab on the ruler, hold down the left mouse button, and drag the tab to the new position. When you release the mouse button, the tab appears in the new place. To remove a tab, do the same thing except drag down below the ruler and release the mouse button.

Setting Tabs with the Keyboard

Press CTRL-SHIFT-F10 to activate the ruler. A flashing rectangle appears at the left. Use the → and ← keys to move the marker to the desired location, then press L, R, C, or D (for left, right, center, or decimal) to place the tab. Enter all your tabs, and then press ENTER. In addition to → and ←, you can also use ↑ and ↓ to move to tabs that are already set and HOME and END to move to each end of the ruler.

To move a tab, press CTRL-SHIFT-F10 to activate the ruler, then select the tab by pressing ↑ or ↓. Use CTRL-→ and CTRL-← to move the tab to the new position, then press ↑ or ↓ to select the next tab to be moved. To remove a tab, press DEL.

Set up the following table for practice. The second column is right-aligned, the third column is left-aligned, and the fourth column is decimal-aligned:

Terrence	80	Regular	80.00
Connors	150	Senior	125.00
Long	130	Regular	130.00
Yee	50	New	67.50

(If you need help, the three tab stops are a right-aligned tab at 2.1 inches, a left-aligned tab at 3.1 inches, and a decimal tab at 4.5 inches.)

LESSON 41: USING LEADER CHARACTERS AND MAKING TABLES

You may have noticed another choice in the Format Tabs command, namely, the leader character. Many tables, such as financial summaries, use characters to connect the columns of information across the page. These characters, usually dots, are called *leader characters,* since they lead to the text at the next tab stop. Unless you specify otherwise, Word will assume that you want a blank leader character.

For example, change the first tab stop in the previous example to include a dot leader character. Give the Format Tabs command and select the period leader (number 2):

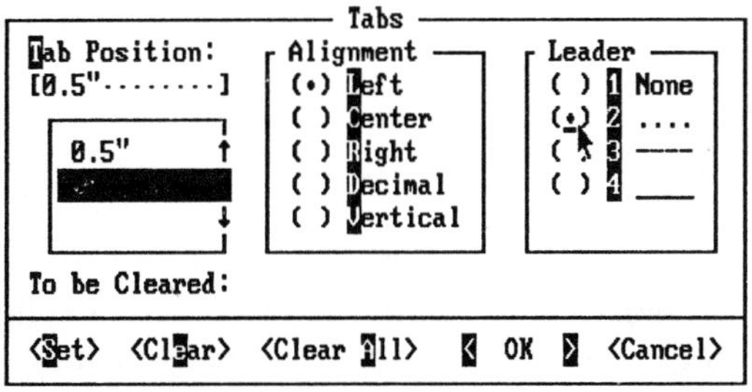

The table will then look like this:

```
Terrence...........88          Regular     88.00
Connors...........150          Senior     125.00
Long..............130          Regular    130.00
Yee................50          New         67.50
```

This is, of course, a great deal easier than typing all the periods yourself. It is also easy to change to another type of leader character in a table since you don't have to erase the old characters and type in the new characters for each entry. For instance, change the leader character to a dash. The table now looks like this:

```
Terrence-----------88          Regular     88.00
Connors-----------150          Senior     125.00
Long--------------130          Regular    130.00
Yee----------------50          New         67.50
```

You can also use underscores as leader characters.

When making a complex table, it is a good idea to use graph paper and pencil before setting your tabs. Figure out where on the line you want each item to appear and mark that place; then use the Format Tabs command.

When you are changing tabs on the ruler with the keyboard, you can press the keys for the type of leader (period, dash, or underscore) that you want to set.

The table shown in Figure 8-1 uses a number of different tab styles; see if you can figure out which ones were used.

Note that the table makes use of underlining and boldfacing to make the report clearer. The dots before the first tab stop were produced as leader characters.

Feel free to experiment with the different types of tabs to determine which will be most useful in your report writing. Try moving tabs around in a table to determine the best amount of room between columns. You will find that editing tables is fairly easy and that the more you experiment with tab settings, the better your tables will look.

LESSON 42: WORKING WITH COLUMNS

If you are editing a table, you may want to move or delete a column of data. For example, in the table in Figure 8-1 you may want to have the current

Financial Report Excerpts
Ice Nine Publishing

Annual Report for 1990

Consolidated Statement of Earnings
for the year ended December 31:

(Dollars in millions)		1990		1989
Gross income				
Sales.	23,274		16,815	
Rentals	9,203		11,121	
Services.	7,676		6,428	
		40,180		34,364
Costs of sales	9,748		6,682	
Costs of rentals.	3,141		3,959	
Costs of services	3,506		3,047	
Selling, general and administrative expenses.	10,614		9,286	
Research development and engineering expenses.	3,582		3,042	
Interest expense	390		454	
		30,981		26,470
		9,199		7,894
Other income, principally interest.		741		328
Earnings before income taxes.		9,940		8,222
Provision for income taxes		4,455		3,813
Net earnings		**5,485**		**4,409**

FIGURE 8-1. A table with a number of different tab styles

year in the right-most column and the previous year to its left. To make such a move you need a way of selecting a single column.

There are other times when you might want to manipulate columns of text. If you have created a table and you want to add a column in the middle, you need to add a new column of tab characters. To format all the numbers in a column, you could select the whole column and give the Format Character command only once.

To select a column of text:

1. Select a character that is in one corner of the column. Usually, you should select a character in the upper-left corner.

```
Northeast       NE      5530
South           S       4950
Midwest         MW     12150
Pacific         P       8810
                       -----
Total                  31440
♦
```

2. Press CTRL-SHIFT-F8 to activate the column selection feature. In the status line, you will see CS indicated at the bottom of the screen.

3. Extend your selection to the end of the column. If you are editing a table, be sure to include the tab characters in your selection.

```
Northeast       NE      5530
South           S       4950
Midwest         MW     12150
Pacific         P       8810
                       -----
Total                  31440
```

You can select more than one column at a time with this method. Word will simply treat everything that you select as a single column.

Once you have selected a column of text, you can treat it as you would any other text. You can delete it, copy it to the scrap, and so on. Thus, to switch the position of two columns, you would select the right column, delete it to the scrap, point to the first character of the remaining column, and insert from the scrap.

LESSON 43: CREATING SIDE BY SIDE PARAGRAPHS

So far, you have learned how to create paragraphs that sit on lines by themselves. Frequently, you'll want two paragraphs to be next to each other, however. For example, imagine that you are preparing a list of events and participants. You could create the list of participants before each event:

Keller, Stanley, Anderson, Thatcher

Customer service seminar for all C.S. staff. Receptionists are invited to this seminar.

Nolan, Timmer, Fellston

Group dynamics seminar for engineering staff and technicians.

But it might be more useful to list the participants to the side:

Keller, Stanley, Anderson, Thatcher	Customer service seminar for all C.S. staff. Receptionists are invited to this seminar.
Nolan, Timmer, Fellston	Group dynamics seminar for engineering staff and technicians.

You cannot do this easily with the techniques you have learned so far, because here you need Word to wrap text separately within each of the two columns.

Instead, use the Side by Side option of the Format Paragraph command. Before you do, however, you must determine the width of both paragraphs and their placement between the page margins. Word does not make this particularly easy, because you must know what the line length for your document is when you make these decisions. You will learn more about determining the page margins in Chapter 9; the following discussion assumes a line length of 6 inches.

For this example, you want the left paragraph to be 2 inches wide, the white space between the paragraphs to be .25 inch, and the right paragraph to be 3.75 inches. Determining the indents for the paragraphs can get a bit tricky. The left paragraph has a left indent of 0 since it is against the left margin, and the right paragraph has a right indent of 0 since it ends against the right margin. However, you need to determine the amount to indent the right side of the left paragraph and the amount to indent the left side of the right paragraph so that you can place them on the same lines. You can see how these margins are set:

Indent from right margin (4")

Keller, Stanley, Anderson, Thatcher	Customer service seminar for all C.S. staff. Receptionists are invited to this seminar.
Nolan, Timmer, Fellston	Group dynamics seminar for engineering staff and technicians.

Indent from left margin (2.25")

The right indent for the left paragraph equals the width of the other (right) paragraph plus the space between the paragraphs. In this case, the right indent is 4 inches (3.75 inches for the right paragraph width plus .25 inches between).

The left indent for the right paragraph equals the width of the other (left) paragraph plus the space between the paragraphs. In this case, the left indent is 2.25 inches (2 inches for the left paragraph width plus .25 inches between).

Follow these steps when you want to create side by side paragraphs:

1. Type in the text for both paragraphs.
2. Determine the layout of the page, deciding on the number of columns and their widths, as in the previous example.
3. Select the left paragraph and give the Format Paragraph command. Set the left indent to 0, the right indent to the amount calculated above, and select the Side by Side option.
4. Select the right paragraph and give the Format Paragraph command. Set the amount calculated above, the right indent to 0, and select the Side by Side option.

Notice that the two paragraphs are not aligned on the screen. When you print your document or use layout mode, Word will align the columns properly. You can use the Side by Side option to put up to six paragraphs on the same line. The method is similar to the one used here, but you must set both the left and right indents for all the middle paragraphs.

Using the Side by Side option does not prevent you from using Word's paragraph formatting. In the previous example, both paragraphs are left-aligned. You can just as easily specify other formatting. For example, if you format the left paragraph in the example with right-alignment, you would get

Keller, Stanley, Anderson, Thatcher	Customer service seminar for all C.S. staff. Receptionists are invited to this seminar.
Nolan, Timmer, Fellston	Group dynamics seminar for engineering staff and technicians.

To see your paragraphs laid out correctly, give the View Layout command. This changes the view to layout mode. You can edit in this mode, but it is often slower than editing in regular mode.

LESSON 44: VERTICAL TABS

The tab settings you have seen up to now were used for aligning text. Word has an additional type of tab, called a *vertical tab,* which allows you to draw vertical lines in your paragraphs. For example, if you want to draw a vertical line in a table, set a vertical tab at the position where you want the line.

Northeast	NE	5530
South	S	4950
Midwest	MW	12150
Pacific	P	8810

Total		31440

To add a vertical line after the abbreviations, select the paragraphs, and then give the Format Tabs command. Specify a vertical tab at 3.5 inches.

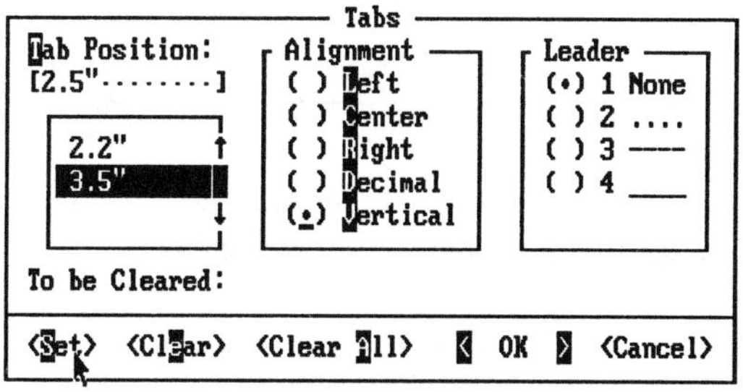

The result is shown here:

```
Northeast          NE |   5530
South              S  |   4950
Midwest            MW |  12150
Pacific            P  |   8810
                      |  -----
Total                 |  31440
```

Vertical tabs are useful when you are designing forms, especially if you also make boxes around paragraphs, which you'll learn to do in the next lesson.

LESSON 45: BOXES AND BORDERS

With Word's Format Borders command, you can put a box or a border around any paragraph. Simply select the paragraph, give the Format Borders command, and specify the border type.

Assume you want to add emphasis to the following paragraph:

```
The next manufacturing staff meeting will be Tuesday, March 22 at
3:00. This week's meeting is in Meeting Room B.
♦
```

The Format Borders dialog is shown here:

```
┌──────────────────── Paragraph Borders ─────────────────────┐
│ ┌ Border Type ─────────────┐  ┌ Line Style ─────────────┐  │
│ │ (•) None                 │  │ (•) Normal              │  │
│ │ ( ) Box Each Paragraph   │  │ ( ) Bold                │  │
│ │ ( ) Lines:               │  │ ( ) Double              │  │
│ │     [ ] Top   [ ] Bottom │  │ ( ) Thick               │  │
│ │     [ ] Left  [ ] Right  │  │ Color: [Black······]↓   │  │
│ └──────────────────────────┘  └─────────────────────────┘  │
│ ┌ Background Shading ─────────────────────────────────────┐│
│ │ Percentage: [0···]↓          Color: [Black······]↓      ││
│ └─────────────────────────────────────────────────────────┘│
├────────────────────────────────────────────────────────────┤
│                                        < OK >  <Cancel>    │
└────────────────────────────────────────────────────────────┘
```

Select "Box Each Paragraph" and execute the command. The text is automatically moved in from the border to accommodate the box.

```
┌──────────────────────────────────────────────────────────────┐
│The next manufacturing staff meeting will be Tuesday, March 22│
│at 3:00. This week's meeting is in Meeting Room B.            │
└──────────────────────────────────────────────────────────────┘
♦
```

Depending on your printer, the box may come out either thin or hairline.

The Format Borders command also lets you put lines around a paragraph without drawing a full box. For example, to put a line on either side of the paragraph, specify "Left" and "Right" in the Lines border type.

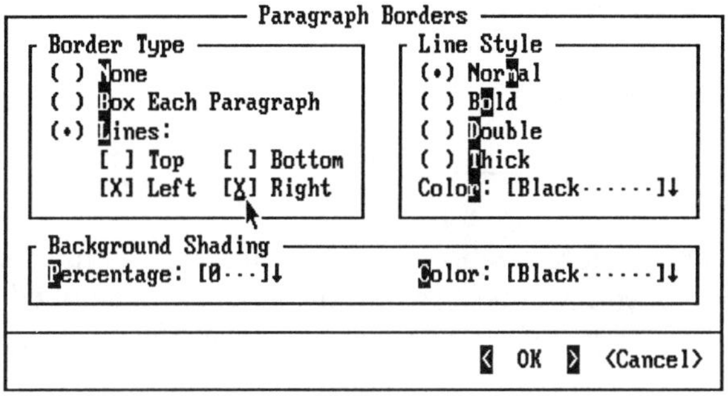

The result will look like this:

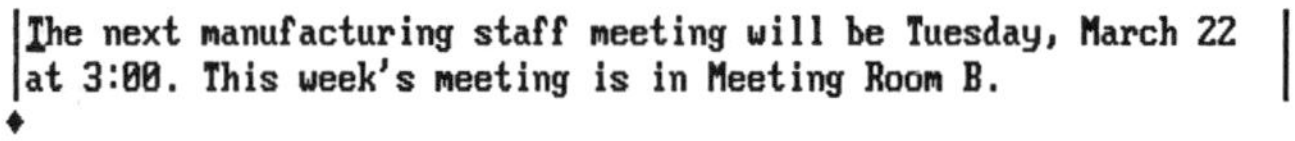

LESSON 46: ABSOLUTELY POSITIONED PARAGRAPHS

In a normal Word document, paragraphs follow one another on the page. However, there are many times when you will want a paragraph to appear in a particular spot on the page and have other paragraphs flow around it. That is, you want to specify an *absolute position* for the paragraph, such as "in the middle of the page, 3 inches from the left margin and 4 inches from the top margin" or "at the bottom of this column."

Absolutely positioned paragraphs are often used to add interesting layout elements such as pictures or excerpts from your text. For instance, a picture in a two-column document can make the page look more interesting. (If you are using a picture, that picture should be the only character in the paragraph.) You can easily do this using the Format Position command. You can also use absolutely positioned paragraphs to highlight information or important quotations.

Any paragraph in Word can be an absolutely positioned paragraph. You can do this easily using the Format Position command.

```
┌──────────────── Position ─────────────────┐
│ ┌ Horizontal ──────┐  ┌ Vertical ────────┐ │
│ │ [Left.·······]↓  │  │ [Inline·····]↓   │ │
│ │                  │  │                  │ │
│ │ Relative to:     │  │ Relative to:     │ │
│ │ ( ) Margin       │  │ (•) Margin       │ │
│ │ ( ) Page         │  │ ( ) Page         │ │
│ │ (•) Column       │  │                  │ │
│ └──────────────────┘  └──────────────────┘ │
│ Distance from Text:   [0.167"··········]  │
│ Paragraph Width:      [Single Column···]↓ │
├───────────────────────────────────────────┤
│ <Reset>                < OK >  <Cancel>   │
└───────────────────────────────────────────┘
```

When you set an absolutely positioned paragraph, you will not see the result on the screen unless you are in "view layout" mode, as described in Chapter 9. For now, use the Format Position command to set the paragraph and then give the Print Preview command to see the result. The different views of the screen are explained more fully in Chapter 9.

You need to specify the horizontal and vertical positions of the paragraph. These measurements can be relative to the margin or to the edge of the page; the horizontal position can also be relative to the column. For instance, to center a picture in the bottom of the text area, you would specify a horizontal position centered relative to the top and bottom margins and a vertical position centered relative to the side margins. You can also specify a measurement for the position, such as "3.25 inches from the left margin."

The choices for horizontal position are Left, Centered, Right, Inside, and Outside. Inside and Outside refer to even- and odd-numbered pages, as described in the next chapter. You can also enter a measurement that is relative to the left edge of the paper (such as "4 in").

The choices for vertical position are In line, Top, Centered, and Bottom. In line puts the paragraph in the vertical position it would normally occupy, following the previous paragraph. You can also enter a measurement that is relative to the top or bottom edge of the paper, or center the paragraph vertically.

The Paragraph Width choice sets the width of the absolutely positioned paragraph; this affects where text will flow around the text. You can set the paragraph width either with the indents in the Format Paragraph command or in the Format Position dialog. For a graphic, the width should be just enough to show the graphic plus any space you want to the left and right of the graphic. For text, you many want to set the indents to give some white space around the paragraph's text. Once you have positioned the paragraph on the page, use the Format Paragraph command to nudge the indents of the paragraph for the best look.

Absolutely positioned paragraphs make the design of your document more interesting. For more ideas about how to use them, see Chapter 23, "Desktop Publishing with Word."

LESSON 47: SEARCHING FOR PARAGRAPH FORMATS

Searching for paragraph formats is similar to searching for character formats. The Edit Search command lets you choose the format of the paragraph to be searched.

In the dialog, choose "Search for Formatting Only," select "Paragraph," specify the type of formatting you are searching for, and then execute the command. The options in the dialog are shown here:

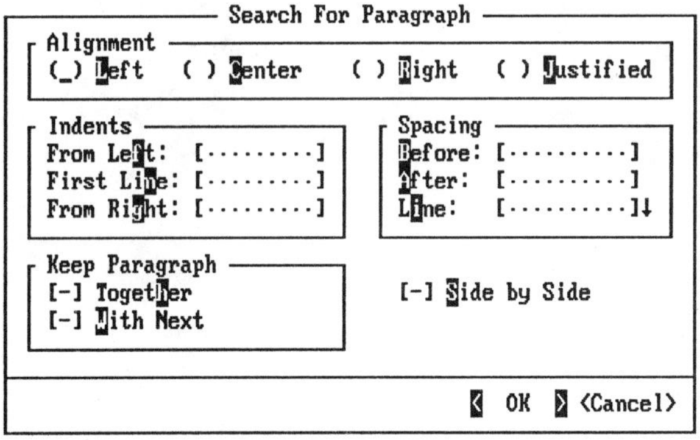

note You cannot search for tab positions.

REVIEW

1. *Formatting paragraphs*
   Which of the following characteristics is changed with the Format Paragraph command?

REVIEW (*continued*)

a. Fonts

b. Single- and double-spacing

c. Page margins

d. Indentation

e. Justification

2. *Indenting paragraphs*
Describe how paragraphs with the following formatting would look:

a. Left indent 1.2 in., first line 0 in., justified

b. Left indent 3 in., right indent 3 in., centered

c. Left indent 1 in., first line –1 in., left-aligned

3. *Centering text*
Enter the following text:

```
WARNING!
Do not operate this equipment before completely reading the
instruction manual. Improper use of this generator can void the
warranty and cause damage to other electrical devices attached to
it.
```

What steps would you use to make the paragraph look like this?

```
              WARNING!
Do  not  operate   this   equipment
before   completely   reading   the
instruction manual. Improper use of
this   generator   can   void   the
warranty and cause damage to  other
electrical devices attached to it.
```

4. *Changing the line spacing of paragraphs*
When would you use triple-spaced paragraphs?

REVIEW (*continued*)

5. *Aligning paragraphs with the margins*
If a paragraph is 12 lines long when formatted with left alignment only, how long will it be if you change to justified format?

6. *Keeping a paragraph together on a page*
Should you use the Together option of the Format Paragraph command to be sure that Word does not split a paragraph after the first line?

7. *Using tabs*
What type of tab stop would be appropriate for:

    a. Dollar amounts

    b. Column headings

    c. Lists of numbers

8. *Making tables*
Enter the following table:

```
Service options:

Limited (A).........25,000.00
Limited (B).........75,000.00
Full (A)...........100,000.00
Full (B)...........125,000.00
```

What type of tab would you use for this table?

9. *Vertical tabs and boxes*
How would the following paragraph be formatted?

Time Date Length	Standard Military Standard	

10. *Absolutely positioned paragraphs*
What command would you use to set a paragraph in the middle of the page?

chapter 9

FORMATTING PAGES AND FOOTNOTES

Lesson 48: Setting Page Margins
Lesson 49: Using Print Preview
Lesson 50: Creating Multi-Column Text
Lesson 51: Using Headers, Footers, and Page Numbering
Lesson 52: Page Breaks and Repaginating
Lesson 53: Using Footnotes
Lesson 54: Numbering Pleadings

So far you have learned how to format characters and paragraphs to improve their appearance. The third unit of formatting is the *section,* which allows you to specify the page formatting of your text when it is printed out. (You can think of a section as a chapter.) Page layout generally consists of the page margins and the position of running heads (the text at the top and bottom of each page, such as the page number and the chapter name).

You normally use the same page layout throughout a document. Sometimes, however, you may use a few different page layouts in one document; for instance, the preface of a report may have a different style than the main text. Word lets you change the page layout for each section.

Use the Format Section commands to change any of the formats for each section. The formatting characteristics of each section are kept in the section marker at the end of the section, just as paragraph characteristics are stored in the markers at the end of paragraphs. To create a new section, give the Insert Break command and choose "Section." Word will display a series of colons as shown here:

::

It is important to remember that these formatting characteristics only show up when you print out your text or when you use layout mode; except for the section marker, none of them appears on the screen. For instance, if you specify the placement of the page number at the top of each page, you won't see the number on the screen, only on the printed page or in layout mode.

A concept basic to many of the choices in the Format Section commands is that of odd and even pages. If you examine books and magazines, you will find that they always begin on the right page (for example, look at the beginning of this book). This means that all right-hand pages have odd numbers (1, 3, 5 . . .) and all left-hand pages have even numbers (2, 4, 6 . . .). Knowing whether a page is odd or even often helps in formatting your pages, as you will see in this chapter.

When you give the Format Section command, you see the following menu:

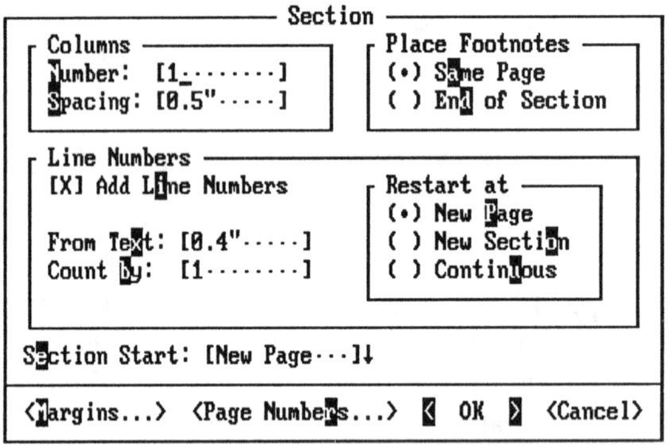

Because you choose where to begin the section, you can select whether the section will continue on the same page as the previous section or start on a different page. These choices are defined in Table 9-1.

Option	Result
Continuous	Continue from previous section without break
Column	Start section in the next column (for multi-column text)
Page	Start section on the next page
Odd	Start section on the next odd page
Even	Start section on the next even page

TABLE 9-1. Choices for Beginning a New Section

Figure 9-1 is a summary of a funding proposal. It will be used to illustrate formatting throughout this chapter and the next one. You do not need to type the report into Word; however, you may want to type in parts of it when trying out the examples.

LESSON 48: SETTING PAGE MARGINS

The Format Margins command options you use to set the general page margins are Page Size Width and Height, and Margins Top, Bottom, Gutter, Left, and Right.

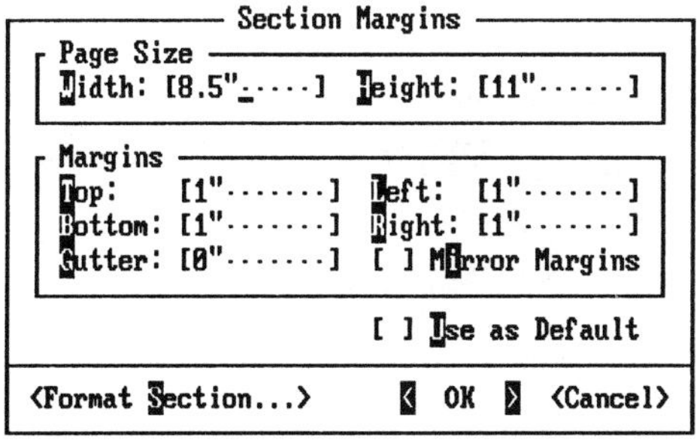

Excerpts from a Proposal for Bank Funding

I. Introduction

National Generators has the opportunity over the next five years to take a commanding lead in our established markets and to penetrate a new market, the construction industry, where our products will be particularly attractive. This report is intended to provide an overview of the company's business development strategies along with a description of those areas for which we require funding.

National Generators can become the premier producer of electrical generation equipment for the entertainment and exposition industries. Our portable yet sturdy generators have acquired a solid reputation in these fields. As the number of outdoor concerts, large conventions, and other events that use portable generators continues to increase each year, we will be better able than our competitors to satisfy the demand for reliable equipment.

While accelerating efforts aimed at our existing base of industrial users, we propose to enter the construction industry. We have already begun developing a small, quiet generator for this market. Research is also underway to design a larger, more efficient generator for heavy construction projects that can replace several smaller ones.

II. Market Analysis

National Generators currently has a 42% share of the markets we now serve. Our nearest competitor, Regional Outdoor Electricity, has 34%, with the rest divided among other manufacturers. We believe that our superior products will insure that we will increase our share of the entertainment and exposition industries' needs for portable generators. Some of our smaller competitors will be unable to match our new technology, and we will pick up their business.

Over the next five years we anticipate gaining 15% of the market for generators in the construction industry.[1] Two important trends favor our planned new products over any now available or known to be coming on the market. Anti-noise pollution legislation restricts the level of noise at urban construction sites, while OSHA legislation protects workers from damage to their hearing caused by equipment.

III. Expansion Costs

In order to carry out the entrance into the construction industry and to keep ahead of growth in the entertainment and exposition industries, we will require $4MM to be allocated in three areas:

1. Research and development of new products
2. Marketing for new business opportunities
3. Additional staffing for R and D and for marketing.

We will need to add one senior mechanical engineer and two technicians in R and D. We will also need a technical services manager, two product managers, and a

[1]Based on trends andgrowth in the construction industry, detailed in U.S. Department of Labor projections for 1985-1990.

FIGURE 9-1. Sample proposal

merchandising manager in marketing. The advertising budget will include campaigns in trade magazines and attendance at national trade shows.

IV. Current and Projected Earnings

National Generators has shown a profit each year since its founding in 1974. Pretax profits in 1987 were $3.25MM on sales of $17.5MM (20%). This year sales are expected to reach $19MM and a pretax profit of $4.2MM (22%). Five year projections call for $50MM in sales and pretax profit of $12MM (25%) by 1993.[2]

V. Company Directors

National Generators is a privately held company. The founders have a controlling interest (70%), and the remainder of the stock is held by the Joffee Group and Japanese-American Enterprises. The members of the board of directors are:

Samuel Ross, President (founder)
Albert Normandy, V.P., research and development (founder)
Irene Yashimoto, V.P., operations
Philip Bushnell, V.P., marketing
Hon. Louise B. Dart, The Joffee Group
Yuji Ko, Japanese-American Enterprises

[2]Based on constant 1987 dollars, using U.S. Department of Commerce inflation and growth estimates.

FIGURE 9-1. Sample proposal (*continued*)

It is important to remember that there is a difference between the left and right page margins and the left and right paragraph margins. The page margins are measured from the edge of the paper (determined by the paper length and width); the paragraph margins are measured from the left and right page margins.

The standard page width and length are 8.5 inches and 11 inches, respectively, since this is the standard size of paper used with Word. You can change these numbers if you are using different-sized paper (such as half-sheets, European-sized paper, or the paper used with a wide-carriage printer).

The top and bottom margins are set by default to 1 inch, and the left and right margins are set to 1.25 inches. These four values are the ones you are most likely to reset. Word gives you wide margins so that your running heads do not appear too near the edge of the page. You can now see how Word decides on the line length of a page:

line length = page width − (left margin + right margin)

In all of the examples so far, the page width has been 8.5 inches, and the left and right margins 1.25 inches, so the line length is 6 inches.

You may, however, need different settings. For example, many publishers insist on a 1.5-inch border around text submitted for publication. To create this margin, you would set the characteristics in the Format Margins command, as shown here:

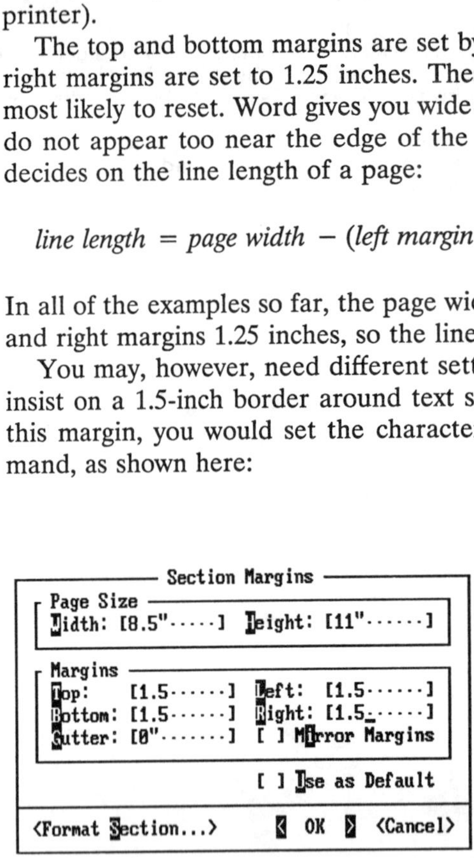

If you are going to bind the document, you may want to set a gutter width. The *gutter* is the space on a page that is not used in printing; in this case, it is the amount of space that is used in binding the document. Since binding a document takes up a certain amount of space where the pages are joined, you need extra paper along the left side of odd-numbered pages and the right side of even-numbered pages. Word allows you to move the margins over, alternating between left and right pages. Set the gutter width to the amount that would be lost in binding: when your pages are printed and bound, the text will not run into the gutter and will thus be easier to read.

LESSON 49: USING PRINT PREVIEW

Word's print preview and layout modes let you see exactly how your document will look when it is printed. Even though what you see on the screen in *galley* view (the normal view) is generally what your document will look like, it is not exact. For instance, you cannot see what the margins look like, or how absolutely positioned paragraphs will appear.

Using the File Print Preview command or the View Layout command is faster than printing out your document and it doesn't waste paper. You can use the commands at any time. The difference between the two commands is that the View Layout command (called *layout* mode) lets you edit your document, while the File Print Preview command (called *print preview* mode) only lets you look at it. If you need to see how your page will look as you edit, layout mode is very useful, although it reduces Word's performance.

To switch from galley mode to layout mode, give the View Layout command. Your screen will look similar to the screen in galley mode.

In layout mode, you can edit text as well as other parts of the page, which you cannot see in galley mode. For example, you can edit the headers and page numbers, which are described later in this chapter. In addition, you can see the position of absolutely positioned paragraphs. This helps you place these paragraphs exactly where you want them.

The major difference in layout mode is the addition of boundary lines around text items. The boundaries surround the parts of text such as tables, absolutely positioned paragraphs, and so on.

If you have a high-resolution screen, you may find it useful to split the screen into two windows, one in galley mode and the other in page view mode. This can help you enter text quickly in galley mode but still see the exact results in page view mode.

The File Print Preview command has a much more limited use. Generally, you only use it if you want to check the positioning on one or a few pages. When you give the File Print Preview command (or press CTRL-F9), Word opens a new window.

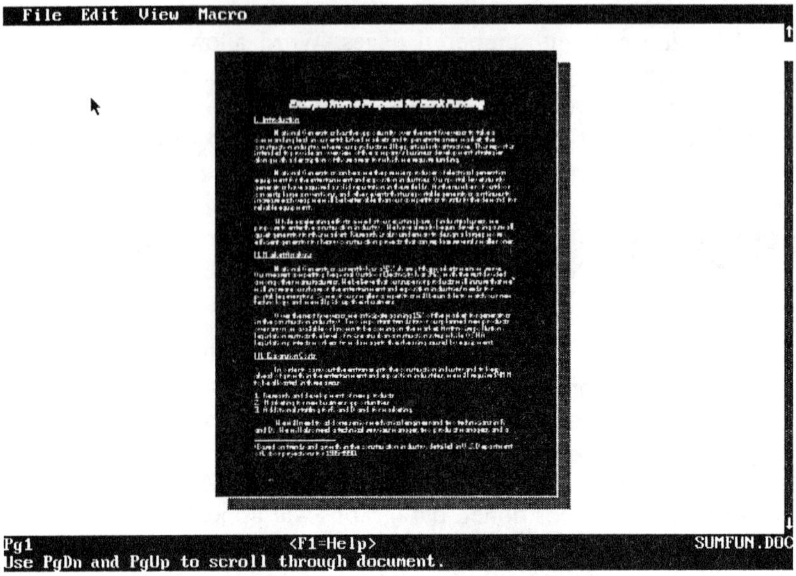

If you have a document that is more than one page, Word will show you two pages at a time.

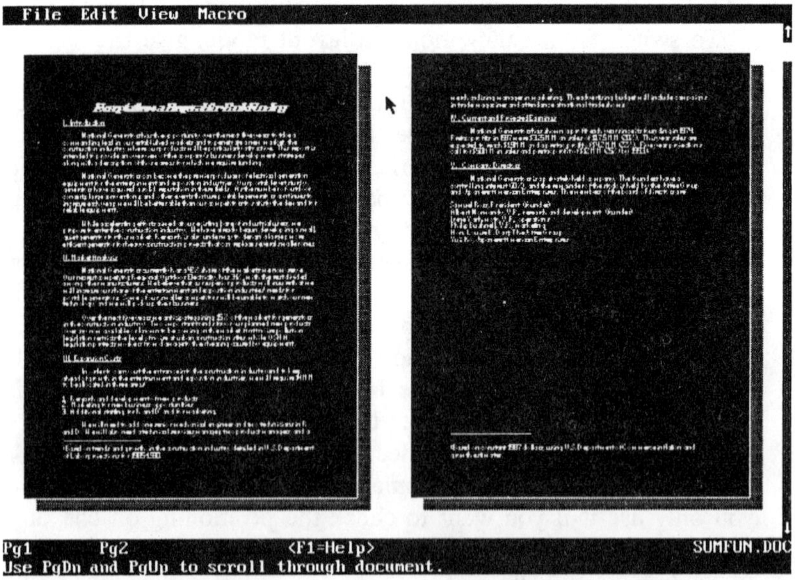

To scroll through the pages, use PGUP or PGDN.

While you are in print preview mode, you can still use the Edit Go to command to find a specific page or bookmark (bookmarks are described in Chapter 16). You can also print with the File Print command. When you want to go back to galley or page view mode, give the File Exit Preview command or press ESC.

LESSON 50: CREATING MULTI-COLUMN TEXT

Word can be used to print out newsletters and other material that is formatted with two or more columns on a page. If you decide to use the multi-column option, all of Word's formatting commands adjust themselves to work within the columns.

The options you set to produce multi-column text are Number of Columns and Spacing (the amount of white space between two columns). For example, to make a three-column document with .25 inch between each column, set the characteristics in the Format Section command as follows:

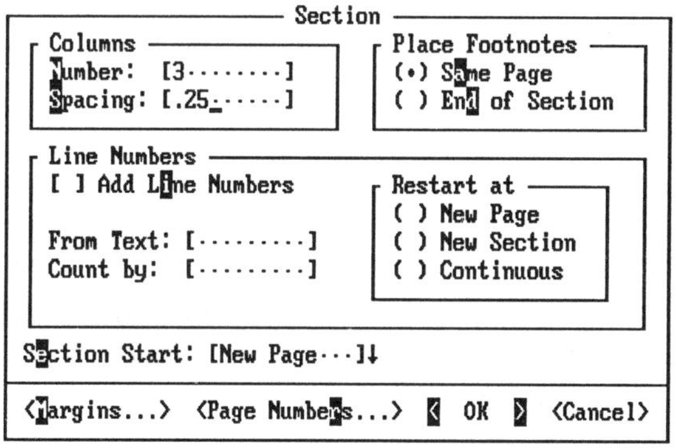

Remember that you won't see the multiple columns on the screen unless you use layout or print preview mode; however, the screen displays each individual column as it will appear on the page.

Splitting a page into columns greatly reduces the number of words per line, so you should probably format the paragraphs with left alignment. You will also want to use as many nonrequired hyphens as you can to make the lines more even. Justifying narrow columns usually results in a great deal of white space between words. For example, compare the paragraph here:

```
This is an example of
text with very thin
margins. Since three
columns were specified,
each column is only 24
characters wide.
Although the text looks
somewhat strange on the
screen, when it is
printed, you will see
that it looks like you
would expect in a
newsletter.
```

with the paragraph here:

```
This is  an  example  of
text  with   very   thin
margins.   Since   three
columns were  specified,
each column is  only  24
characters         wide.
Although the text  looks
somewhat strange on  the
screen,   when   it   is
printed,  you  will  see
that it looks  like  you
would   expect   in    a
newsletter.
```

Even though multi-column text is not often used in business documents, you may find that it enhances the appearance of some reports. Figure 9-2 shows part of the report printed in two columns.

LESSON 51: USING HEADERS, FOOTERS, AND PAGE NUMBERING

Word allows you to put headers and footers at the top and bottom of the page, and to change their text as often as you want. If you wish, your headers

Excerpts from a Proposal for Bank Funding

I. Introduction

National Generators has the opportunity over the next five years to take a commanding lead in our established markets and to penetrate a new market, the construction industry, where our products will be particularly attractive. This report is intended to provide an overview of the company's business development strategies along with a description of those areas for which we require funding.

National Generators can become the premier producer of electrical generation equipment for the entertainment and exposition industries. Our portable yet sturdy generators have acquired a solid reputation in these fields. As the number of outdoor concerts, large conventions, and other events that use portable generators continues to increase each year, we will be better able than our competitors to satisfy the demand for reliable equipment.

While accelerating efforts aimed at our existing base of industrial users, we propose to enter the construction industry. We have already begun developing a small, quiet generator for this market. Research is also underway to design a larger, more efficient generator for heavy construction projects that can replace several smaller ones.

II. Market Analysis

National Generators currently has a 42% share of the markets we now serve. Our nearest competitor, Regional Outdoor Electricity, has 34%, with the rest divided among other manufacturers. We believe that our superior products will insure that we will increase our share of the entertainment and exposition industries' needs for portable generators. Some of our smaller competitors will be unable to match our new technology, and we will pick up their business.

Over the next five years we anticipate gaining 15% of the market for generators in the construction industry.[1] Two important trends favor our planned new products over any now available or known to be coming on the market. Anti-noise pollution legislation restricts the level of noise at urban construction sites, while OSHA legislation protects workers from damage to their hearing caused by equipment.

III. Expansion Costs

In order to carry out the entrance into the construction industry and to keep ahead of growth in the entertainment and exposition industries, we will require $4MM to be allocated in three areas:

1. Research and development of new products
2. Marketing for new business opportunities
3. Additional staffing for R and D and for marketing.

We will need to add one senior mechanical engineer and two technicians in R and D. We will also need a technical services manager, two product managers, and a merchandising manager in marketing. The advertising budget will include campaigns in trade magazines and attendance at national trade shows.

IV. Current and Projected Earnings

---

[1]Based on trends andgrowth in the construction industry, detailed in U.S. Department of Labor projections for 1985-1990.

FIGURE 9-2. Text printed in two columns

Format	Meaning	Examples
1	Normal numbering	1,2,3,4, . . .
I	Roman numerals, uppercase	I,II,III,IV, . . .
i	Roman numerals, lowercase	i,ii,iii,iv, . . .
A	Alphabetic, uppercase	A,B,C,D, . . .
a	Alphabetic, lowercase	a,b,c,d, . . .

TABLE 9-2. Page Number Formats

and footers can each be more than one line.

There are two ways to get page numbers in your Word document: with the Insert Page Numbers command and with headers or footers. If you use the Insert Page Numbers command, the page numbers appear on every page in the same place and you cannot have other text next to the page numbers (such as the word "Page"). You have much more flexibility if you use headers and footers for your page numbers. Both commands only affect the current section.

With either type of numbering, you can choose a format for page numbers. This is useful when you submit articles and reports for publication since many publishers have guidelines about the format of page numbers. If you are preparing a long report, it is common to use lowercase Roman numerals for the pages up to the introduction, then normal numbering thereafter. Table 9-2 shows the page number formats available in Word.

You can also specify what number you want Word to start numbering with. If you want to continue from the previous pages' number, enter **Auto** instead of a number.

Insert Page Numbers Command

The Insert Page Numbers command lets you specify where the page numbers go on the page. The dialog is shown here:

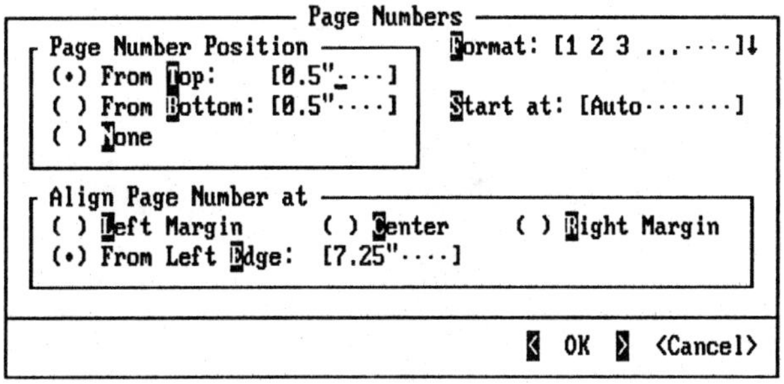

Choose how far you want the page number from the top or bottom of the page, and how you want it aligned with the side of the page. For example, if you want your page numbers to appear near the bottom of the page at the right margin, select "From Top," enter a measurement, and choose "Right Margin."

Headers and Footers

If you like, headers and footers can appear on only odd or only even pages, or only on the first page of a section. Depending on your requirements, you can have up to six different running heads in a section. Often, however, you will have similar or identical text at the top or bottom of even or odd pages, or no text at all.

Word allows you to include the current page number as part of the text on a page (for instance, if you want to print the number 5 on page 5), by using the glossary feature described in Chapter 6. You do this in a header or footer by using the *page* term from the glossary. When you expand this abbreviation, Word prints out "(page)" on your screen but substitutes the page number when you print or preview your document; the number is printed in the format you choose in the Insert Page Numbers dialog.

To see the use of page, type the following:

```
This sentence appears on page number page
```

Now press the F3 key to expand the glossary abbreviation.

```
This sentence appears on page number (page)♦
```

When you print this out, Word prints

This sentence appears on page number 17

You can now see the advantage of using headers and footers for page numbering. Instead of just a number, you can include text to go with the number (such as "Page 5" or "-5-"). You can also set the positioning of the page number differently for different types of pages. For example, it is common to have the page number near the left margin on even pages and near the right margin on odd pages (as it is in this book).

Positioning headers and footers is fairly easy. First, decide what information you want to present; then decide which part of that information should be at the top or bottom of the page. For instance, if you want to show just the page number and chapter name, you may want the chapter name at the top and the page number at the bottom.

Next, decide if there should be a distinction between even and odd pages. If your text will be printed back-to-back (on both sides of the paper), you should position the header and footer text on the right side of odd-numbered pages and the left side of even-numbered pages, so that the information will appear on the outside edge of the printed document.

Finally, decide whether you want headers and footers on the first page of the section. You usually will not, since this distracts the reader from the main title. Once you have decided on a layout, you can easily incorporate it.

To create a header or footer, type in the text you want, select it, and then give the Format Header/Footer command. Each type of header or footer must be its own paragraph.

note You cannot give this command in layout mode; you must be in galley mode.

The dialog will look like the following:

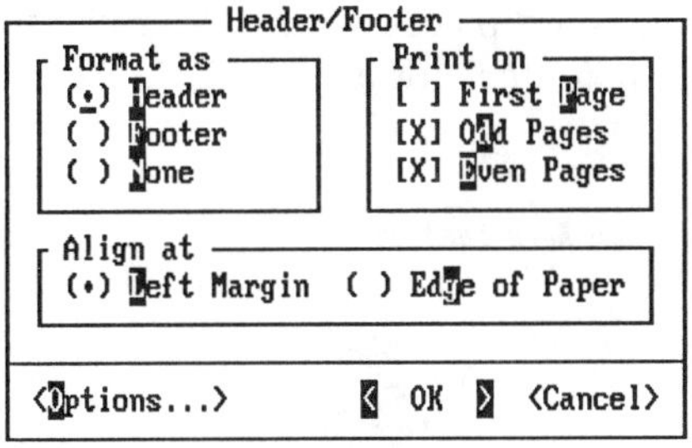

Specify whether your paragraph is a header or footer and what type of pages it will appear on.

You also need to specify where the header or footer will appear. You set the horizontal distance from the left edge of the page with the normal paragraph formatting, but you must also specify whether that formatting is relative to the left margin of the page or the edge of the paper. Select the "Options" button to tell Word how close to the top or bottom of the page the header or footer appears.

To make a paragraph that is a header or footer a normal paragraph again, give the Format Header/Footer command and choose "None."

For instance, to create a header that says "Funding proposal, page (page)" on the right side of the page (for odd pages), first enter the text in Word and use the glossary to enter the page number code, and then select it.

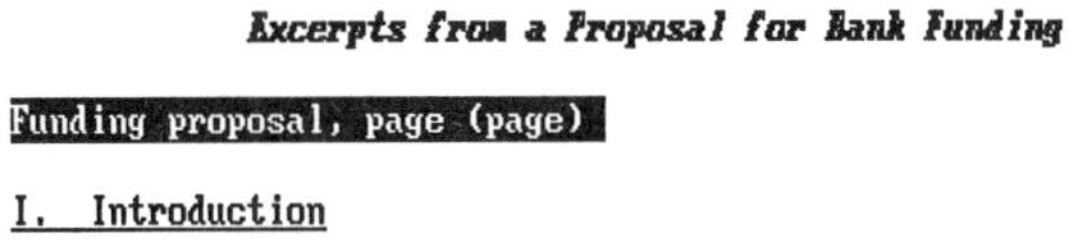

Give the Format Header/Footer command. Choose whether you want the selected paragraph to be a header or footer, and which pages it should appear on. In this case, you would choose Header and Odd Pages. If you want the same head to appear on all pages, select both even and odd pages. You can also choose whether to align the heading relative to the edge of the paper or to the page margin.

After you format a paragraph, Word places a caret (^) in the selection bar to indicate that this is a header or footer, not a normal paragraph.

```
            Excerpts from a Proposal for Bank Funding

^Funding proposal, page (page)

 I.  Introduction
```

You can put both a header and a footer on a page. For example, assume that you want the report to show some text at the top and the page number at the bottom. You want the text in boldface type against the outside margin (you will later be printing the report on both sides of the paper) and the page number centered at the bottom of the page, with a dash on each side of the number. The first page shows the report title, so it will not have a header or footer.

Enter **Funding Proposal** for the header, and use the Format Character command to make it boldface. Since you are going to want the header at the right margin on odd pages and at the left on even pages, you will have to make two copies of the header:

```
            Excerpts from a Proposal for Bank Funding

^Funding proposal

^Funding proposal

 I.  Introduction
```

Use the Format Paragraph command to left-align the first head and to right-align the second head.

```
            Excerpts from a Proposal for Bank Funding

^Funding proposal

^                                       Funding proposal

 I.  Introduction
```

Now select the first paragraph, give the Format Header/Footer command, and make the following selections:

```
┌──────────────── Header/Footer ─────────────────┐
│ ┌ Format as ──────┐   ┌ Print on ─────────┐    │
│ │ (•) Header      │   │ [ ] First Page    │    │
│ │ ( ) Footer      │   │ [ ] Odd Pages     │    │
│ │ ( ) None        │   │ [X] Even Pages    │    │
│ └─────────────────┘   └───────────────────┘    │
│ ┌ Align at ───────────────────────────────┐    │
│ │ (•) Left Margin  ( ) Edge of Paper      │    │
│ └─────────────────────────────────────────┘    │
├────────────────────────────────────────────────┤
│ <Options...>          < OK >  <Cancel>         │
└────────────────────────────────────────────────┘
```

Now select the second header, give the Format Header/Footer command again, unselect Even Pages, and select Odd Pages and First Page.

On a new line, type a dash and then **page**; press the F3 key to expand the definition to the page number and then type another dash. Format the paragraph as center-aligned.

```
               Excerpts from a Proposal for Bank Funding

^Funding proposal

^                                          Funding proposal

                              -(page)-_

 I.  Introduction
```

Give the Format Header/Footer command, and select "Footer" and all three page types. Click "OK" button.

LESSON 52: PAGE BREAKS AND REPAGINATING

The Format Section command does not allow you to go to a new page without creating a new section. However, pressing CTRL-ENTER or using the

Insert Break command inserts a page break wherever you enter it (this is similar to using NEWLINE to go to a new line without making a new paragraph). Word prints a line of dots across the screen to indicate the forced page break:

....

If you want to move from page to page, you can use the Edit Go to command or press F5. When you give the command, Word prompts you for the page number you want to go to. Enter a page number, and Word moves the selection indicator to the beginning of that page. You can also specify a section instead of a page by entering the letter **S** followed by the number of the section (such as **S2**). Word shows you page marks after it prints or repaginates your text. The Edit Go to command will use these page marks as well as those you specify with CTRL-ENTER to determine which page to move to.

When you print or repaginate your text, Word determines where it should start each new page based on the amount of text you have. It then marks the page breaks. The page marks appear as widely spaced dots as shown here:

```
     We will need to add one senior mechanical engineer and two
technicians in R and D.  We will also need a technical services
manager, two product managers, and a merchandising manager in
. . . . . . . . . . . . . . . . . . . . . . . . . . . . . . . .
marketing.  The advertising budget will include campaigns in
trade magazines and attendance at national trade shows.
```

If you add lines of text to a file, you will notice that these marks are not updated. There may be times when you want to see where the current page breaks occur in your document without printing it out. You can use the Utilities Repaginate Now command to tell Word to read through the whole document and set these markers in the correct place or use the Utilities Customize command to constantly repaginate.

In galley mode, Word does not normally keep track of where each page break in your document is unless you tell it to. This makes the program run faster, but it can be somewhat frustrating to you if you want to know where pages will break as you enter your text. You could use view layout mode, but this also adds a great deal of overhead to running Word.

The Utilities Repaginate Now command is confusing for many people. If you have used other word processing programs, you may expect that the page marks will always be correct. Word does not keep them current, however; you need to give the Utilities Repaginate Now command to update them. This may not always be a problem, but it can take a very long time on a large document, especially if you have used many fonts or character styles.

The Confirm Page Breaks option of the Utilities Repaginate Now command lets you change Word's page breaks, so that you can decide where to break pages in your file. You will generally not select this option, however, because, unfortunately, it is clumsy and difficult to use.

The second method for repagination is to tell Word to always repaginate while you edit. To do this, give the Utilities Customize command and select "Background Pagination." Although Word will run more slowly, you will always know where the page breaks will appear without having to go into print preview or page view mode.

LESSON 53: USING FOOTNOTES

You may have noticed the footnotes in the sample report. Many writers find footnotes hard to incorporate into text correctly; however, Word lets you include footnotes easily. In general, footnotes are used for two purposes: to give the reference for a quotation or an idea, or to give a supplementary note. They are most commonly used in academic and scholarly papers, but they are becoming more common in financial reports.

Footnotes consist of the reference mark (usually an asterisk or a number) and the footnote text. To enter these parts, use the Insert Footnote command. Most people prefer to use sequentially numbered footnotes: Word will keep track of the current footnote number and will even renumber your footnotes if you take one out. When you later print your document, you can choose if you want the footnotes to be printed on the page where they are referenced or at the end of the text (using the Format Section command).

To insert a footnote, position the selection indicator at the place where you want the reference mark. When you give the Insert Footnote command, Word prompts you for the reference mark. If you type a character or characters, Word will use that as the reference mark; if you leave it blank, Word will automatically number the footnote in sequence.

The dialog is shown here:

```
─────────── Footnote ───────────
[X] Auto-numbered Reference
           or
Footnote Reference Mark: [_·····]
─────────────────────────────────
          < OK >   <Cancel>
```

When you execute the Insert Footnote command, Word jumps to the end of the text and creates a footnote area (this follows the diamond that normally finishes the text). You can enter and edit the footnote text in this area, and then go back to your normal text. To return to where you were before you entered the footnote, use the Edit Go to command and click "OK." You can also use the Edit Go to command to jump to the last footnote that you edited or to a specific footnote.

To make your document look more professional, you should probably use a superscript for the footnote reference mark. Use the Format Character command to do this. If you delete a footnote, simply remove its reference. Word will renumber the other footnotes if you use automatic numbering.

LESSON 54: NUMBERING PLEADINGS

Lawyers who use Word often need to prepare legal papers (called *pleadings*) that have each line numbered. Word's line numbering capabilities make this a fairly easy task. To add line numbers to a document, use the Format Section command. That part of the dialog is shown here:

```
Line Numbers ──────────────────────────────────────
[X] Add Line Numbers            Restart at ──────
                                (•) New Page
From Text: [0.4"·····]          ( ) New Section
Count by:  [1········]          ( ) Continuous
```

Generally, you will want to restart the numbers on each page. You can also change the increment so only selected line numbers are shown. For instance, if you specify an increment of 5, only lines 5, 10, 15, and so on are numbered.

If you added line numbers to the report, this is how the top of the second page would look:

We will need to add one senior mechanical engineer and two technicians in R and D. We will also need a technical services manager, two product managers, and a merchandising manager in marketing. The advertising budget will include campaigns in trade magazines and attendance at national trade shows.

<u>IV. Current and Projected Earnings</u>

National Generators has shown a profit each year since its founding in 1974. Pretax profits in 1987 were $3.25MM on sales of $17.5MM (20%). This year sales are expected to reach $19MM and a pretax profit of $4.2MM (22%). Five year projections call for $50MM in sales and pretax profit of $12MM (25%) by 1993.[1]

You'll notice that Word does not number the lines in footnotes or in running heads.

REVIEW

1. *Setting up page characteristics*
   Which of the following can be set with the Format Section command?

   a. Number of columns

   b. Underlining of running heads

   c. Justification

   d. Type of numbers used in page numbers

2. *Adjusting page margins*
   Why might you set the top margin of each page to 2 inches?

3. *Formatting multi-column text*
   Reformat the report into two columns with a half-inch space between them. What steps did you use? What things should you do to your text if you are using multi-column printing?

REVIEW (*continued*)

4. *Using headers and page numbering*
   How would you specify a centered running head like "(page 33)"?

5. *Page breaks*
   What does Word do when it sees a CTRL-ENTER character while it is printing a document?

6. *Footnotes*
   How do you choose between showing footnotes on the bottom of each page or at the end of a document?

7. *Formatting front matter*
   Make a title page for the report that includes the report title, company name, and date. Each line should be centered. Give two methods for separating such a title page from the text.

chapter 10

FORMATTING WITH STYLE SHEETS

Lesson 55: Creating a Style Sheet
Lesson 56: Saving, Loading, and Printing Style Sheets
Lesson 57: Using Styles in Your Documents
Lesson 58: Getting the Most Out of Style Sheets

Up to this point you have had to specify the formatting characteristics for each paragraph in your text. Microsoft Word also allows you to define a general style sheet for your documents that is automatically used when you format. When you use style sheets, instead of formatting each paragraph, you specify the style for each type of paragraph (such as "normal paragraph" or "section heading"), and Word formats the paragraph by finding the corresponding style in the style sheet.

The term *style sheet* is Microsoft's own jargon for this feature. Word is one of the few word processors offering style sheets, so even if you are familiar with many other word processing packages, this concept is probably unfamiliar to you. (If you use IBM mainframe computers, you may have used the Generalized Markup Language [GML], which is similar to style sheets.)

A style sheet can be thought of as a formatting guide that contains a list of types of paragraphs and the formats associated with them. For example, to format a "normal paragraph" in your text, your instructions might be "justified text, indent the first line .5 inch, and skip a line before the paragraph." Instead of having to format each paragraph this way when you enter or edit the text, you simply tell Word that you are entering a "normal paragraph." When you print the text, Word looks up the formatting for your "normal paragraph" in the style sheet.

Using style sheets in Word consists of two steps. First, you must create the style sheet by defining the types of styles you want. After you design the style sheet, you format your document by labeling its elements with styles. As you will see, you use the CTRL-SHIFT key combination and two letters to specify the style in your documents. The Format Attach Style Sheet command will tell Word which style sheet you want to use.

In order to format a document with a particular style sheet, you tell Word the name of the style sheet you want to use. This is called *attaching* the style sheet to the document. One of the excellent features of formatting with style sheets is that you can have many different style sheets that use the same style elements but format them differently. Thus, a "normal paragraph" in one style sheet might be double-spaced and ragged right, but single-spaced and justified in another. You might use the first style sheet to print rough drafts so you can correct mistakes easily, and then use the second style sheet to print your final document.

Word lets you specify the types of styles you want and allows you to modify and add styles easily; you do not need to stick to predefined styles. You might have styles for "normal paragraph," "long quotation," "normal running head," "section heading," and so on. In fact, you can even define styles for different types of characters (like "emphasized" and "book title") and divisions (like "normal division," "preface," and "index").

Using style sheets does not prevent you from using direct formatting; however, you will probably find that using style sheets almost exclusively will make writing and printing easier. If you have used only style sheets and want to change the format of one type of paragraph in all of your different documents, you do not need to change any of them: simply change your style sheet. When you print the document, your new formatting will automatically be used. Of course, you cannot do this with direct formatting.

While you can use style sheets for most of your text, you can also use some direct formatting when it is faster or when you are sure you will not want to change the format. For instance, putting foreign words in italics with CTRL-I is easier than defining a style for foreign words and then using this style for the words you italicize.

Another big advantage of style sheets is that you can easily change a format without having to change anything in your documents. For example, you may have a character style called "normal heading" that corresponds to boldface and centered text. If you later want all the normal headings to be underlined and left-aligned, you only need to change the style sheet, not search through all of your files to change the headings.

If you want to begin using style sheets but do not want to create your own at first, you can use the ones supplied by Microsoft. Of course, you can modify these style sheets if you wish.

The next lesson shows you how to create a style sheet from scratch and how to specify your own style elements. The lesson after that shows how to save your style sheets on disk, which is very similar to saving files on disk. You will then learn how to specify styles in your documents.

LESSON 55: CREATING A STYLE SHEET

Now that you understand the concept behind style sheets, the next step is to build a small style sheet that you can experiment with.

Style sheets are kept in files with the extension .STY. You create and modify style sheets in their own windows, which have an editing environment similar to Word's normal text editing screen. In style windows, however, you do not edit text: instead, you edit definitions of styles. You use commands to load, save, and modify style sheets that are similar to Word's commands for handling text.

The first few times you use style windows, you may become confused about what commands will work there, since they look so much like Word's text editing screen. Remember that you can switch to an editing window anytime you want.

The rest of this chapter will use the report shown in Chapter 9 for its examples. You may want to enter the first section heading and the first few paragraphs of the report so you can try out examples as they are presented. When you enter the text, be sure not to use any direct formatting commands.

There are four commands in the Format menu that you use when you are using styles:

```
Apply Style...
Record Style...
Define Styles
Attach Style Sheet...
```

To start a style sheet, use the Format Define Styles command. Once you have your styles defined, you can use the Format Apply Style command (or other keyboard and mouse shortcuts shown later in this chapter). Format

Record Style lets you define a style based on formatting you already have in your document. To tell Word which style sheet to associate with your document, use the Format Attach Style Sheet command.

Give the Format Define Styles command to start a new style sheet. Word brings up the NORMAL.STY sheet:

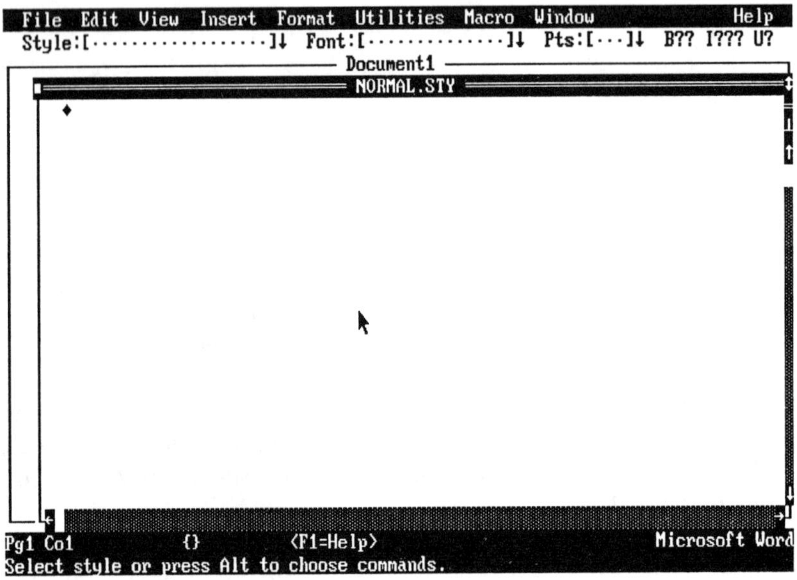

When you are editing a style sheet, the menus are still active but there are far fewer commands available. Browse through the menus to see what commands there are.

You will create four styles for this sample sheet: a character style used for footnote reference numbers (which you learned about in Chapter 9), a paragraph style for section headings, another paragraph style for normal paragraphs, and a section style for corporate reports. These are shown in Table 10-1; the terms in the table are described later in this lesson.

To begin creating a style, you first give the Insert New Style command. You will see the following:

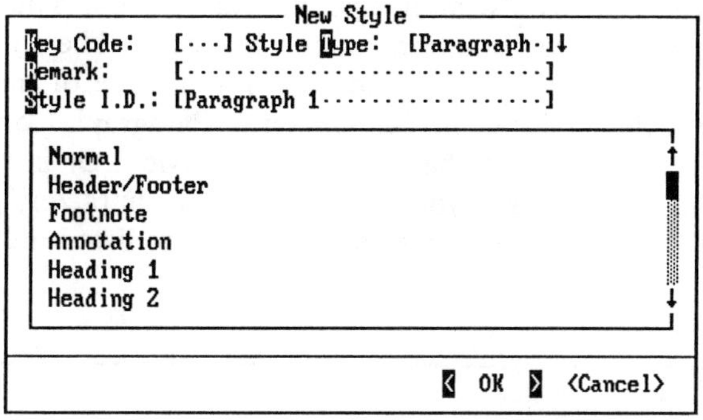

The *key code* is a one- or two-character symbol that you will use in your document to specify this style. The key code is usually an easy-to-remember abbreviation for the style you are describing. Thus, "fr" could stand for

Style	Key Code /Style Type	Style I.D.	Formatting
Footnote	fr/Character	Footnote ref	Superscript reference numbers
Section head	sh/Paragraph	Heading level 1	Bold, underlined, left-aligned, heading 2 lines above, 1 line below
Normal	np/Paragraph	Standard	First line indented .5 inch, justified, single-spaced
Corporate report	cr/Section	Section 1	Top margin 2 inches (to allow room for a letterhead), other margins 1 inch, gutter width .3 inch, running head .5 inch from bottom

TABLE 10-1. Characteristics of the Sample Style

"footnote reference," "sh" for "section heading," and so on. You can use a single letter or two-letter combination for the key code. The *style type* and *style I.D.* make up Word's internal designation for the use of the style you are defining. The style type can be "Character," "Paragraph," or "Section." This defines what the scope of the style is. The style I.D. is an internal designation for the style so that you can have many character, paragraph, and section styles. The style I.D.s for each style type are listed in Table 10-2.

Style Type	**Style I.D.s**
Character	Page number
	Line number
	Footnote Ref
	Annotation Ref
	Line Draw
	Summary Info
	Character 1-23
Paragraph	Normal
	Header/Footer
	Footnote
	Annotation
	Heading level 1-7
	Index level 1-4
	Table level 1-4
	Paragraph 1-55
Section	Normal Section
	Section 1-21

TABLE 10-2. Style Types and I.D.s

The *remark* can store a brief description (for your own use) of the style you are creating. Word ignores this entry, so you can fill in anything you want, up to 28 characters.

To see how these are used, start by defining the first of the sample styles, the footnote reference. Use the Insert New Style command and fill in the key code as **fr**.

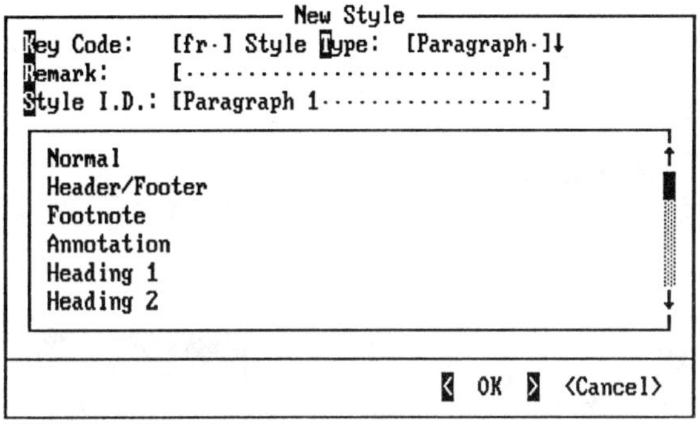

Next, move to the Style Type scroll box and select Character. In the list box at the bottom, choose the style I.D. In this case, there is a usage that matches the style you are defining, Footnote Ref. (In most other cases, however, there won't be such a good match, and you will have to use your own numerical designations.)

Fill in a brief remark about the intended use for this style, for example, **All numbered footnote refs**. Execute the command, choose "OK," and the new style is placed in the current style sheet:

Notice that Word filled in some of the formatting characteristics for you; you will change these in the following steps.

So far you have only named the style, not given it a format. To do this, use the Format Menu commands. The choices presented should look familiar: they are the same as the Format menu you see when you edit.

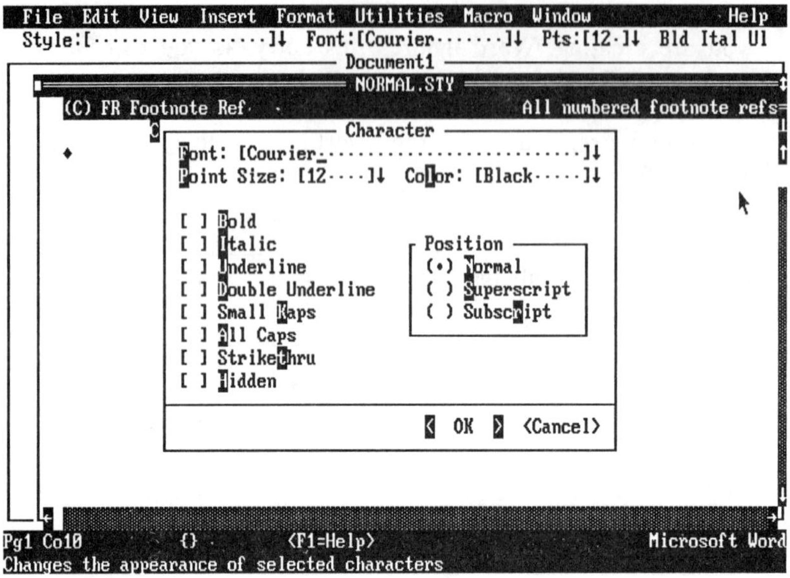

Word knows that you are creating a character style, since you chose a style of Type "Character." Give the Format Character command and select the format just as you would in direct formatting (in this case, only superscript), and then select "OK."

You can now create the other three sample styles—the section heading, the normal paragraph, and the corporate report section style—using the Insert New Style and Format menu commands. For the section heading, you have to give two formatting commands: Format Character (for bold and underlining) and Format Paragraph (for the paragraph formats). For the normal paragraph you only need to give a Format Paragraph command, and you only need a Format Section command for the corporate report style. Remember that Word will give you default format settings when you insert a new style; for sections this is usually a few lines of information, since you have so many choices with section formatting.

When you finish creating these four styles, your style sheet will show the following:

```
NORMAL.STY
(P) NP Normal
        Courier 12. Justified (first line indent 0.5").
(S) CR Section 1                          Corp. reports on letterhead
        Page break. Page length 11"; width 8.5". Page # format Arabic. Top
        margin 2"; bottom 1"; left 1"; right 1". Header at 0.5" from top.
        Footer at 0.5" from bottom. Gutter 0.3". Footnotes on same page.
(P) SH Heading 1                          Section headings
        Courier 12 Bold Underlined. Flush left, space before 2 li, space
        after 1 li.
(C) FR Footnote Ref                       All numbered footnote refs
        Courier 12.
```

LESSON 56: SAVING, LOADING, AND PRINTING STYLE SHEETS

To save your style sheet on disk, use the File Save As command. This and all the other File menu commands in the Insert Style window are like the regular File menu commands. For now, call this style sheet "FIRST.STY."

Word will suggest the name "NORMAL.STY" in the file name area; you can simply type over it. Now return to the editing part of Word by choosing the document window.

After saving your style sheet, you can edit a different style sheet; close the first sheet and start or open a second one. Word also lets you merge the styles from a style sheet on disk with those currently in memory by using the Insert Style Sheet command. Merging styles is helpful if you have created a set of specialized styles for a particular project and want to quickly add the "normal" style elements that you usually use.

Each document can have a default style sheet associated with it. You attach a style sheet with the Format Attach Style Sheet command, which is explained in the next lesson. When you print a document after attaching a style sheet, that sheet is attached as the document's default style sheet. You cannot "detach" a style sheet from a document; instead, when you attach a new style sheet, the old one is forgotten.

If you often use a particular style sheet, you should name that sheet NORMAL.STY (Word comes with a NORMAL.STY file, and you should first rename that to something else). When you run Word, it always looks for

NORMAL.STY and attaches it if it is found and the document does not have its own style sheet.

You can print out the style sheet's contents on your printer with the File Print command. When you do this, the output will look like what you see on the style window. It is often useful to have printouts of your various style sheets; you can then estimate how your document will be formatted before printing with a particular sheet.

LESSON 57: USING STYLES IN YOUR DOCUMENTS

Now that you have a style sheet, you can start applying styles to your documents. When you use Word, you can either set up a style sheet and then enter the styles as you type in new text, or you can convert a directly formatted document to styles.

If you convert a directly formatted document to styles, you must first unformat the entire document. Word requires that you do this since you cannot use both style sheets and direct formatting at the same time. To unformat a document, select the entire document by pressing F8 five times, press CTRL-X to make all paragraphs normal, and then press CTRL-SPACEBAR to remove all character formatting. You now have a very plain document that is ready to have styles applied.

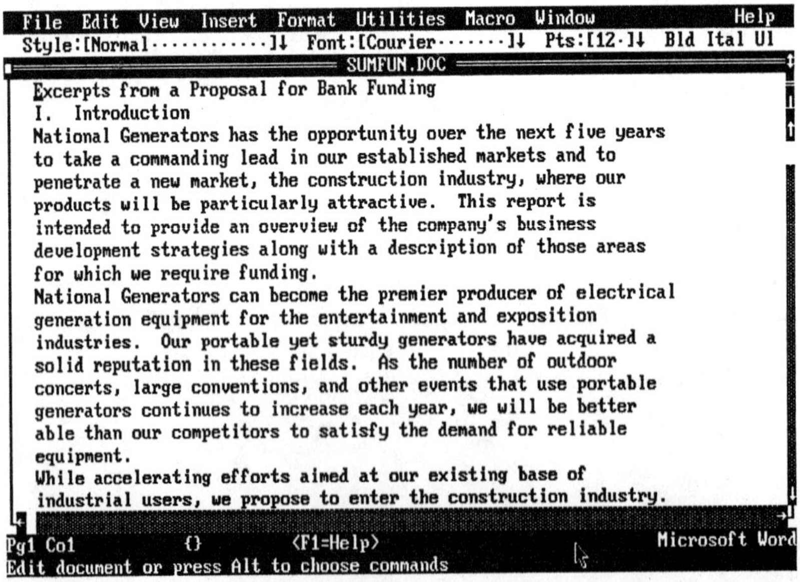

When you use style sheets, it is always useful to see the names of the styles you have applied. To see these, give the View Preferences command and select "Style Bar" in the "Show" section. When you execute this command, Word makes room on the left side of the window for displaying the key codes:

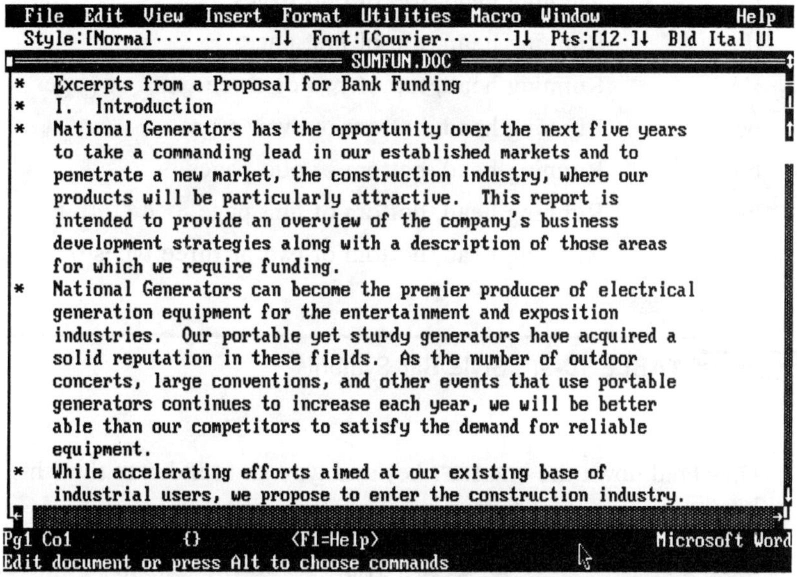

Character and section formats do not appear in the style bar. Table 10-3 shows the style bar symbols that do appear.

Now give the Format Attach Style Sheet command and attach the FIRST style sheet to this document. You are now ready to start applying styles. One way to give text a style is by selecting the text, holding down the CTRL-SHIFT key, and typing the one or two letters of the style you want to apply.

For example, select any part of the first section heading, "I. Introduction":

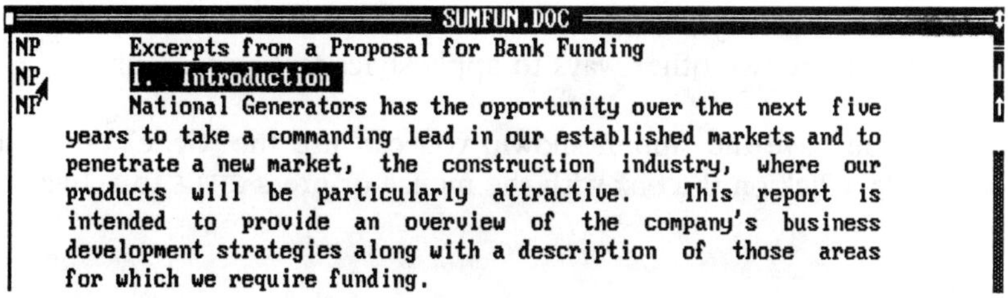

Symbol	**Meaning**
key code	The CTRL key sequence for the paragraph
*	A paragraph style that is not defined in the current style sheet
te	Running head, top of even pages
to	Running head, top of odd pages
tf	Running head, top of first page
t	Running head, top of two or three types of pages
be	Running head, bottom of even pages
bo	Running head, bottom of odd pages
bf	Running head, bottom of first page
b	Running head, bottom of two or three types of pages

TABLE 10-3. Style Bar Symbols

Now hold down the CTRL-SHIFT key and type **sh** to indicate that this is a section heading.

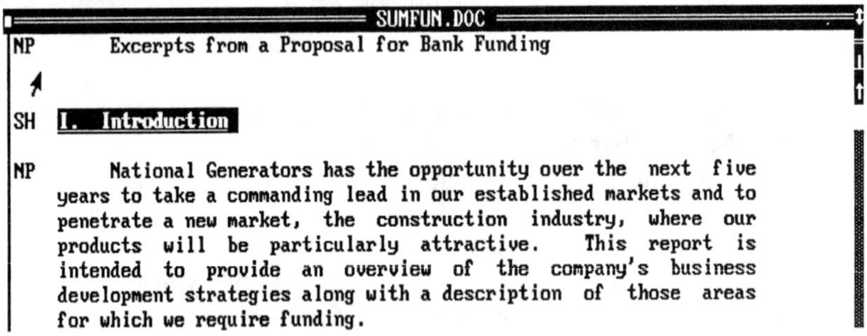

Notice that the paragraph is now formatted properly and that the "SH" now appears in the style bar.

There are two other ways to apply styles to a paragraph:

- If you have the ribbon shown, you can use the "Style" box to choose the style. Click on the box with the mouse or press CTRL-S to activate it from the keyboard (CTRL-S works even if the ribbon is not shown). You can then either type in the style name or choose it from the list.

- Use the Format Apply Style command. Its dialog looks like this:

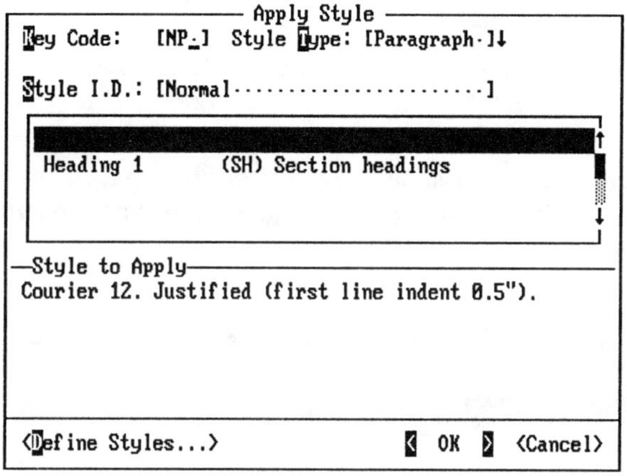

To see the power of style sheets, suppose that you decide not to justify the normal paragraphs and want to change them to left-aligned. Simply give the Format Define Styles command and change the formatting of NP to left-aligned.

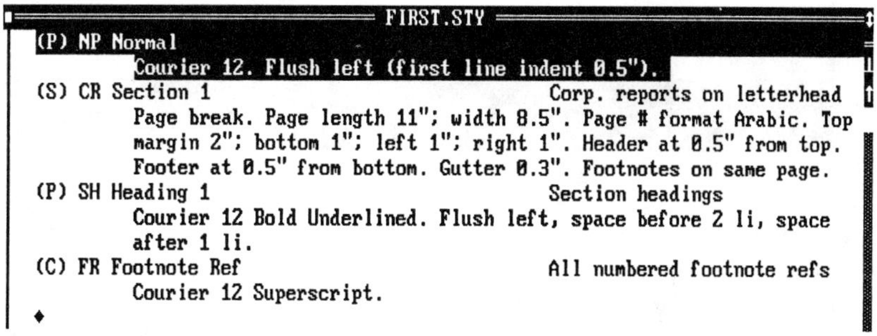

As soon as you return to editing, your document has changed to the new style shown here:

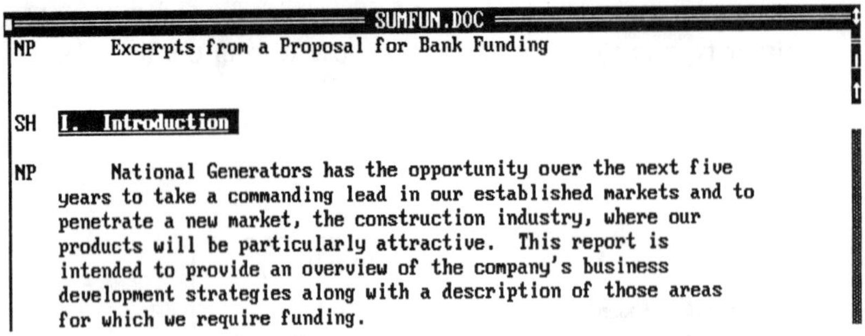

You can now easily make a style sheet for double-spaced drafts of reports. Select the FIRST.STY window and change the line spacing of normal paragraphs to two lines .

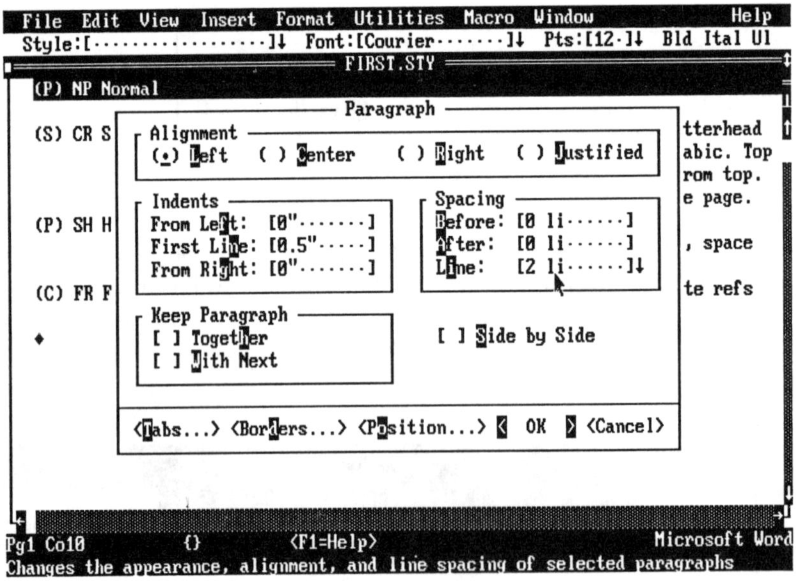

Save this style sheet as DOUBRPT.STY. Now whenever you want to print a draft of a report, it takes almost no effort to double space it, since all you have to do is give a new Format Attach Style Sheet command.

Copying styles from one piece of text to another is identical to copying direct formats. It is thus easy to convert files that use direct formatting to style-sheet formatting simply by applying a style to one paragraph and then copying that style to all other paragraphs to which it applies.

LESSON 58: GETTING THE MOST OUT OF STYLE SHEETS

Style sheets can make formatting all your documents, from letters to entire books, a much easier task. Even for large reports it is unlikely that your style sheet will contain more than 15 styles, and only 5 or so will probably be used with any frequency. If you want, you can rearrange the order of the styles in a style sheet by using the Delete and Insert commands in the gallery. You can also search for styles with the Format Search Style command.

You will find that style sheets have many advantages over direct formatting, and in the few places where style sheets are not appropriate, you can still format directly. Once you start thinking in terms of style elements ("this is a heading," "this is a normal paragraph," and so on), you will find that your printed documents will be much clearer, since they will be presented in a more organized manner.

REVIEW

1. *Using style sheets*
   Briefly describe the advantages of style sheets over direct formatting.
2. *Creating new styles*
   What are the four parts of a style? Create a new style for the title of the sample report.
3. *Saving, loading, and printing style sheets*
   Give the steps for creating a style sheet and attaching it to a document.
4. *Applying styles*
   Explain three ways to specify the style elements in a document.

part III

ADAPTING WORD TO YOUR SPECIAL USES

Printing Your Text
Using Merge for Form Letters
Choosing Word's Custom Options

chapter 11

PRINTING YOUR TEXT

Lesson 59: Selecting a Printer Driver
Lesson 60: Setting Up Your Printer for Word
Lesson 61: Setting the Printer Options
Lesson 62: Using the Print Queue
Lesson 63: Saving Printed Output in a File

Word has many advanced features that make printing easier. When you edit and format text, for example, you do not need to know what type of printer your text will be printed on. Instead, when you are ready to print you simply tell Word what type of printer you are using, and it will determine what it needs to do in order to use as many of the formats you specify as it can.

This is important, since there is no standard method for instructing different printers how to perform certain tasks, such as printing superscripts. Most of the instructions are complex and involve strange character codes. However, Word does not require you to remember these arcane codes; it stores the text formatting with your file, and when you print, it reads a special file called a *printer driver* to determine how to use your printer's special features so they correspond to the format. The printer drivers are the files on your Printer Disks that have file extensions of .PRD.

January 11, 1990

Chris Richford, Vice President
Manufacturer's Bank of the Northeast
1000 First Avenue
Millerton, CT 06492

Dear Ms. Richford:

I am pleased to send you the latest update on the results of our expanded product line. The enclosed summary documents our increased profit margin (7%) for the fourth quarter of 1989, which is largely due to the successful introduction of our new model, the DC50. In 1990 we expect to continue increasing our profitable inroads into this new area.

As you can see, we are well within the projections we outlined to you when you helped us obtain short-term financing. Thank you again for all your assistance. If you have any questions regarding this information, please feel free to call me.

Sincerely,

Thomas Mead, Controller
National Generators
1275 Oak Glen Industrial Park
Oak Glen, CT 06410

January 11, 1990

Chris Richford, Vice President
Manufacturer's Bank of the Northeast
1000 First Avenue
Millerton, CT 06492

Dear Ms. Richford:

I am pleased to send you the latest update on the results of our expanded product line. The enclosed summary documents our increased profit margin (7%) for the fourth quarter of 1989, which is largely due to the successful introduction of our new model, the DC50. In 1990 we expect to continue increasing our profitable inroads into this new area.

As you can see, we are well within the projections we outlined to you when you helped us obtain short-term financing. Thank you again for all your assistance. If you have any questions regarding this information, please feel free to call me.

Sincerely,

Thomas Mead, Controller
National Generators
1275 Oak Glen Industrial Park
Oak Glen, CT 06410

FIGURE 11-1. Examples of printed output

Figure 11-1 shows typical output from two printers. Different printers, of course, produce output of different quality; they also print at different speeds, have different special features, and range in cost from around $250 to over $5000.

Although you learned a bit about printing in Chapter 1, this chapter gives you the rest of the information you need to tell Word what type of printer you have and to use the options of the Print command.

LESSON 59: SELECTING A PRINTER DRIVER

Microsoft has printer drivers for dozens of brands of printers. If you are printing with one or more of the printers that are supported, you can copy the printer driver(s) from your Printer Disks to your Program Disk. It is better, however, to use the Word SETUP program, since some drivers consist of many files.

Many printers that are not included in Word respond to the same codes from your computer as those on the list; for instance, many printers take the same codes as the Epson MX-80. If your printer has an equivalent on the list, you can use the indicated printer driver. You can find out if your printer acts like some other printer by asking your dealer.

If you have a printer from a listed manufacturer with a model number that is slightly different from the one that is supported, try the listed driver before following the suggestions given here. Note that some printer manufacturers supply Microsoft Word drivers for their printers.

Don't worry if your printer does not appear to be supported by Word and you do not know whether it emulates one of the listed printers. You can use one of Word's all-purpose printer drivers, the TTY drivers discussed earlier in Chapter 1, for the type of printer you have. The only difference is that some formatting features (such as italics or subscripts) will not appear on your output. Also, if you use character formats a great deal, it may take slightly longer to print with all-purpose drivers.

If you have a dot-matrix printer, the TTY driver will probably work just fine for you. If your dot-matrix printer can back its head up when a program sends it a BACKSPACE character, you should use the TTYBS driver, which is slightly faster than the TTY driver. If you have a daisy-wheel printer, you should use the TTYWHEEL driver.

Microsoft is constantly adding new printer drivers to Word. To find out about the latest drivers on your Printer Disk, read the file on that disk called README.DOC or PRINTERS.DOC.

LESSON 60: SETTING UP YOUR PRINTER FOR WORD

Depending on your type of printer, you may need to do some preparation in MS-DOS before printing with Word. A printer is either *parallel* or *serial,* depending on the type of connection it has with the PC. If you do not know whether it is parallel or serial, check with the dealer from whom you bought the printer.

If you are using a serial printer (sometimes also called an *RS-232* printer), you need to tell MS-DOS about some of the printer's characteristics before running Word. You need to give the MS-DOS MODE command to specify how the printer communicates. For example, your MODE command may look like this:

C>MODE COM1:9600,N,8,1,P

For convenience, you should also give the following command:

C>MODE LPT1:=COM1:

If you are not familiar with this process, see the discussion of the MODE command in your IBM PC-DOS reference manual. If you have a parallel printer, you do not need to use the MODE command.

Regardless of the type of printer you have, be sure that it is turned on and that it has paper before giving the Print command. Also be sure the cable between the printer and the computer is attached properly.

LESSON 61: SETTING THE PRINTER OPTIONS

Before you give the Print command, you should tell Word about your printer with the File Printer Setup command. The dialog looks like this:

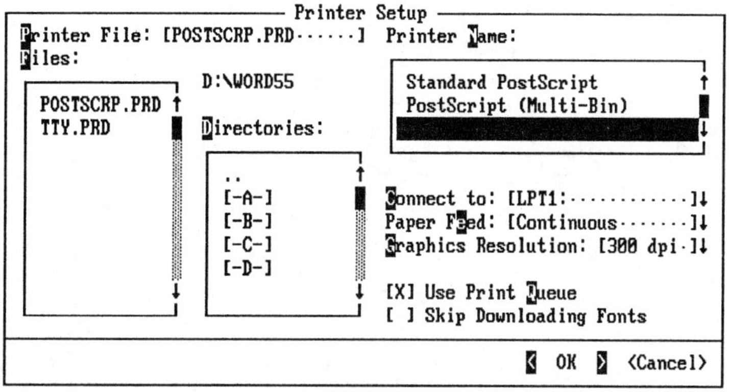

During the process of installing Word, you may already have specified a printer driver. If so, its name will appear after printer in the menu, as POSTSCRP.PRD does in the previous illustration. If you have not specified a printer driver during installation, your first task is to enter the name of the printer driver you are going to use.

If the driver is not on the Program Disk, you can specify a drive with the name. For example, if your Program Disk is in drive A: and you are using the TTYBS driver in B:, you can specify **B:TTYBS**. If you don't specify a printer driver, Word attempts to use the TTY driver from the Program Disk.

The printer driver you are using may include many printer names. Be sure to choose the correct name from the list at the right of the dialog.

The "Connect To" choice tells Word how your printer is attached to your computer. The list has the names of the standard connection ports. Depending on the type of printer you have, there may also be choices for paper feed, graphics resolution, and whether to download fonts. See your printer's manual for more information on how these choices affect your printer.

The Paper Feed option tells Word how your printer handles the paper you are printing on. Table 11-1 explains the different options. Use the Bin1, Bin2, or Mixed option only if your printer has a sheet-feeder attached to it.

Word has an internal print queue so you can resume editing while a document is printing. The print queue is discussed in the next lesson.

After you have made your choices in the File Printer Setup command, choose "OK" and then give the File Print command. This offers you more options:

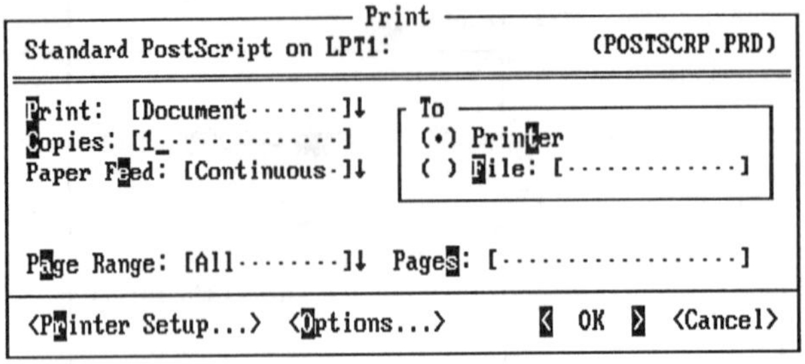

Normally, you want to print the document, but you can also specify to print the summary information (described in Chapter 19), the glossary, or the style sheet attached to the document.

If you want to print more than one copy of the file, use the "Copies" option. This is a convenient way to print many copies of a letter or memo without having to give the File Print command over and over.

You can change the paper feed here in the same way you did in the File Printer Setup command. The "To" choice is described later in this chapter.

Choice	Meaning
Manual	This is used for individual sheet feeding. Each time Word finishes a page, it prompts you to insert the next page and press **Y** when you are ready.
Continuous	If you have continuous-form paper, Word prints without pausing for paper changes.
Bin1	Print from sheet-feeder bin 1 only.
Bin2	Print from sheet-feeder bin 2 only.
Bin3	Print from sheet-feeder bin 3 only.
Mixed	Print the first page from bin 1 and all other pages from bin 2. This is used when you have a multi-page document and want to print the first page on special paper, such as letterhead.
Envelope	Print from the envelope bin.

TABLE 11-1. Paper Handling with Feed Option

You can choose to print only certain pages from your document by using the Page Range and Pages options. With the Page Range option, you can instruct Word to print the entire document (All is the normal setting), to print only the currently-selected text, or to print the text on particular pages. If you choose Pages, enter the page numbers. You can specify a range of pages with a hyphen or colon (as in "2-6" or "2:6"), specify individual pages ("7, 9, 15"), or both.

As you are printing, Word tells you which page it is printing or formatting:

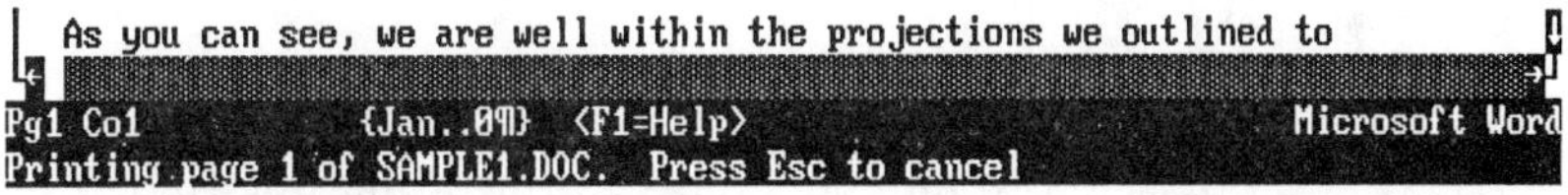

LESSON 62: USING THE PRINT QUEUE

Word's print queue is very much like MS-DOS's PRINT command. You put files into the queue by selecting "Use Print Queue" in the File Printer Setup dialog, and then you print the files normally with the File Print command.

If you want to stop printing the files in the queue, use the File Print Queue command. The following dialog appears:

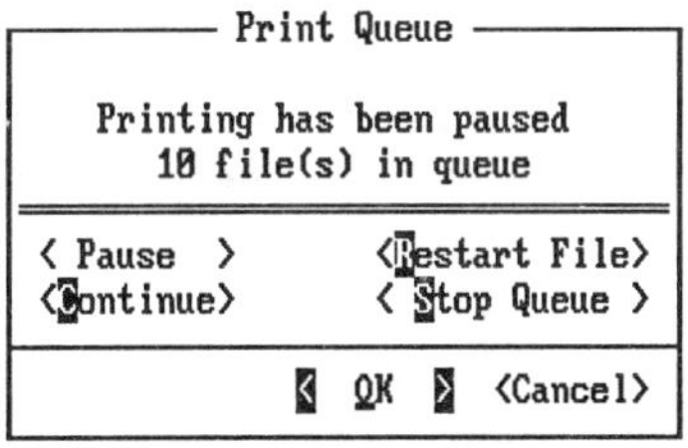

If you want to terminate the printing of files in the queue, choose the Stop Queue button; this cancels the printing altogether. If you only want to stop printing for a while but want to continue again later, use the Pause button (and use the Continue button when you want to resume printing).

While you are printing a file from the queue, you can start printing the file again from the beginning by using the Restart File button. You may want to do this, for example, if the printer jams or runs out of ribbon or toner.

LESSON 63: SAVING PRINTED OUTPUT IN A FILE

There are occasions when you want to print a file but your printer may be unavailable. For instance, many people in your office might share the same printer, and it is usually in demand when you want to use it. If your printer is very slow, you may not want to tie it up with a long document.

You can use the "To" option of the File Print dialog to have Word format your text for the printer and then save it in a file instead of printing it. When your printer is available, you do not need to run Word; instead, use the MS-DOS PRINT or COPY command to send the file to the printer.

Enter a name for the file that is different from the other file names on your disk. For instance, if you are printing SAMPLE1, you may want to call the output either SAMPLE1.OUT or SAMPLE1.PRN.

It is important to remember that the output from the File Print command is formatted only for the printer you specify in the File Printer Setup command. If you try to print out a file that was formatted for a different printer, you may get unpredictable results. If you do not know what type of printer the output will be printed on (for instance, if an associate will be printing the file), you should use the TTY driver.

In some circumstances, you want Word to print to a file that can be read by other programs. For instance, you may want the printed output (including running heads, footnotes, and so on) to be read by another text processing program. That program will not recognize the special printer commands Word imbeds in files with the File Print command. To prevent Word from imbedding printer commands, use the TTY.PRD printer driver. This printer driver is specially designed to suppress "strange" characters in the output of the File Print command.

REVIEW

1. *Selecting a printer driver*
   What printer driver do you use if Word does not provide a driver designed for your printer?

2. *Setting up your printer*
   What setup do you need to perform if you have a serial printer?

3. *Choosing other print options*
   How do you tell Word that you are not using continuous-form paper?

4. *Using the print queue*
   How do you temporarily halt printing from the queue?

5. *Saving printed output in a file*
   How do you make a Word file that can be sent to the printer with PC-DOS's PRINT command?

chapter 12

USING MERGE FOR FORM LETTERS

Lesson 64: Using Merge Fields
Lesson 65: Using the Datafile Format
Lesson 66: Printing Your Document
Lesson 67: Using Merge Instructions

Some five years ago, only a few word processing programs included features that let you create form letters from a file of names and addresses. This feature is sometimes referred to as *mail merge.* Today, many programs give you this capability in a limited fashion. The merge feature in Word is more sophisticated than in most other word processing programs and produces letters that look much more personalized.

The basic concept behind Word's merge feature is fairly simple. Your *main document* contains the letter you want to send to many people, with special place holders (*fields*) for the parts that change from letter to letter (like the recipient's name and address). Your *datafile* contains the information that Word puts into the fields in the main document; all the fields for each letter are on one line (called a *record*) of the datafile.

Your main document tells Word which file is to be the datafile. You create the main document with Word and create the datafile either with Word, a data base management system, or a programming language like

BASIC. The format of the datafile is very easy to understand, so it is easy to set up datafiles to go with your main documents.

When you print your file with the File Print Merge command, Word reads the first record from the datafile, substitutes the fields into your main document, formats your letter, prints it, reads the next record from the datafile, and so on. You can have as many as 64 fields in a letter, as long as each field matches the information in the datafile.

You can include fields in the middle of a paragraph, and Word will format the paragraph with the new information in it (almost all other programs will not format the paragraph after putting in the new information). Thus, if you have a field called "amount," and that field in one record of your datafile is equal to 1533, one of your form letters would print the sentence "You still owe us $1533, which we would like you to send immediately."

LESSON 64: USING MERGE FIELDS

Each field has a name of as many as 64 letters or hyphens, such as "name" or "amount"; the field name cannot contain spaces. The field name is used in both the main document and the datafile, and the names must match. However, the order in which the names are used in the main document does not need to match the order in which the fields appear in the datafile. In fact, you can use the data in a field many times in your main document.

The body of your main document is entered just as you would normally enter text with Word. When you want to enter a field name, you surround it with « and » symbols (called *chevrons*), which you enter by pressing CTRL-[and CTRL-], respectively. You also enclose all merge instructions and keywords with the « and » symbols. Note that you must enter these symbols with CTRL-[and CTRL-], not by using the less-than and greater-than keys, < and >.

Type in the following example, which is a main document that could be used to inform customers of balances due. The fields are company, name, address, city, state, zip, amount, and lastpayment.

```
«DATA PAYLET1.DAT»
                                         February 15, 1991
«company»
«name»
«address»
«city», «state»  «zip»

Dear «name»:

Our records show that your outstanding balance is $«amount», and
that we have not received any payment from you since
«lastpayment». If there is a disagreement about this amount,
please feel free to call us about it.

                                         Sincerely,

                                         Sharon Myers
                                         National Manufacturing
```

Each main document must begin with a DATA instruction, which names the datafile. For example, if the name of your datafile is PAYLET1.DAT, your data statement is "«DATA PAYLET1.DAT»." In general, the datafile should have an extension that indicates that the file is data. If you do not include an extension in the DATA statement, Word will assume that the extension is .DOC.

LESSON 65: USING THE DATAFILE FORMAT

The first record in a datafile, the *header,* is a list of fields in the order in which they appear in all the other records, with the field names separated by commas. Do not confuse this header record with headers that appear on every page, which you learned about in Chapter 9. The other records contain the data, with each field separated by a comma. Enter the datafile for the main document shown in the last lesson.

```
company, name, address, city, state, zip, amount, lastpayment
Industrial Mining Co., Michael Townsend, P. O. Box 4110,
Cambridge, MA, 02139, 127.53, 1/3/91
Maxwell Publishing, Tamara Fine, "91 Oak Avenue, Suite 119",
Chicago, IL, 60606, 118.18, 12/16/90
Charles' Computer Supplies, Charles Gifford, 4545 17th Avenue,
Los Angeles, CA, 90441, 18.00, 12/27/90
California Computer Center, "Augustus ""Jim"" Dornbrook", 92
North Barrington Ave., San Francisco, CA, 94711, 89.42, 1/7/91
♦
```

When you create your datafile, it is often useful to see the main document at the same time; this is a perfect use for Word's windows (discussed in Chapter 4).

Since commas in the datafile indicate the boundaries of fields, commas in your data could cause Word to be confused. However, Word allows you to enclose any field with quotation marks, so that a comma in a quoted field will not be considered a field boundary. (You should also use quotes in any field that contains a TAB character.) The second record in the datafile shows this use.

Since any text field might have a comma in it, it cannot hurt to enclose all text fields in quotation marks. If you are preparing your datafile with Word, however, this is not necessary as long as you are careful to enclose all fields containing a comma with quotes.

The WRITE# statement in most BASIC programming languages, including IBM's BASICA, will enclose all strings in quotes for you. If your quoted fields have quotation marks in them, you need to put two quotation marks instead of one inside the field. This is shown in the fourth record of PAYLET1.DAT.

Some applications programs that can write out datafiles may not be able to write out the header record. In this case, Word lets you have two datafiles: one with just the header record, the other with the data. If you use this scheme, you need to alter your DATA instruction to indicate both files: you would give the name of the header file first and then the name of the datafile. For instance, if the file PAYLET1.HD has the header record and another file PAYLET1.DAT has the data, your DATA instruction would read "«DATA PAYLET1.HD, PAYLET1.DAT»."

LESSON 66: PRINTING YOUR DOCUMENT

Printing with merge is very similar to regular printing. Choose the File Print Merge command after setting up your printer. You should see something like this:

```
┌──────────────── Print Merge ──────────────────┐
│ (•) All:                                      │
│ ( ) Records: [.........................]      │
├───────────────────────────────────────────────┤
│ <Print...>  <New Document...>  <Cancel>       │
└───────────────────────────────────────────────┘
```

Click the "Print" button.

Figure 12-1 shows the letters Word prints out when you merge the PAYLET1 letter. As you can see, Word fills in the fields in the body of the paragraph and correctly wraps and justifies the text.

The New Document button is similar to the Print button except that instead of printing the merged output, Word saves it in a file. This allows you to print the document later or edit it prior to printing.

The Records box lets you specify which records to print. For instance, you may want to merge only the first two records in the datafile. You can specify ranges of record numbers in a format similar to that used for page ranges specification in the File Print command (for example, 3:7 would cause Word to print records 3 through 7).

LESSON 67: USING MERGE INSTRUCTIONS

The previous example showed a simple merge file with a DATA instruction and many fields. A unique feature of Word that makes letter writing even

February 15, 1991

Industrial Mining Co.
Michael Townsend
P. O. Box 4110
Cambridge, MA 02139

Dear Michael Townsend:

Our records show that your outstanding balance is $127.53, and that we have not received any payment from you since 1/3/91. If there is a disagreement about this amount, please feel free to call us about it.

Sincerely,

Sharon Myers
National Manufacturing

February 15, 1991

Maxwell Publishing
Tamara Fine
91 Oak Avenue, Suite 119
Chicago, IL 60606

Dear Tamara Fine:

Our records show that your outstanding balance is $118.18, and that we have not received any payment from you since 12/16/90. If there is a disagreement about this amount, please feel free to call us about it.

Sincerely,

Sharon Myers
National Manufacturing

FIGURE 12-1. Output from the Print Merge command on the PAYLET1 letter

February 15, 1991

Charles' Computer Supplies
Charles Gifford
4545 17th Avenue
Los Angeles, CA 90441

Dear Charles Gifford:

Our records show that your outstanding balance is $18.00, and that we have not received any payment from you since 12/27/90. If there is a disagreement about this amount, please feel free to call us about it.

Sincerely,

Sharon Myers
National Manufacturing

February 15, 1991

California Computer Center
Augustus "Jim" Dornbrook
92 North Barrington Ave.
San Francisco, CA 94711

Dear Augustus "Jim" Dornbrook:

Our records show that your outstanding balance is $89.42, and that we have not received any payment from you since 1/7/91. If there is a disagreement about this amount, please feel free to call us about it.

Sincerely,

Sharon Myers
National Manufacturing

FIGURE 12-1. Output from the Print Merge command on the PAYLET1 letter (*continued*)

Instruction	Use
ASK	Has Word prompt you to fill in a field when each letter is printed.
DATA	Identifies the datafile.
IF. . .ENDIF or IF. . .ELSE. . .ENDIF	Conditionally inserts text if a field in the datafile has a particular value. You can use the =, >, or < operators for numeric fields or the = operator for string fields.
INCLUDE	Inserts another Word file in the main document.
NEXT	Has Word read the next record in the datafile.
SET	Sets the contents of a field or has Word prompt you for the value once at the beginning of printing.

TABLE 12-1. Word Merge Instructions

easier is *conditional insertion.* You can check the value of a field and insert different text depending on the value of the field. For instance, if the amount field is over 1000, you can insert a sentence describing the dire consequences of not paying promptly. Or your datafile can have a field called "regularcustomer" that contains a Y or N; you can use this to automatically give your regular customers a different salutation, shown later in this lesson.

The merge feature has a number of options that you can use; these are listed in Table 12-1. The main paragraph of the following letter is similar to the previous example except that it has an IF instruction used with a text field. The IF instruction checks the value of the salesrep field and prints one of two possible sentences, depending on whether salesrep is none or some other value.

```
Our records show that your outstanding balance is $«amount», and
that we have not received any payment from you since
«lastpayment». «IF salesrep="none"»Our accounts receivable
manager, Holly Watson, will call you about this.«ELSE»Your sales
representative, «salesrep», will call you about this.«ENDIF»
```

The datafile is also similar to the previous one:

```
company, name, address, city, state, zip, amount,
lastpayment,salesrep
Industrial Mining Co., Michael Townsend, P. O. Box 4110,
Cambridge, MA, 02139, 127.53, 1/3/90, Jan Phillips
Maxwell Publishing, Tamara Fine, "91 Oak Avenue, Suite 119",
Chicago, IL, 60606, 110.10, 12/16/89, none
Charles' Computer Supplies, Charles Gifford, 4545 17th Avenue,
Los Angeles, CA, 90441, 10.00, 12/27/89, Bill Tyler
California Computer Center, "Augustus ""Jim"" Dornbrook", 92
North Barrington Ave., San Francisco, CA, 94711, 90.42, 1/7/90,
none
```

Figure 12-2 shows the new output. Notice the results of the IF instruction.

You can also use the IF instruction with integer fields to test whether a number is greater than, less than, or equal to a field value. For instance, if your datafile has a field "custyears" that is the number of years a customer has done business with your firm, you might include a sentence like this in a letter: "«IF custyears>5»We value your long-standing relationship with us.«ENDIF»."

The IF instruction can be used to check whether there is anything in the field or not. For example, the following command determines if there is any value in the owner field: "Dear «IF owner»«owner»«ELSE»Store Owner «ENDIF»." This prints the contents of the owner field if it exists or the phrase "Store Owner" if it does not.

The SET and ASK instructions allow you to enter information from the keyboard when you merge-print. The SET command sets a field once for all letters, while the ASK command prompts you for a new value for each letter. You can include a string that Word will prompt you with.

For instance, instead of typing the date into a main document, you could include an ASK instruction:

```
«DATA PAYLET2.DAT»
«ASK date=?Enter today's date:»

                              «date»

«company»
«name»
«address»
 ...
```

This would prompt for the definition of the date field. You would then position the date field at the place you want the date in your main document, just as if it were a field in your datafile.

February 15, 1991

Industrial Mining Co.
Michael Townsend
P. O. Box 4110
Cambridge, MA 02139

Dear Michael Townsend:

Our records show that your outstanding balance is $127.53, and that we have not received any payment from you since 1/3/91. Your sales representative, Jan Phillips, will call you about this.

Sincerely,

Sharon Myers
National Manufacturing

February 15, 1991

Maxwell Publishing
Tamara Fine
91 Oak Avenue, Suite 119
Chicago, IL 60606

Dear Tamara Fine:

Our records show that your outstanding balance is $118.18, and that we have not received any payment from you since 12/16/90. Our accounts receivable manager, Holly Watson, will call you about this.

Sincerely,

Sharon Myers
National Manufacturing

FIGURE 12-2. Output from the Print Merge command on the PAYLET2 letter

February 15, 1991

Charles' Computer Supplies
Charles Gifford
4545 17th Avenue
Los Angeles, CA 90441

Dear Charles Gifford:

Our records show that your outstanding balance is $18.00, and that we have not received any payment from you since 12/27/90. Your sales representative, Bill Tyler, will call you about this.

Sincerely,

Sharon Myers
National Manufacturing

February 15, 1991

California Computer Center
Augustus "Jim" Dornbrook
92 North Barrington Ave.
San Francisco, CA 94711

Dear Augustus "Jim" Dornbrook:

Our records show that your outstanding balance is $90.42, and that we have not received any payment from you since 1/7/91. Our accounts receivable manager, Holly Watson, will call you about this.

Sincerely,

Sharon Myers
National Manufacturing

FIGURE 12-2. Output from the Print Merge command on the PAYLET2 letter (*continued*)

The INCLUDE instruction allows you to bring the contents of other files into your Word document. This is useful if you want to include some standard information in a letter but do not want to copy the information until the file is printed. For instance, if you have a table that is updated often, instead of inserting it in the file, use the INCLUDE instruction so the table will be current every time you print the file.

You can use the NEXT instruction to read in more than one record for each main document, for example, if you are using Word to read a list of data to make a report. The following is a main document that reads five records from a file and prints a report of the data in one document:

```
«DATA ASSETS.DAT»

The following is a summary of our current assets, based on the
latest figures:

Division       Division head      Assets   Reporting date

«division»     «divhead»         «assets»  «repdate»
«NEXT»
«division»     «divhead»         «assets»  «repdate»
«NEXT»
«division»     «divhead»         «assets»  «repdate»
«NEXT»
«division»     «divhead»         «assets»  «repdate»
«NEXT»
«division»     «divhead»         «assets»  «repdate»
♦
```

Here is the datafile, ASSETS.DAT, that goes with the report.

```
division, divhead, assets, repdate
Pacific, Anita Yee, 1315000, 8/15/90
Mid-West, Sam Horn, 875000, 8/14/90
South, Margaret Miller, 1105000, 8/14/90
North-East, Kim Taylor, 2660000, 8/15/90
Foreign, Noriko Takayama, 397000, 8/12/90
♦
```

Figure 12-3 shows the output of the report. Notice that all the records appear on the same output.

The following is a summary of our current assets, based on the latest figures:

Division	Division head	Assets	Reporting date
Pacific	Anita Yee	1315000	8/15/90
Mid-West	Sam Horn	875000	8/14/90
South	Margaret Miller	1105000	8/14/90
North-East	Kim Taylor	2660000	8/15/90
Foreign	Noriko Takayama	397000	8/12/90

FIGURE 12-3. Output from the NEXT instruction

REVIEW

1. *Printing documents with merge features*
   Briefly describe what you need in order to use the merge feature.

2. *Typing in merge instructions and field names*
   Which keys do you use to enter the « and » characters?

3. *Using fields*
   Create a merge letter for an insurance firm to remind clients to renew their auto insurance policies. In addition to standard form-letter fields (name, address, and so on), add fields for expiration date and policy type. How would you

   a. Tell clients about a home insurance policy if they don't already have one?

   b. Explain new features of their policies?

REVIEW (*continued*)

4. *Setting up a datafile with fields*
   What precautions must you take if your data contains commas?

5. *Using merge instructions*
   Which merge instruction do you use

   a. To insert text from another file?

   b. To set a field before printing each letter?

   c. To test a field's value?

chapter 13

CHOOSING WORD'S CUSTOM OPTIONS

Lesson 68: Using the View Preferences Command
Lesson 69: Using the Utilities Customize Command

Word has many commands that allow you to customize the program. These commands set various options that affect, for example, the way Word's screen looks and the amount of information that Word gives you. Other custom options allow you to start Word in a number of different ways, depending on the type of monitor and adapter board in your IBM PC. The primary commands that change the way Word displays information on the screens are the View Preferences and Utilities Customize commands. You can move easily between these two commands with buttons in their dialogs.

When you leave Word, it remembers the settings that you made with these two commands. The next time you start Word, it starts with those settings so that you do not need to give the commands again.

LESSON 68: USING THE VIEW PREFERENCES COMMAND

The View Preferences command is used to change what you see on the screen and how you see it. The dialog is shown here:

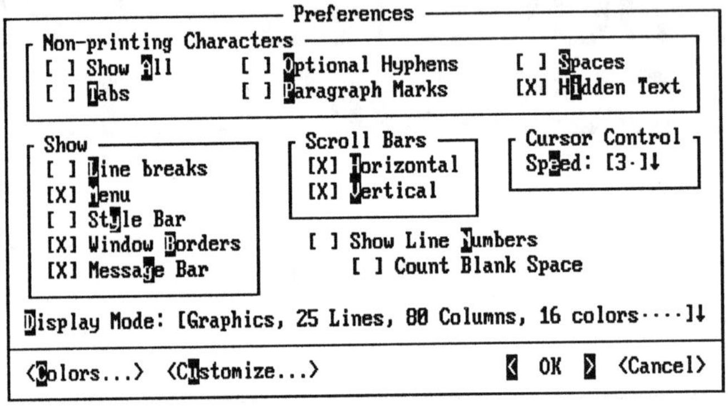

You can choose which non-printing characters you want to see on the screen in the first section. Usually, you will want to leave all choices unselected or have only hidden text shown (hidden text is explained in Chapter 15).

The other choices let you view specific kinds of characters so that you can see which characters are in your document. The "Show All" choice causes the other five choices to be selected for you. This is especially useful if you are reformatting tables, since you can quickly tell which lines are connected in a paragraph.

Tabs show as right-pointing arrows (→); spaces show as dots(.). Paragraph marks are shown as the traditional paragraph symbol (¶) and newlines are shown as down-pointing arrows (↓).

The choices in the "Show" section let you see additional information on the screen.

- "Line Breaks" causes the lines on the screen to be set as they will be in the printed document. This may be different than what you normally see if you are using proportional fonts since the letters in proportional fonts have different widths.

- "Menu" causes the menu bar to be at the top of the screen at all times. If you unselect this, the menu bar only appears when you press the ALT key.

- "Style Bar" shows the style codes at the left of the paragraphs as described in Chapter 10.
- "Window Borders" shows the borders of the windows. Unselecting this adds the width of two more characters to your windows but makes it hard to use more than one window at a time.
- "Message Bar" shows the message bar at the bottom of the screen. Unselecting this gives you an additional line of space in your windows.

Like the choices in the "Show" section, the "Scroll Bars" section let you choose whether or not to view the horizontal or vertical scroll bars. Removing these gives you a bit more room in your windows.

You can set the speed that the cursor moves, from very fast (9) to very slow (0). Many people prefer to set the speed midway, to around 5.

"Show Line Number" lets you see in the status bar the number of the line that the cursor is in. This is useful when you have to find a specific line on a particular page.

The display mode tells Word how you want to see characters on the screen. The choices in this option depend on the type of display adapter you are using. For example, with a color VGA adapter, you can choose between text and graphics mode, at 25, 43, 50, or 60 lines, all in 16 colors. Other adapters may have more or fewer choices. You will usually only make the selection in this menu once and leave it set from then on.

The "Colors" button takes you to a special dialog that lets you assign a different color to each of the parts of the window. If you have a color monitor, this can be a very important choice since you can choose combinations that are easier for *your* eyes; if you are going to be using Word often, it is very important to set it up so that it puts the least amount of strain possible on your eyes.

The "Customize" button takes you directly to the Utilities Customize command, described in the next lesson.

LESSON 69: USING THE UTILITIES CUSTOMIZE COMMAND

The Utilities Customize command is used to change the way Word acts (as opposed to the way that it looks). The dialog is shown here:

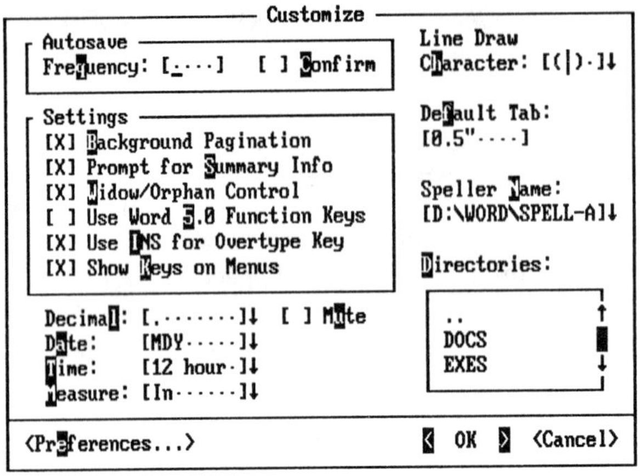

The "Autosave" feature lets you tell Word to save your document every so often for safety. This prevents any loss from power failures. Set the frequency to the number of minutes you want between automatic saves; specify "Confirm" to have Word confirm before each automatic save.

The line drawing character is used when you use the Utilities Line Draw command (which will not be very often).

The choices in the Settings section follow:

- "Background Pagination" causes Word to always repaginate. This is described in Chapter 9.
- "Prompt for Summary Info" tells Word to ask you to fill in the summary sheet every time you create a new file. Summary sheets are described in Chapter 19.
- "Widow/Orphan Control" tells Word how to break pages. This is described in Chapter 8.
- "Use Word 5.0 Function Keys" is valuable to people familiar with Word 5.0. This will make Word recognize the old key combinations.
- "Use INS for Overtype Key" is also for people who are familiar with Word 5.0. When this is not selected, the INS key inserts the scrap like versions of Word before 5.5.
- "Show Keys on Menus" shows the shortcut keys on the menus so that, when you pull a menu down, you can quickly see how to activate a particular command. With this, you do not need to remember all of the keystrokes for all of Word's commands.

The default tab width is the amount of space that Word uses between tab stops when you haven't specified your own tabs (see Chapter 8). If there are no tab positions set for a paragraph, pressing the TAB key will advance the cursor by this amount. If you have some tab positions set but you are past all of them, Word will also use this amount to establish the next position.

The Speller Name is the file that Word uses for spell checking (see Chapter 17). If you use a different dictionary (such as one supplied by other manufacturers), you change this setting to tell Word which dictionary to use.

The decimal character should generally be left as the period (.). Although you can change it to a comma for European format, this requires you to change other parts of documents (such as the characters that separate fields in merge documents).

The mute option does not affect how the screen looks, but instead specifies whether or not you want to hear Word's beep when you make an error (such as using the ↑ key when you are at the beginning of a file). Selecting this turns the beep off. It is safe to turn the beep off since it does not signal serious errors; it only signals when you try to do something that Word cannot do.

The date and time format options let you select how to show the date and time in the date, dateprint, time, and timeprint glossary entries. MDY shows the month first (such as March 21, 1990) while DMY shows the day first (21 March 1990). Setting the time format to 12 uses a 12-hour clock and an A.M. or P.M. indicator (such as 4:31 P.M.). Setting the format to 24 shows the time in 24-hour format (16:31).

The "Measure" option lets you set the units that Word uses when it prompts you for linear measurement, as in the Format Paragraph and Format Section menus. You select the choice you want to use when you give measurements. Table 13-1 shows the meaning of each choice.

Choice	Meaning
In	Inches (1 in. = 2.5 cm.).
Cm	Centimeters (1 cm. = .4 in.).
P10	10-pitch characters (one 10p character = 1/10 in.). This measure is useful if you are printing with a 10-pitch printer.
P12	12-pitch characters (one 12p character = 1/12 in.). This measure is useful if you are printing with a 12-pitch printer.
Pt	Points (1 point = 1/72 in.). Points are used for measurement by typesetters.

TABLE 13-1. Measurement Choices in the Options Command

REVIEW

1. *Custom options*
   Which commands do you use to set the following:
   a. Background color
   b. Word's measurements
   c. Whether or not you see the menu
   d. Cursor speed
   e. The beep

part IV

ADVANCED WORD FEATURES

Outlining
Generating Tables of Contents and Indexes
Annotations, Bookmarks, and Cross-References
Spelling Correction, Hyphenation, and Thesaurus
Sorting
Retrieving Documents
Macros
Linking Documents
Revision Marks
Desktop Publishing with Word

chapter 14

OUTLINING

Lesson 70: Introduction to Word's Outlining Features
Lesson 71: Creating an Outline
Lesson 72: Text Edit and Outline Edit Modes
Lesson 73: Collapsing and Expanding
Lesson 74: Rearranging Your Outline
Lesson 75: Numbering Your Outline

There are many circumstances where outlines help you organize your thinking. Outlines can assist you in determining how important various thoughts are relative to each other. Writing an outline is also a good way to be sure you have covered all the topics that are relevant to your subject.

Of course, you can use the features of Word you have already learned to make an outline. If you set the tabs for a document at half-inch increments, you can enter text in a standard outline format. You can use Word's selection features to move groups of items around; you can even use an outline style sheet to specify a different emphasis for each level of your outline. However, Word's new outlining features allow you to do much more.

This chapter shows you how to create and modify outlines using special outlining features. With these new features you can even turn existing documents into outlines. If you are familiar with other outlining programs for the IBM PC, you may see similarities between those programs and Word. Once you've learned how to outline with Word, you will find many situations in your daily work where outlines are very useful. In the next chapter, for example, you will learn how to use an outline to generate a table of contents.

LESSON 70: INTRODUCTION TO WORD'S OUTLINING FEATURES

Every document in Word can also be viewed as an outline. Up to now, you have used the document view exclusively; since you haven't used any of Word's outlining features, you haven't needed to see your document in outline view.

It is important to understand that outlines are not separate documents in Word. Most outline programs create files that can only be used as outlines. Word, on the other hand, lets you create an outline, then fill in its parts with text. When you want to see the text, you use document view; when you want to see the outline, you use outline view. Outline view is just a different, more streamlined way to look at your document.

The outline view and the document view are used for different purposes. Editing and formatting are done in document view, as you have seen. Outline view is used to review and change the structure of your text, just as you might decide to switch the position of two major ideas after writing an outline on paper.

In Word's outline view, when you move a heading, all the text under that heading moves too. To achieve this result in document view, you would have to select a huge amount of text, delete it to the scrap, move to the new location, and insert the text there. In outline view, you just move the heading, and the associated text moves with it.

If you have a complicated and detailed outline, you may have dozens of subheads under a main heading. When you are working with this kind of outline, you can get lost in the lower-level headings and miss the overall picture. Word lets you *collapse* an outline so that lower-level headings are invisible. For example, suppose your outline looks like the following:

```
Contract preparation
    Use standard contract as basis
    Add union work clause
        Local 112 for installing
        Local 112 and 427 for maintenance
    Add outdoor setting clause
Contract signing
    Phillips at National Generators
    Martinez and Washington at fair
Site preparation
    Verify space requirements
    Erect shelters
    Cable to main sections
        4 500' spans
        Check with Martinez for exact locations
```

Collapsing the subheads under the "Contract preparation" first-level head gives you the following result:

```
+ Contract preparation
  Contract signing
      Phillips at National Generators
      Martinez and Washington at fair
  Site preparation
      Verify space requirements
      Erect shelters
      Cable to main sections
          4 500' spans
          Check with Martinez for exact locations
```

When you are viewing the structure of a large outline, you will often find it useful to look at only the first- and second-level headings, collapsing the outline so that all headings below the second level are hidden. Of course, you can always expand the outline again to show all head levels.

There is a price for the convenience of using the outline view: you cannot select text across paragraph boundaries. Because of this limitation, you are usually restricted to editing a single paragraph. (In outlines, each heading is a separate paragraph.)

A further requirement is that you have to use two different modes in outline view: *text edit* mode lets you edit your headings but not move them, while *outline edit* lets you move headings but not edit them.

Moving between document view and outline view is very easy. Use SHIFT-F2 to switch from one view to the other—SHIFT-F2 toggles between them. You can also switch to outline view with the View Outline command.

You can tell which view you are in by looking in the lower-left corner of the screen. In document view, the page number is displayed.

```
Pg1 Co1          {·}         <F1=Help>                    Microsoft Word
Edit document or press Alt to choose commands
```

In text edit mode of outline view, the message area looks like this:

```
Level 1          {·}         <F1=Help>                    Microsoft Word
Edit document or press Alt to choose commands
```

In outline edit mode of outline view, you will see the following:

```
ORGANIZE         {·}         <F1=Help>                    Microsoft Word
Edit document or press Alt to choose commands
```

When you move from document view to outline view, Word always puts you in text edit mode. Switching between text edit mode and outline edit mode is easy also. You toggle between the two modes by pressing SHIFT-F5.

Outlines can have both headings and *body* text (body text is like regular text). Each heading has a level, starting with level 1. (Body text does not have a level.) As you make an outline, Word remembers the level of headings by saving a paragraph style with each one. In the gallery, these styles are Heading 1, Heading 2, and so on. Body text is formatted as Normal. As long as you enter your outline in outline view, you do not have to add these styles; Word does it for you.

Because outlines are just like regular documents, Word treats them very similarly. You can print an outline with the File Print command, and you can save it with the File Save command. In fact, you will find that handling outlines is almost identical to handling regular text files.

LESSON 71: CREATING AN OUTLINE

You can enter the text for a new outline in either document or outline view. The advantage of using document view mode is that you have a wider range of editing commands. The disadvantage is that you cannot see the structure of your outline as you enter it. It is usually better to enter and edit outlines in outline view.

Create a new outline with the File New command. Switch from document view to outline view by pressing SHIFT-F2. Your screen will show the following:

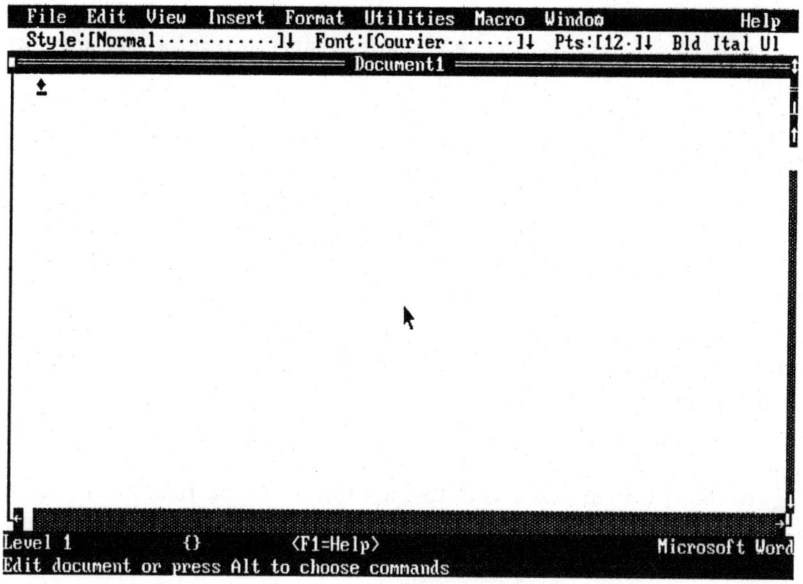

Word automatically puts you in text edit mode so that entering and making small changes is easy.

The following shows the outline you will work with in this chapter. It shows the steps needed for a project.

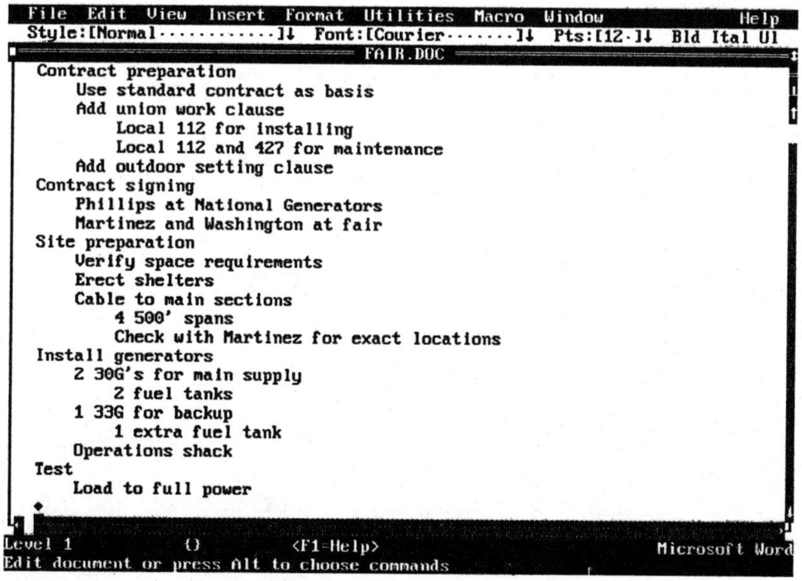

You can begin entering it by typing in **Contract preparation** and pressing ENTER. Word assumes that you want to start at level 1 (see the level indicator in the lower-left corner of the screen).

Next you want to enter the line, **Use standard contract as basis**. However, this is a level-2 entry, not a level 1. To tell Word that this line is level 2, press CTRL-0 (zero, not capital "O"). Word indents the line, and the level indicator reflects the level you have chosen. Type in the line and press ENTER. Continue with the next line, **Add union work clause**, and then press CTRL-0 again to tell Word that the next line will be level 3.

After you add the two level-3 lines, you will want to go back to level 2. To do so, press CTRL-9. You can see how CTRL-0 and CTRL-9 move the levels up and down. Finish entering all the text and save the file as FAIR.DOC with the File Save command.

So far, you have only entered headings. Many outlines will contain body text as well, such as paragraphs under headings or a title. For this example, use body text to add a title to the outline. To do this, move to the top of the outline, press ENTER twice to add some space, and type **Millerton Art Fair** on the first line, as shown here:

```
Millerton Art Fair_

Contract preparation
    Use standard contract as basis
    Add union work clause
        Local 112 for installing
        Local 112 and 427 for maintenance
    Add outdoor setting clause
```

To tell Word that this is body text, press CTRL-X. Word displays a "T" on the screen in the selection bar, as shown here:

```
T Millerton Art Fair_

  Contract preparation
      Use standard contract as basis
      Add union work clause
          Local 112 for installing
          Local 112 and 427 for maintenance
      Add outdoor setting clause
```

You can insert topics in the middle of an outline by moving to the beginning of a line, typing in new characters, and pressing ENTER. You can change the level of a heading by selecting any part of the heading and pressing CTRL-9 or CTRL-0. Note, however, that Word will not let you move a heading more than one step to the right of the heading above it. You can change a heading into body text by selecting any part of the heading and pressing CTRL-X.

It is important to remember to use CTRL-9 and CTRL-0 to shift headings. You cannot use the TAB key to do this; Word will not recognize it.

LESSON 72: TEXT EDIT AND OUTLINE EDIT MODES

As you have seen, editing in text edit mode is very similar to normal editing in document view. The major restriction is that you cannot select more than one paragraph.

Outline edit mode is far more restrictive, but it does make certain processes go much more quickly. Switch from text edit mode into outline edit mode by pressing SHIFT-F5. Move the cursor around with the ← and → keys. Notice that the entire line is selected in outline edit mode.

The selection movement keys work differently in outline edit mode than they do in text edit mode. They allow you to skip around in a way that suits the process of outlining. To see this, move the selection to the "Contract preparation" heading using the ← and → keys. Now press the ↓ key. Notice that the selection skips directly to "Contract signing." Press ↓ again and it jumps to "Site preparation."

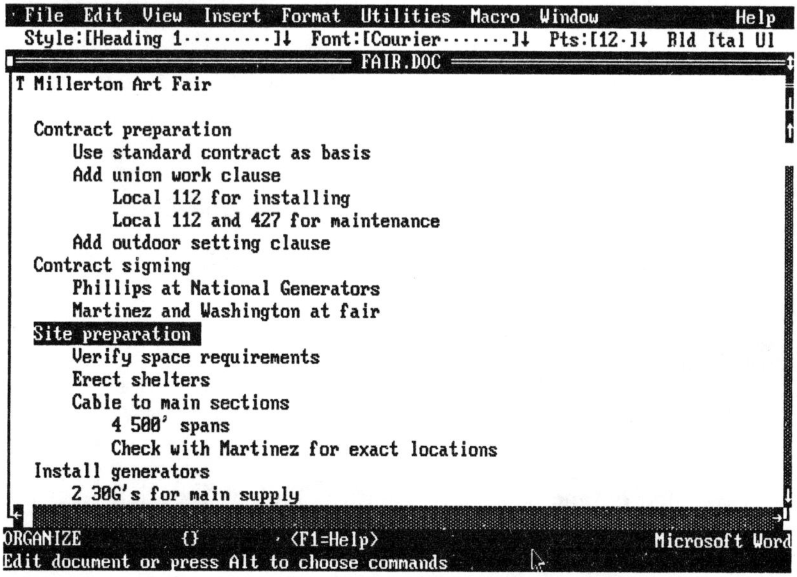

The ↑ and ↓ keys move around the outline by jumping to the next heading that is at the same level, regardless of the headings between. If you try to move beyond the beginning or end of a section of headings, Word will beep at you. For instance, use the ← and → keys to move to "Use standard contract as basis." Press the ↓ key to move to the next level-2 heading, and the next. Pressing the ↓ key once more does not move the selection.

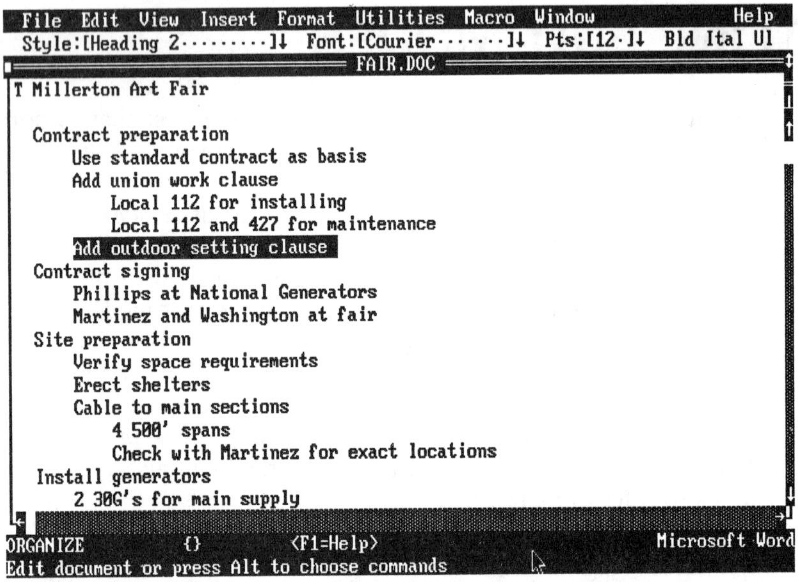

As you could tell, the ← and → keys move up and down regardless of the paragraph level. The HOME and END keys act differently. HOME moves the selection to the previous heading that is one level higher; END goes to the next lower level. The F8 key causes Word to select all of the subheads under the currently selected head. Table 14-1 shows the key actions.

LESSON 73: COLLAPSING AND EXPANDING

A detailed outline can be very hard to follow, especially if it includes body text. When outlining a complex business report, for example, you can quickly lose track of the outline among all the text.

Key	Where Selection Is Moved
←	Up one line
→	Down one line
↑	Previous paragraph at same level
↓	Next paragraph at same level
HOME	Up one heading level
END	Down one heading level
F8	This heading and all subordinate headings

TABLE 14-1. Selection Movement Keys in Outline Edit Mode

To avoid this problem, you will often want to see only higher-level portions of an outline. Word allows you to hide lower-level heads and body text with its collapse feature. To collapse all of the headings below a particular one, simply select that heading (or any part of it) and press the MINUS (–) key on the numeric keypad. To restore these headings, press the PLUS (+) key on the numeric keypad.

Because you generally want to collapse headings in order to see more of your outline, it is convenient to do this in outline edit mode. In fact, you must be in outline edit mode if you want to collapse and expand headings with the mouse. Switch from text edit mode to outline edit mode by pressing SHIFT-F5. Select the first level-1 heading, "Contract preparation."

```
T Millerton Art Fair

  Contract preparation
     Use standard contract as basis
     Add union work clause
        Local 112 for installing
        Local 112 and 427 for maintenance
     Add outdoor setting clause
  Contract signing
     Phillips at National Generators
     Martinez and Washington at fair
```

Press the MINUS key to hide the subordinate headings. When you collapse a heading, Word puts a "+" mark in the selection bar to remind you that there is more under that heading.

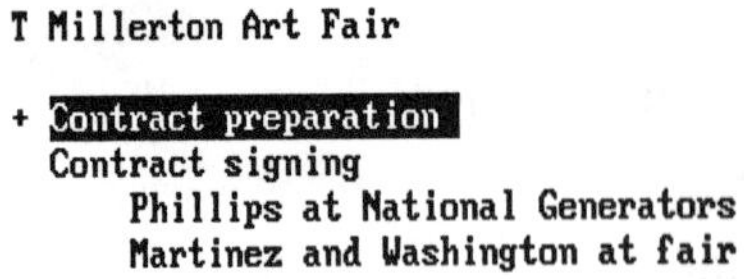

You can also collapse and expand headings with the mouse, but only in outline edit mode, as mentioned earlier. (You can use the PLUS and MINUS keys in either mode.) To collapse a heading, simply point at it and press both buttons.

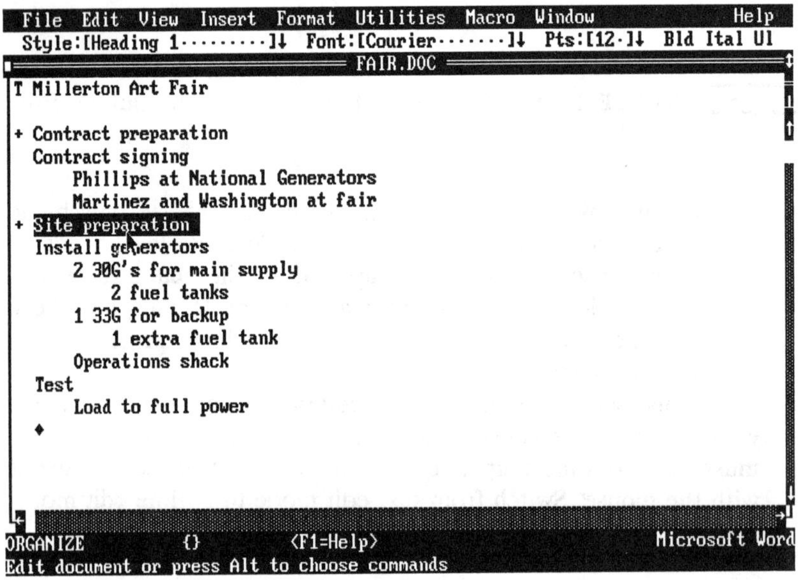

You can expand a heading by using the right-hand button alone.

Expanding a heading shows only the level immediately below it. For example, if you collapse a level-1 heading and some of the level-2 heads below it have subheads, expanding the level-1 heading will not expand the level-2 heads at the same time. If you have collapsed different levels of headings and you want to expand them all at once, use the ASTERISK (*) on the numeric keypad. This will expand all the headings below the one currently selected.

Word treats body text differently than it does subheads when you use the Collapse feature. If you collapse a heading that has body text under it, Word puts a "t" in the selection bar. When you expand that heading, Word does not automatically expand the body text: you have to tell it explicitly to do so.

To see how this works, add the following text lines after the heading "Add union work clause."

```
T Millerton Art Fair

  Contract preparation
      Use standard contract as basis
      Add union work clause
T Although not all fair workers will be union members, all
  concession and novelty sellers will have union cards._
          Local 112 for installing
          Local 112 and 427 for maintenance
      Add outdoor setting clause
  Contract signing
      Phillips at National Generators
      Martinez and Washington at fair
```

Press SHIFT-F5 to get into outline edit mode, select the "Add union work clause" heading, and press the MINUS key. You'll see the following:

```
T Millerton Art Fair

  Contract preparation
      Use standard contract as basis
+     Add union work clause
      Add outdoor setting clause
  Contract signing
      Phillips at National Generators
      Martinez and Washington at fair
```

Now press the PLUS key and your outline will look like this:

```
T Millerton Art Fair

  Contract preparation
      Use standard contract as basis
t     Add union work clause
          Local 112 for installing
          Local 112 and 427 for maintenance
      Add outdoor setting clause
  Contract signing
      Phillips at National Generators
      Martinez and Washington at fair
```

Notice that Word did not expand the text, but instead marks the paragraph with a lowercase "t."

To expand both the subheads and the body text, you must press SHIFT-PLUS instead of PLUS. Select the "Add union work clause" heading again, and press the MINUS key. Now press the SHIFT-PLUS key and your text reappears:

```
T Millerton Art Fair

  Contract preparation
      Use standard contract as basis
+     Add union work clause
T Although not all fair workers will be union members, all
  concession and novelty sellers will have union cards.
      Add outdoor setting clause
  Contract signing
      Phillips at National Generators
      Martinez and Washington at fair
```

Although a fair amount of work, this actually makes it easier for you to view and manipulate your outline without being distracted by underlying text. Word even lets you collapse only the lower-level body text; use SHIFT-MINUS.

The keys and key combinations used to collapse and expand outlines are summarized in Table 14-2. Note that using the ASTERISK key does not expand body text; to expand everything, you must first select the entire document and then press the ASTERISK key.

LESSON 74: REARRANGING YOUR OUTLINE

If you could write an outline correctly the first time you tried, there would not be much use for Word's special outlining commands. Because outlines

Key	Action
MINUS	Collapse subheads and text
PLUS	Expand subheadings
SHIFT-MINUS	Collapse text only
SHIFT-PLUS	Expand subheads and text
ASTERISK	Expand headings throughout document

TABLE 14-2. Collapsing and Expanding Keys in Outline Edit Mode

are used to organize your thoughts, you need to rearrange headings as you decide to change their position or importance. The outline edit mode makes these adjustments especially easy.

If you are moving a heading, it is likely that you also want to move all the ideas associated with it. Word lets you do this. In outline edit mode, deleting and sending a heading to the scrap includes all subheads and body text under that heading, so moving whole ideas is easy.

Suppose that you want to move "Add union work clause" and its related subheads and text to follow "Add outdoor setting clause." Instead of having to select each subhead, just select "Add union work clause."

```
T Millerton Art Fair

  Contract preparation
      Use standard contract as basis
+     Add union work clause
T Although not all fair workers will be union members, all
  concession and novelty sellers will have union cards.
      Add outdoor setting clause
  Contract signing
      Phillips at National Generators
      Martinez and Washington at fair
```

Now give the Edit Cut command to cut this to the scrap.

```
 File  Edit  View  Insert  Format  Utilities  Macro  Window          Help
 Style:[Heading 2·········]↓  Font:[Courier·······]↓  Pts:[12·]↓  Bld Ital Ul
================================ FAIR.DOC ===================================
T Millerton Art Fair

  Contract preparation
      Use standard contract as basis
      Add outdoor setting clause
  Contract signing
      Phillips at National Generators
      Martinez and Washington at fair
  Site preparation
      Verify space requirements
      Erect shelters
      Cable to main sections
          4 500' spans
          Check with Martinez for exact locations
  Install generators
      2 30G's for main supply
          2 fuel tanks
      1 33G for backup
          1 extra fuel tank
ORGANIZE          {Add..e¶}  <F1=Help>                          Microsoft Word
Edit document or press Alt to choose commands
```

"Add outdoor setting clause" is now selected. Move the selection to the next heading, "Contract signing," and give the Edit Paste command. Press PLUS.

```
T Millerton Art Fair

  Contract preparation
      Use standard contract as basis
      Add outdoor setting clause
  Add union work clause
T Although not all fair workers will be union members, all
  concession and novelty sellers will have union cards.
      Local 112 for installing
      Local 112 and 427 for maintenance
  Contract signing
      Phillips at National Generators
      Martinez and Washington at fair
```

Word pasted the heading in as a level-1 heading because "Contract signing" is level 1. To make the selection a level 2, simply press CTRL-0:

```
T Millerton Art Fair

  Contract preparation
      Use standard contract as basis
      Add outdoor setting clause
      Add union work clause
T Although not all fair workers will be union members, all
  concession and novelty sellers will have union cards.
          Local 112 for installing
          Local 112 and 427 for maintenance
  Contract signing
      Phillips at National Generators
      Martinez and Washington at fair
```

This feature is especially useful if you have a lot of body text. Instead of scrolling through many screens of text, you can simply select the heading, knowing that the Delete and Insert commands will include all subordinate material.

LESSON 75: NUMBERING YOUR OUTLINE

Up to this point, all the outlines discussed have been simple outlines without numbers and letters. If you create an outline with numbered headings, you cannot move a heading somewhere else in the outline without affecting the numbering. Word gives you a simple way of numbering and renumbering outlines.

Word will, in fact, number anything, not just outlines. You can select a section of text in document view and have it numbered. This procedure is described in detail in the Word reference manual. This section shows you how Word numbers and renumbers outlines; numbering regular text is very similar.

All numbering is done with the Utilities Renumber command. This command comes with a preset system for numbering, which you can change easily. The preset system conforms to standard outline numbering: level-1 heads in Roman numerals, level-2 heads in capital letters, level-3 heads in regular numerals, and so on. Word can also number in *cascading numeral* format: 1, 1.1, 1.2, 1.2.1, and so on. If you are numbering an outline, Word will not number body text.

To see how the Utilities Renumber command works, select a single paragraph, such as the title:

```
T Millerton Art Fair

  Contract preparation
      Use standard contract as basis
      Add outdoor setting clause
      Add union work clause
T Although not all fair workers will be union members, all
  concession and novelty sellers will have union cards.
          Local 112 for installing
          Local 112 and 427 for maintenance
  Contract signing
      Phillips at National Generators
      Martinez and Washington at fair
```

Give the Utilities Renumber command:

```
┌──────────── Renumber ────────────┐
│ ┌ Renumber Paragraphs ┐          │
│ │ (•) All  ( ) Remove │          │
│ └─────────────────────┘          │
│ [X] Restart Sequence             │
├──────────────────────────────────┤
│       < OK >  <Cancel>           │
└──────────────────────────────────┘
```

Both the "All" and "Restart Sequence" options are correct, so execute the command. The outline is now numbered as shown here:

```
 File  Edit  View  Insert  Format  Utilities  Macro  Window              Help
 Style:[Normal············]↓  Font:[Courier·······]↓  Pts:[12·]↓  Bld Ital Ul
═══════════════════════════ FAIR.DOC ══════════════════════════════════════
T Millerton Art Fair

  I. Contract preparation
      A. Use standard contract as basis
      B. Add outdoor setting clause
      C. Add union work clause
T Although not all fair workers will be union members, all
  concession and novelty sellers will have union cards.
          1. Local 112 for installing
          2. Local 112 and 427 for maintenance
  II. Contract signing
      A. Phillips at National Generators
      B. Martinez and Washington at fair
  III. Site preparation
      A. Verify space requirements
      B. Erect shelters
      C. Cable to main sections
          1. 4 500' spans
          2. Check with Martinez for exact locations
Text              {Add..e¶}  <F1=Help>                         Microsoft Word
Edit document or press Alt to choose commands
```

The Utilities Renumber command works on the whole document, regardless of whether portions are collapsed.

If you want to use a different form of numbering, you have to indicate what form you want. To do this, switch to outline text edit mode, then enter numbers in the desired format on a heading at the beginning of your outline. For example, to have Word number your outline with cascading numerals, enter the following:

```
T Millerton Art Fair

  Contract preparation
      1.1 Use standard contract as basis
      Add outdoor setting clause
      Add union work clause
          Local 112 for installing
          Local 112 and 427 for maintenance
```

When you give the Utilities Renumber command, Word figures out the numbering system you've requested.

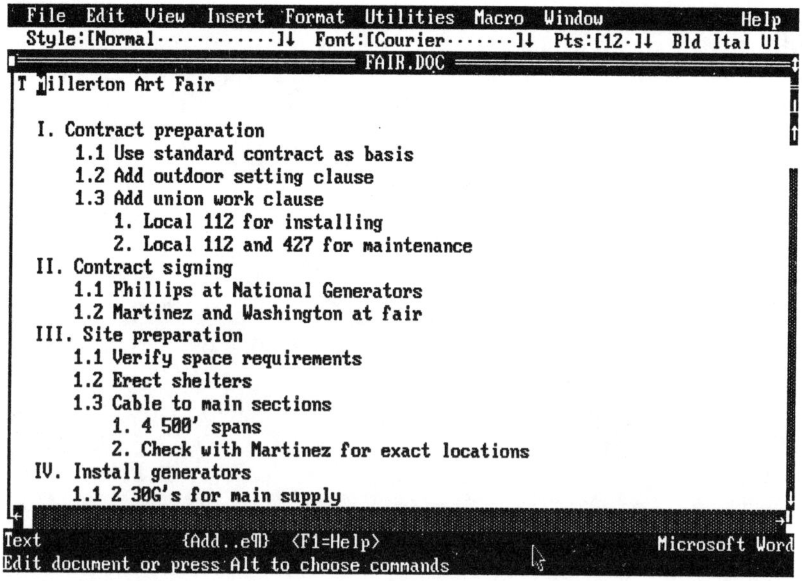

Word also renumbers your documents if you move headings around. For example, if you move the "Add union work clause" heading and give the Utilities Renumber command, Word will correctly renumber that heading and all subsequent heads.

REVIEW

1. *Editing*
   What is the difference between outline edit and text edit modes?
2. *Outline view*
   How do you switch between outline view and document view?
3. *Collapsing and expanding*
   Which keys do you use to collapse and expand text?
4. *Numbering*
   How do you get Word to number your outline?

chapter 15

GENERATING TABLES OF CONTENTS AND INDEXES

Lesson 76: Hidden Text
Lesson 77: Introduction to Tables of Contents
Lesson 78: Specifying Entries
Lesson 79: Creating the Table of Contents
Lesson 80: Advanced Use of Tables of Contents
Lesson 81: Creating an Index

Not only are tables of contents and indexes time-consuming and tedious to prepare, but they must be updated whenever you add to or rearrange your document. Very few word processing packages automatically compile tables of contents or indexes. Those that do usually restrict you to a preset style of printout that may not meet your needs.

With Word, on the other hand, you can easily create entries for the table of contents or index, and you have great flexibility in styling your printout. In addition, you can generate a new table of contents or index whenever you choose. These features make Word one of the most popular programs for business and academic use.

This chapter shows you how to create a table of contents and assemble an index. Specifying the text for either one is similar, so read this chapter even if you only want to generate indexes.

Making a table of contents from an outline is significantly easier than making one from regular text. You simply give the Insert Table of Contents command (discussed later in this chapter), indicate that you are working on an outline, and Word does the rest. Instead of requiring you to identify headings in the text, Word takes them from the outline and assembles the table of contents automatically. Thus, if your document is based on an outline, you do not need to "mark" your headings, a procedure that is described later in this chapter.

LESSON 76: HIDDEN TEXT

To create a table of contents, you must tell Word what you want in the table. You do this by flagging the headings you want included with a special marker that is formatted on the screen as hidden text.

Hidden text is similar to other text that has a character format applied to it. You can use the Format Character command to make text bold; you can also use the command to make text hidden. To make a section of text hidden, simply select it and give the Format Character command with the "Hidden Text" option enabled, or use CTRL-H.

Once you mark something as hidden, you cannot see it on the screen (as you might have guessed). For example, select the word "Vice" in the SAMPLE1 file.

```
January 11, 1985

Chris Richford, Vice President
Manufacturer's Bank of the Northeast
1000 First Avenue
Millerton, CT  06492
```

Format it as hidden, and your screen will look like the following:

```
January 11, 1985

Chris Richford, President
Manufacturer's Bank of the Northeast
1000 First Avenue
Millerton, CT  06492
```

Word gives you two ways of seeing your hidden text after you have formatted it. To see all the hidden text in a document, use the View Preferences command and select the Hidden Text option. If you are using a graphics screen, you will see the hidden text with a dotted underline (on a monochrome screen, it appears bold):

```
January 11, 1985

Chris Richford, Vice President
Manufacturer's Bank of the Northeast
1000 First Avenue
Millerton, CT  06492
```

Do not get into the habit of showing hidden text on the screen. Should you print or repaginate a document that has hidden text showing, Word would include that text in its calculations for the ends of pages and so on. Then, were you to generate a table of contents or an index, Word would enter incorrect page numbers.

If you want to see hidden text, you can open up a second window and use the View Preferences command in that window to do so. This lets you see the document both with and without the hidden text. Be careful, though, not to repaginate the document when this second window is the selected window, or Word will include the hidden text in its page calculation. You will get used to typing hidden text fairly quickly, and most of the time you won't need to see it.

LESSON 77: INTRODUCTION TO TABLES OF CONTENTS

Before you start using Word to generate tables of contents for your documents, you should consider the purpose and structure of a table of contents. Generally, a table of contents appears at the beginning of a document. It tells the reader what is presented in the document, and in what order. A document that is only one or two pages long generally does not need a table of contents.

A table of contents can be a simple list of where each section of the document begins, or it can be a detailed roadmap of the document. Some tables of contents are meant to show almost the entire contents of a document. These are much longer than simple tables of contents and are often hard to browse through. Of course, someone looking for a particular subject will be more likely to find it in a detailed table of contents. However, many authors prefer to create an index for detailed listings and keep the table of contents brief.

The format of a table of contents is also important. If you list two or more levels of headings in a table of contents, Word's paragraph and character formatting will make the table of contents significantly easier to read. Compare this unformatted table of contents:

```
Installation   1
   Unpacking  2
      Checking the crates   2
         In case of damage 3
      Removing the main unit     4
      Other units 8
   Connecting to equipment   10
   Adding fuel     10
Testing   13
   Starting for the first time    14
```

to this formatted one:

```
Installation..............................................1
   Unpacking.......................................2
      Checking the crates..........................2
         In case of damage.........................3
      Removing the main unit.......................4
      Other units..................................8
   Connecting to equipment........................10
   Adding fuel....................................10

Testing..................................................13
   Starting for the first time....................14
```

Compiling a table of contents for a document is quite easy. There are basically two steps:

1. Mark all paragraphs that you want to appear in the table of contents. The methods you use are shown in the next lesson.

2. Give the Insert Table of Contents command. Word creates a table of contents in a new section at the end of your document.

There are rules and suggestions for both steps, but you do not need to do much more for Word to create a full table of contents.

LESSON 78: SPECIFYING ENTRIES

There are two distinct methods for specifying what the Insert Table of Contents command should treat as table entries. You must use either one of the methods, but not both. The two methods are

- Use "Heading" paragraph styles for the entries.
- Mark each entry with **.c.** (a period before and after a lowercase "c") in hidden text before the entry.

Many people prefer the first method because they do not need to worry about keeping the hidden text off the screen when repaginating. If you are already using styles in your work (as advocated in Chapter 10), the paragraph style method is very simple.

Other people prefer the hidden **.c.** method since they can tailor the text that appears in the table of contents better than with the styles method. Using the styles method, the entire tagged paragraph appears in the table. With the hidden **.c.** method, you can specify exactly what you want to appear in the table of contents; in fact, you can even specify text that does not appear in your document.

Using the Heading Styles for Entries

To mark table of contents entries with the first method, using styles, simply select the headings and apply paragraph styles to them. You must first define these styles in your style sheet using the style I.D.s "Heading 1," "Heading 2," and so on.

Use the methods described in Chapter 10 to add at least three levels of headings to the style sheet you have attached to the document. If you have many style sheets, you may want to define just the heading styles in a separate style sheet and use the Insert Style Sheet command when editing your style sheets. This command lets you easily merge your headings style sheet into your existing style sheets.

Once you have a style sheet with the defined styles, simply select a heading and apply the appropriate paragraph style using any of the three methods described in Chapter 10.

Using Hidden Text for Entries

To specify which text should appear in the table of contents using hidden text, enter **.c.** before the text and make the **.c.** hidden. The entry itself can be either hidden or regular text. Word assumes that the first character after the **.c.** is the first character of the entry, unless the first character is a colon (the use of the colon is described later in this section).

Word ends the entry when it sees a semicolon, a paragraph mark, or a division mark. Because most tables of contents contain headings from the document, and most headings are paragraphs, you can generally just add the hidden **.c.** at the beginning of lines you want included in the table.

Assume that you want this heading to appear in the table of contents:

Excerpts from a Proposal for Bank Funding

I. Introduction

National Generators has the opportunity over the next five years to take a commanding lead in our established markets and to penetrate a new market, the construction industry, where our products will be particularly attractive. This report is intended to provide an overview of the company's business development strategies along with a description of those areas for which we require funding.

Move the selection to the first character. Press CTRL-H to turn on hidden formatting, type **.c.**, and press CTRL-SPACEBAR to turn off hidden formatting. The line looks the same, but Word's marker has been added. (This insertion is more easily performed with a glossary entry or a macro.)

If the text you want in the table of contents is not a heading, and does not end with a paragraph mark, you can still specify it easily. To indicate the end of your desired entry, add a hidden semicolon. Of course, you will want this semicolon to be hidden so that it does not appear in your text.

Assume that you want the words "National Generators" from the first sentence of the following paragraph to be an entry:

Excerpts from a Proposal for Bank Funding

I. Introduction

National Generators has the opportunity over the next five years to take a commanding lead in our established markets and to penetrate a new market, the construction industry, where our products will be particularly attractive. This report is intended to provide an overview of the company's business development strategies along with a description of those areas for which we require funding.

Move the selection to the first letter, press CTRL-H to turn on hidden formatting, type **.c.**, and press CTRL-SPACEBAR to turn off hidden formatting. Now move to the space after "Generators," press CTRL-H to turn on hidden formatting, type the semicolon (;), and press CTRL-SPACEBAR again to turn off hidden formatting once more.

So far, you have only learned how to put level-1 entries into a table of contents with hidden text. As you saw earlier, however, it is often desirable to have more than one level in your table of contents. To tell Word that an entry is level 2, precede the text of the entry with a colon. Thus, to make the previous example a level-2 head, you would insert this hidden text:

```
.c.:
```

To make it a level-3 head, you would insert this hidden text:

```
.c.::
```

Unfortunately, when you are specifying entries with hidden text, there are many special cases. If your heading contains a semicolon or a colon, you have to tell Word exactly what text you want included. Any entry that has either a semicolon or a colon must have quotation marks at the beginning and end of the entry. Of course, these quotation marks should be formatted as hidden characters or they will show up in your document. For example, suppose you wanted to make the following heading an entry:

```
The Future: More Growth
```

At the beginning of the line, press CTRL-H to turn on hidden formatting. Type **.c."** and press CTRL-SPACEBAR to turn off hidden formatting. At the end of the line, press CTRL-H to turn on hidden formatting. Type " and press CTRL-SPACEBAR to turn off hidden formatting again.

If your entry contains quotation marks, the situation is even trickier. First, you must surround the entire entry with quotation marks, just as if it contained a semicolon or a colon. Next, you must precede any quotation mark in the entry by another quotation mark. Again, use hidden formatting for all of these special quotation marks. For instance, if your desired entry is

Finding the "Best" Solution: Optimization

you must put

.c."

at the beginning of the line, a hidden quotation mark before the first real quotation mark, a hidden quotation mark before the second real quotation mark, and a hidden quotation mark at the end of the line. Needless to say, this can be a bit tedious.

LESSON 79: CREATING THE TABLE OF CONTENTS

Once you have entered all the hidden marks for Word, you can create a table of contents with the Insert Table of Contents command. Briefly, this command will automatically do the following:

1. Repaginate your document (remember to hide hidden text in the View Preferences dialog).
2. Search through your document from the beginning for marked entries.
3. Collect copies of those marked entries and their associated page numbers. (Word uses the page number of the first visible text after the heading.)
4. Create a new section at the end of your document containing the entries.

The Insert Table of Contents command has many interesting features that are described in this lesson and later in the chapter. Even if you skip these descriptions, you can quickly generate a simple table of contents just by giving the Insert Table of Contents command and printing your document. With a bit more planning and work, however, you can create more complex tables of contents and figure lists.

The Insert Table of Contents command's dialog looks like this:

```
Table of Contents
Create Table of Contents from
( ) Outline                         (•) Codes: [C·]

Page Numbers                        Indent Each Level
[X] Show Page Numbers               (•) By: [0.4"·····]
Separate by: [^t···]                ( ) Use Style Sheet

                                    < OK >  <Cancel>
```

The first option, "Create Table of Contents from," is the most important. This tells Word which method you used to mark your entries. Be sure that the correct choice is selected so Word can find your entries.

You can create a new table of contents at any time. If you change your document by adding, deleting, or moving text, you should give the command before you print your document so that the table of contents reflects the most current revision. If you have already created a table of contents, Word replaces the old copy with the new one after verifying that you want this done.

When you execute the command, Word creates a new section at the end of your document containing the table of contents. If you jump to that section, you will see something similar to this:

```
:::::::::::::::::::::::::::::::::::::::::::::::::::::::::::
Installation                                     1
   Unpacking                                     2
      Checking the crates                        2
         In case of damage                       3
      Removing the main unit                     4
      Other units                                8
   Connecting to equipment                      10
   Adding fuel                                  10
Testing                                         13
   Starting for the first time                  14
♦
```

Word puts the table of contents at the end of your document so that it doesn't affect the numbering of the pages in the main part. Unless you have a specific reason to move it, it is best to leave the table of contents at the end of your document.

Once you have this text at the end of your document, you can format it any way you want. (In general, you will not want to use Word's default formatting.)

note You can use normal character, paragraph, and section formatting on the table; however, if you regenerate the table of contents, your formatting changes are lost.

One of the most obvious changes you may want to make is to add leader characters between the entries and the page numbers. Word's default setting simply puts a tab between them. To change this, select all of the paragraphs in the table and give the Format Tabs command. Replace the existing tab with one that has right alignment and a dot leader character. The result could look similar to this:

```
::::::::::::::::::::::::::::::::::::::::::::::::::::::::::::::
Installation.............................................1
    Unpacking............................................2
        Checking the crates..............................2
            In case of damage............................3
        Removing the main unit...........................4
        Other units......................................8
    Connecting to equipment.............................10
    Adding fuel.........................................10
Testing.................................................13
    Starting for the first time.........................14
♦
```

Other items you might want to change are the spacing, margins, and page numbering.

You can change a few of Word's default formatting characteristics when you give the Insert Table of Contents command.

- The "Separate by" option has a default of "^t" that separates the entry and the page number by a tab. It is unlikely you would want anything else, but you can specify other characters.

- The "Indent Each Level" option lets you specify the default indentation for each level of subhead. You can instead choose to use a style sheet.

Of these options, using a style sheet is the most useful. With a style sheet, you can specify formatting for the heads in the table of contents. These styles will be implemented automatically as Word adds entries to the table of contents. The paragraph styles "Table 1," "Table 2," and so on are used for the entries. Using a style sheet means that you do not have to reformat the paragraphs each time you regenerate the table of contents.

LESSON 80: ADVANCED USE OF TABLES OF CONTENTS

Microsoft made Word's features flexible so that you would be able to do more than just create a table of contents. This section describes how you can use these features to make advanced documents.

Word knows where previous tables of contents are in your document by looking for special hidden text that it enters at the beginning and end of the table. When it creates a table of contents, it inserts in hidden text ".Begin Table C." at the beginning and ".End Table C." at the end. When it re-creates a table of contents, Word only erases the text between these two lines.

It is common to add text at the top of your table of contents, such as the title "Table of contents." If you put that text inside the beginning and end markers, Word automatically deletes it each time it re-creates the table of contents. Instead, put text that you want to keep outside of the markers, like this:

```
::::::::::::::::::::::::::::::::::::::::::::::::::::::::::
                    Table of Contents_
.Begin Table C.
Installation.............................................1
   Unpacking.............................................2
      Checking the crates................................2
         In case of damage...............................3
      Removing the main unit.............................4
      Other units........................................8
   Connecting to equipment..............................10
   Adding fuel..........................................10
Testing.................................................13
   Starting for the first time..........................14
.End Table C.
♦
```

You can also format the section marker for the table of contents after the first time Word creates it; Word won't change it after that.

Many reports have numerous figures and tables. It is often useful to list these elements and let the reader know the page numbers. In the same way that you create tables of contents, you can also create other lists.

For example, assume that you have a figure listing such as the following:

Figure 7. Power indicators at full.

In front of the listing, add the hidden text ".**f.**" (instead of **.c.**). Do the same in front of each figure, following the rules for special characters. Next, give the Insert Table of Contents command. In the "Codes" option, change the "C" to "F". When you execute the command, Word creates a new list consisting of the entries that were marked with **.f.**.

You can use this technique to create lists of figures, tables, charts, and so on. The only letter that you cannot use is "i" because that is the marking character Word uses for indexes (as you will see in the next lesson). All other aspects of creating tables of contents are identical to those for creating other lists.

LESSON 81: CREATING AN INDEX

The steps used to make an index are almost identical to those used for a table of contents, and the results are also similar. Almost everything you learned to create a table of contents applies here.

To mark an entry for the index, use **.i.** instead of **.c.**. The same rules apply for ending the entry: use either a semicolon, a paragraph mark, or a division mark. If you are marking a visible part of your text, you will probably use many hidden semicolons. The rules for special characters apply here as well.

Subentries are created slightly differently. Because there is a predetermined order to an index, you must specify a main entry when you specify a subentry. Separate the two with a colon. For example, to include an index entry for "new models" under "Generators" you would type

```
.i.Generators:new models
```

Word allows up to five levels of entries; however, indexes rarely have more than three levels, and most have only two.

If you use *see references* in your index, specify them as subentries. For instance,

```
.i.Power:see electricity
```

Word does not know the difference between a see reference and a subentry, and the output will therefore have a page reference with it. You'll need to delete the page numbers in see references after Word creates the index.

As you become proficient at determining what a reader needs in an index, you will find that the words and concepts that you want to refer to on a page may not be stated specifically. Thus, many of your index entries will consist entirely of hidden text. For instance, imagine that you are discussing religion and you also want a reference to "theology," although that word does not appear in the text. You can enter **.i.theology** in hidden text to make the entry.

The Insert Index dialog looks like this:

```
┌────────────────── Index ──────────────────┐
│Separate Page Numbers from Entry by: [^t_··]│
│                                            │
│┌ Indent Each Level ┐                       │
││(•) By: [0.2"·····]│  [X] Capitalize Main  │
││( ) Use Style Sheet│      Entries          │
│└───────────────────┘                       │
├────────────────────────────────────────────┤
│                        < OK >  <Cancel>    │
└────────────────────────────────────────────┘
```

- The "Separate Page Numbers from Entry by" option has a default setting of a tab character. Most indexes do not have leader characters between the entries and the page numbers. If you want spaces, however, change this option.

- The "Capitalize Main Entries" option tells Word whether to force the first letter of a main entry to a capital letter. If you do not select it, Word will use whatever case you used in the entry. Word will never capitalize lower-level entries.

- "Indent Each Level" is the same as for tables of contents, although the default is .2 inch. "Use Style Sheet" is also the same. The advantages of using a style sheet are just as strong for indexes as for tables of contents. If you select Yes, Word assigns the levels to "Index 1," "Index 2," and so forth.

When you execute the Insert Index command, Word creates a new section and places the sorted index entries in it. You can format the output any way you want, just as before. Remember, though, that any formatting will be lost if you create the index again.

It is common practice to have multi-column indexes. Recall from Chapter 9 that Word can make columns easily with the Format Section command. Since most index entries are short, a two-column index usually looks fine. However, be careful to check that none of your page numbers wraps around in a confusing fashion.

There are many other changes that you might want to make to standardize the appearance of your index. Remember to make these changes only after you are sure that the index is in final form. Possible changes include

- Adding a title to the page.
- Italicizing see references.
- Removing the superfluous page numbers from see references.
- Changing lists of consecutive pages into ranges. For instance, you may want to change this entry:

Starting 17, 18, 19, 23

into this:

Starting 17-19, 23

REVIEW

1. *Marking for a table of contents*
   How do you mark an entry to be included in the table of contents?

2. *Special characters*
   What are the special characters that affect marking entries? How do you handle them?

3. *Formatting the table of contents*
   How can you format your table of contents?

REVIEW (*continued*)

4. *Other lists*
   How do you create a list of figures?

5. *Marking for an index*
   How do you mark an entry to be included in the index?

6. *Capitalization*
   What choices does Word give you concerning capitalization in the index?

chapter 16

ANNOTATIONS, BOOKMARKS, AND CROSS-REFERENCES

Lesson 82: Creating Annotations
Lesson 83: Using Bookmarks
Lesson 84: Cross-References in Your Documents

Word has three innovative features that make long projects significantly easier to manage.

- *Annotations* allow you to leave notes for yourself in your document and to later reference those notes. You can also use annotations to let other people comment on a document.
- *Bookmarks* make jumping around in your document much faster, since you don't have to remember page numbers when you move within the document.
- *Cross-references* let you refer to parts of your document by pages or by numbers in a series. For instance, if you have a table that you want to refer to, you can put a bookmark at the table and include a special cross-reference. When you print your document, the cross-reference will refer to the table's page.

LESSON 82: CREATING ANNOTATIONS

You can use annotations to leave yourself easy-to-find notes and markers in your text. Since annotations are stored just as footnotes are, you can add them, move them, and edit them in a similar fashion.

When you are writing a long report, there are often times when you do not have complete information. You may want to write the text around the unknown data instead of waiting until you receive the data to add the sentence or paragraph that goes with it. A convenient method for doing this is to write what you can, then select all the text that is uncertain. Give that text a special formatting (such as double underlining) and add an annotation. If you find the missing data before the final draft of the report, simply select the text, unformat it, add the new information, and remove the annotation.

Word treats annotations as it does footnotes, which you learned about in Chapter 9. Instead of using footnote numbers, however, you can use any mark you want. Thus, if many people are annotating a document, each person can use his or her initials (or his or her name, up to 28 characters). If you are annotating your own document, you can use marks that are meaningful for the types of notes you are leaving for yourself. For example, you might use "more" as an annotation mark to indicate that you need more material in a section, and then describe in the annotation what new material you need. After you perform the task the annotation reminded you to do, you can easily remove it.

To enter annotations, use the Insert Annotation command. This command looks a great deal like the Format Footnote command. The Annotation dialog looks like this:

```
┌──────────────────── Annotation ────────────────────┐
│ Annotation Mark: [_...................]            │
│                                                    │
│ [ ] Include Date      [ ] Include Time             │
├────────────────────────────────────────────────────┤
│                         < OK >   <Cancel>          │
└────────────────────────────────────────────────────┘
```

Enter the characters you want for the annotation mark in the mark field. You can set Include Date and Include Time to append the date and time to the end of the annotation. When you execute the command, Word moves you to the annotation area at the end of the document. To get back after entering your text, use the Edit Go to command.

Since annotations are similar to footnotes, you can edit and delete them in the same way. To edit annotation text, move to the end of your document by scrolling or select the mark in your document for the annotation you want to edit and give the Edit Go to command. To delete an annotation, simply delete its mark. Annotations print with footnotes, so you use the Place Footnotes field in the Format Section command to tell Word where you want the annotations.

LESSON 83: USING BOOKMARKS

Bookmarks make jumping around a long document much easier. You don't have to remember page numbers (which might change when you edit your document) or search for specific text. Instead, you simply insert a named bookmark and jump to it by name. For instance, if you have a 250-page document that has 20 chapters, you might put a bookmark at the beginning of each chapter; you might also put bookmarks at tables you refer to often.

Word's bookmarks can mark a selection of text, not just a location. For instance, if you create a bookmark for a table, when you give the Edit Go to command, the entire table will be selected. This is very handy for items that you copy a great deal. When you move the selected text, the bookmark moves with it. A bookmark can be a single character if you wish.

To create a bookmark, select the desired text (or the single character) and give the Insert Bookmark command:

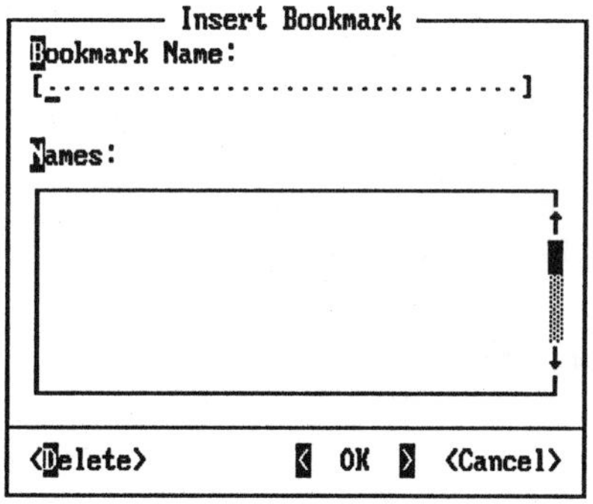

Enter the bookmark's name in the name field (up to 31 characters, no spaces or colons), and press ENTER. To jump to a bookmark, give the Edit Go to command and either type in the name of the desired bookmark or select it in the scroll box.

To remove a bookmark, give the Edit Go to command, select the bookmark you want, and choose the Delete button.

LESSON 84: CROSS-REFERENCES IN YOUR DOCUMENTS

Word can cross-reference any number that is in an automatically generated series. These numbers can be page numbers, paragraph numbers (generated with the Utilities Renumber command you learned about in Chapter 14), footnotes, or series that are specially generated. You then use special codes to refer to the numbered items; when printing, Word replaces the special codes with the numbers to which they referred. You always cross-reference to a bookmark, so be sure you understand the previous lesson before you continue here.

For example, assume that you want to refer to the page number of a specific heading in your document. The heading is "New Operations." You would want its reference to look something like:

This is described in detail in *New Operations* on page 32.

To cross-reference to a section of text, first select the text and make a bookmark for it. At the place where you want to cross-reference to that section, type **page:** followed by the bookmark name, and then press F3. Thus, to generate the cross-reference just given, you would select the "New Operations" heading, make it a bookmark called "newop-head," and enter the following text:

```
This is described in detail in New Operations on page
page:newop-head♦
```

Next, press F3. Your screen will look like this:

```
This is described in detail in New Operations on page
(page:newop-head)♦
```

When you print your text, this will be replaced with the page number.

To cross-reference to a paragraph number that is generated by the Utilities Renumber command, type **para-num:** instead of **page:** in the cross-reference. For example, you might want Word to print the following:

This is described in detail in *New Operations,* which is section 3.2.

To get this, enter the following:

```
This is described in detail in New Operations, which
is section para-num:newop-head◆
```

To cross-reference to a footnote number, type **footnote:** instead of **page:** in the cross-reference.

You can also have Word create a numbered series for you and cross-reference to the series. To start a series, enter the series name (up to 31 characters, no spaces or colons) followed by a colon. For example, use **table:** for a series of tables. Press F3 to tell Word that this is a series label. Use the same label for each entry in the series. When you print your document, Word prints a "1" for the first time it sees a series name, a "2" for the second time, and so on.

If you want a number to be included in the series numbering but not to show up in the printout, follow the name with two colons (such as **table::**). You can even set the numbering yourself by entering the name, two colons, and one less than the number you want to set. For instance, to start a series called "product-code" and start the series at 100, enter **product-code::99** and press F3. You can reset the series anywhere in your document.

For example, you might have a table with a series of seminars:

```
(sem:)    Martin    Finding the Best Commercial Real Estate In
                    Cities
(sem:)    Kress     Marketing To Older Americans
(sem:)    Barrett   Brief Introduction To Radio and TV
                    Advertising
```

This would print out as:

1	Martin	Finding the Best Commercial Real Estate in Cities
2	Kress	Marketing to Older Americans
3	Barrett	Brief Introduction to Radio and TV Advertising

To refer to items in the table, create a bookmark for each row of the table. In the preceding example, you might make the bookmark for the second row "marketing" and refer to it this way:

```
If you work with senior citizens, you might be interested in
seminar #(sem:marketing).◆
```

REVIEW

1. *Annotations*
   What are some of the uses of annotations?

2. *Bookmarks*
   How do you find the list of defined bookmarks?

3. *Cross-references*
   What types of items can be cross-referenced?

Chapter 17

SPELLING CORRECTION, HYPHENATION, AND THESAURUS

Lesson 85: Introduction to Spelling Correction
Lesson 86: Spelling
Lesson 87: Hyphenation
Lesson 88: Using the Thesaurus

Because most people are not perfect spellers, Word has included an easy-to-use spelling checker that works closely with the other parts of Word. You can use the program at any time, and you do not need to exit from Word to do so.

Word also includes a hyphenation program. Justified text looks significantly better if all of the long words in the text have optional hyphens. Of course, inserting these yourself is tedious. The hyphenation program frees you from the task of putting optional hyphens in every word and gives you control over the way hyphens are used in your document.

Word's thesaurus lets you quickly look up words that are similar in meaning to the word you just typed. If, for instance, you find that you are repeatedly using the same word in a paragraph, you may want to have Word suggest a synonym.

LESSON 85: INTRODUCTION TO SPELLING CORRECTION

The second most useful program for writers is a spelling checker (the first, of course, is a word processor). Even if your spelling is nearly flawless, it is likely that your proofreading is not; and a single spelling mistake in a report or memo can have a very negative effect.

The idea behind spelling checkers is fairly simple. When you run a spelling checker, it reads your document file and makes a list of all the words you used. The program compares this list against a list of all the English words it knows and tells you which words it does not recognize. You then change the words either through the program or with your word processor.

Of course, even a good spelling checker is not perfect, since you will probably use words that it does not know, which it will think you have misspelled. For example, most dictionaries that come with spelling programs do not include proper names, so a program may think that you misspelled something if, for example, it sees the word "Jones" in your text. Also, spelling checkers cannot spot words that are used incorrectly in context, as in "I one the race."

The dictionary in Word's spelling checker has a great vocabulary. This makes it less likely that Word will not recognize a correctly spelled word. The dictionary takes up a fair amount of space, however, so you need a separate disk for it unless you are using a hard disk.

If Word thinks you have misspelled a word in your document, it can offer help by checking through its dictionary for a few guesses at what you intended. For example, if you have the misspelled word "postion" in your document, Word will suggest words such as *portion, position,* and *potion.*

The spelling corrector uses three different dictionaries when it corrects a document. It searches these invisibly so that you need not keep track of the names.

- The *standard* dictionary contains all common words. This is the largest of the three dictionaries. You can add words to this dictionary, and delete or edit the words you add.

- *User* dictionaries contain words that are used in certain types of documents. You can tell the speller to check a particular user dictionary before you proof your document. It is likely that you will have one user dictionary just for words that are only used in your field. Words that are perfectly acceptable but are not in the standard dictionary also can be included in a user dictionary.
- *Document* dictionaries contain words that you want to use in only one document. If you are using some abbreviations in a particular document that you know will not be used in anything else, you can enter them into a document dictionary, which will have the same name as the document with an extension of .CMP. Document dictionaries are rarely used.

Word lists the unrecognized words one at a time. For each word, you have the following choices:

- Add the word to one of the dictionaries.
- Correct the word in your document by typing in the correct spelling or by selecting one of Word's guesses.
- Ignore the word, indicating that you know it is not recognized, but you don't care.
- Mark the word so that you can find it easily when you return to editing. Word puts a special mark before the word so that it is easy to find with the Search command.

The spelling checker is easy to use, although some find it slow. If you are creating a large document, you may want to check the spelling after you have entered all the text (but before you edit) and again just before you print the text. If you create a table of contents or index, you should run the spelling checker after doing so; any mistakes made in hidden text will then be found.

Word will also check for doubled words (such as "and and"), since these are rarely desired in your documents, and for some cases of bad punctuation, such as a comma at the beginning of a word ("now ,you").

LESSON 86: SPELLING

When you are ready to check the spelling of a document, give the Utilities Spelling command. If you are on a floppy-based system, Word will prompt you to insert the Spell Disk. After Word loads the spelling program, it looks for the first unrecognized word and displays the following:

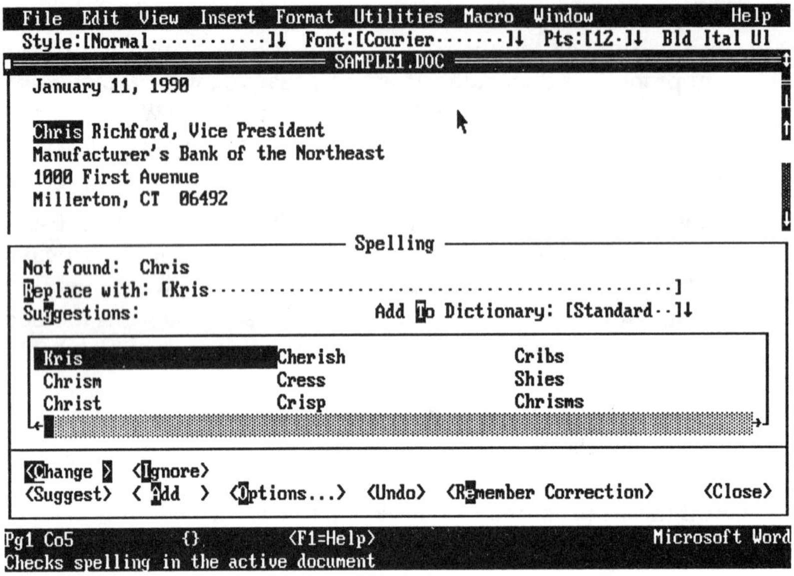

The speller has a few options that make it easier to use in special circumstances. Set these with the "Options" button. Word displays this dialog:

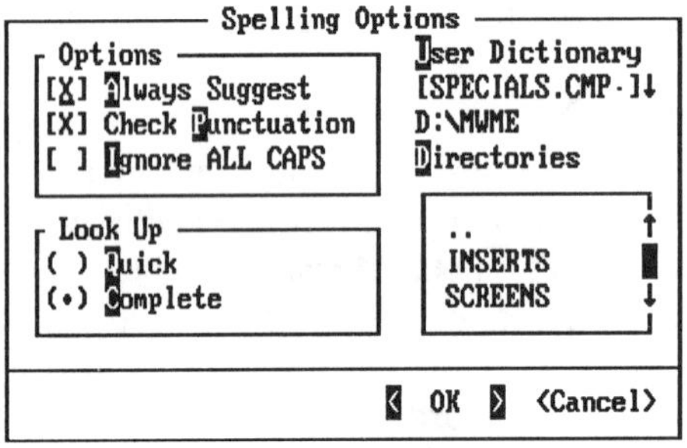

You have many choices here:

- You can tell Word not to automatically list the suggested alternative spellings by unselecting "Always Suggest."
- The "Check Punctuation" option tells Word whether you want it to look for questionable punctuation.
- The "Ignore ALL CAPS" option tells Word not to bother with words that are all capital letters. Since words in all caps are usually acronyms, it is highly unlikely they will be in the standard dictionary. However, it is easy

to mistype these words, so it is a good idea to include the correct versions in your user dictionary and have Word check them.

- You can specify the User Dictionary.
- The Look Up option lets you tell Word how thorough to be when it guesses at misspellings. "Quick" indicates that Word should assume the first two letters of any suspect word are correct. This is almost always the case; people most often misspell words after they type the first two letters. "Complete" means to make no assumptions about the misspelling.

Once you have changed any options you want altered, execute the command. If Word finds words that it does not recognize, it displays the following:

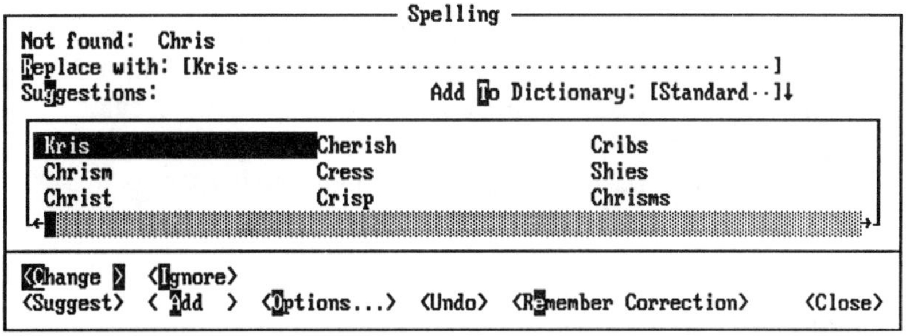

Use the Add button to tell Word this is an acceptable word to add to the dictionary specified in the "Add to Dictionary:" scroll box. Ignore indicates that you want to leave the word as it stands but you do not want to add it to the dictionary. If you correct this document again later, you will see all the ignored words again.

Use the Change button when you know that the word is not what you want in your document. Word will give you a list of its best guesses. You can select from this list with the mouse or the arrow keys. If none of the guesses is correct and you know the correct spelling for the word, you can simply type it in.

LESSON 87: HYPHENATION

You may think that there is only one kind of hyphen. Word, however, has three: normal, nonbreaking, and nonrequired hyphens. Each time you hyphenate a word, you can indicate the kind of hyphen you want so that wordwrap will not produce an effect you do not want.

A *normal* hyphen is one that is always printed. For example, the word "fast-moving" contains a normal hyphen, since you always want the hyphen to appear in the printed text.

A *nonbreaking* hyphen is like a normal hyphen, except that Word will never break the hyphenated word if it occurs at the end of a line. For instance, if you use a normal hyphen, you may end up with a paragraph that looks like this:

```
There are many different spreadsheets that perform "what-
if" calculations.
```

Since there was a normal hyphen between "what" and "if," Word broke the line there. In many cases, this is all right, but in this case it looks a bit clumsy. If you want to prevent Word from ever breaking a word at its hyphen, you use a nonbreaking hyphen, which you enter by pressing CTRL-SHIFT-HYPHEN. The result of using a nonbreaking hyphen is this:

```
There are many different spreadsheets that perform
"what-if" calculations.
```

If a paragraph contains many long words, wordwrap can make the paragraph look a bit sparse, as in the following:

```
His telecommunications discussion was
significantly sidetracked as he started
expostulating about interplanetary associations of
antedeluvian civilizations.
```

To make the lines more even, you will need to hyphenate some of the words. However, the Word program cannot guess where to hyphenate words that do not contain hyphens. If you want Word to hyphenate a word, you have to enter an optional hyphen. You usually do this only when you notice that a particular set of lines is broken unevenly.

An *optional* hyphen is only used when needed. You can include optional hyphens anywhere in a word. To enter an optional hyphen, use CTRL-HYPHEN.

You do not see these hyphens unless they appear because of wordwrap. If you use optional hyphens in the previous example, the result is

```
His telecommunications discussion was signifi-
cantly sidetracked as he started expostulating
about interplanetary associations of antedeluvian
civilizations.
```

Word can help you hyphenate by automatically putting optional hyphens in every word that sits at the end of a line and might be split. The Utilities Hyphenate command will let you decide where the hyphen goes in each word or will hyphenate without confirmation.

The Utilities Hyphenate command will normally hyphenate your whole document from the beginning. If you want to hyphenate only part of the document, select that part before giving the command. This is the dialog:

```
┌──────────── Hyphenate ──────────────┐
│ [X] Confirm   [X] Hyphenate Caps    │
├─────────────────────────────────────┤
│               < OK >  <Cancel>      │
└─────────────────────────────────────┘
```

It is unlikely that you will want to have Word confirm hyphenation for each word, especially in a long document. If you do choose to have Word confirm each hyphenation, Word will change the display as though you were in page view mode. For each word, the program shows you where it thinks the hyphen should go and asks you to enter a response:

```
┌──────────────────── Hyphenate ─────────────────────┐
│Hyphenate at: [in-creased··························]│
│                                                    │
│[X] Confirm   [X] Hyphenate Caps                    │
├────────────────────────────────────────────────────┤
│                  < Yes >  < No >  <Cancel>         │
└────────────────────────────────────────────────────┘
```

Choose "Yes" to confirm the choice or "No" to change the position. If you choose "No," use the ↑ and ↓ keys to move to one of Word's other choices for hyphenation. If you want to force the hyphen to some other position, use the ← and → keys. When you are satisfied, choose the "Yes" button.

LESSON 88: USING THE THESAURUS

Word's thesaurus is a very handy tool for writers. It can help you when you just can't think of the correct word to use. It is also useful for suggesting ideas related to a word that you are using. The thesaurus contains over 220,000 words. The connections between words in the thesaurus are often loose, so the words presented may cover a wide range of related subjects.

To use the thesaurus, simply select a word in your document and give the Utilities Thesaurus command. The thesaurus window will appear, displaying a list of related words. You can then scan the list of definitions and synonyms. After you find a word you like:

- You can replace your selected word with the word from the thesaurus window.

- You can select the word in the thesaurus window and have Word look up additional words related to that word.

For example, select the word "pleased" in the SAMPLE1 file. Give the Utilities Thesaurus command.

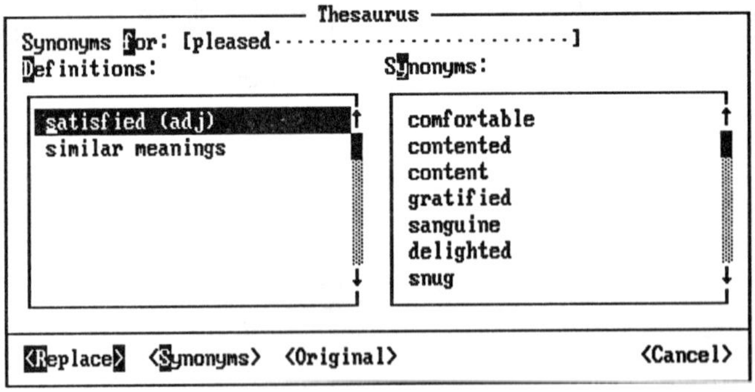

Use the mouse or cursor control keys to select "delighted."

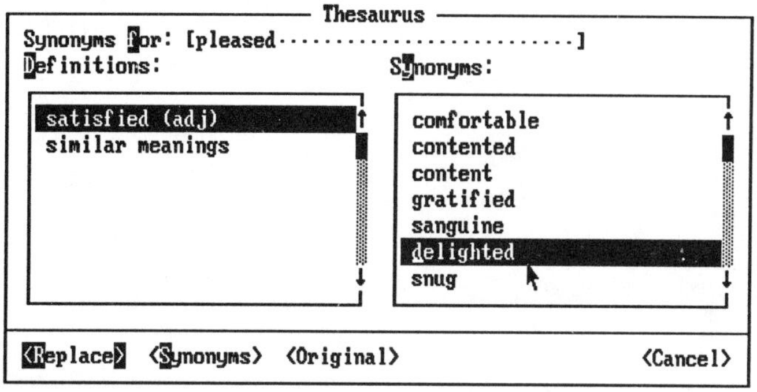

Choose "Replace" and Word will replace "pleased" with "delighted" in your document.

If the word you chose has many definitions, they appear in the list on the left. By selecting a different definition, you see a different group of synonyms.

You can use the thesaurus to explore different meanings. For instance, if you see a word in the list on the right that is close but not exact, select it and click the "Synonyms" button. That word now becomes the definition and other synonyms for the word are shown.

REVIEW

1. *Spelling*
   Describe how Word decides what is misspelled.

2. *Hyphenating*
   Which keys do you use to specify normal, nonbreaking, and nonrequired hyphens?

3. *Thesaurus*
   How would you replace a word in a document with a synonym?

chapter 18

SORTING

Lesson 89: Sorting Text
Lesson 90: Sorting Numbers
Lesson 91: Sorting in Tables

There are often times when you want to sort a list inside one of your documents. If the list is only five or ten lines long, it is fairly easy to sort by hand, but sorting long lists by hand is extremely inconvenient. Word's Utilities Sort command makes sorting any list easy.

Word can sort both text and numbers. This distinction may seem trivial, but most sorting programs cannot sort text in a way useful to people because computers don't store characters the ways humans do.

Computers think in terms of numbers, not of characters such as letters, punctuation, numerals, and so on. Early computer scientists got around this problem by assigning an internal value to each letter. Most computers use a specific system called ASCII to relate characters to internal numbers. Roughly, the ASCII sorting order is

1. Most punctuation marks
2. Numerals (0, 1, 2, . . . 9)
3. Uppercase letters (A, B, C, . . . Z)
4. Lowercase letters (a, b, c, . . . z)

This order, dating back to the sixties, presents some problems, most of which Word overcomes.

The first problem is that sorting numerals is very different than sorting numbers. Look at the following:

```
23
142
5
```

Of course, you would sort it numerically as 5, 23, 142. However, in ASCII code, 1 comes before 2, and 2 before 5. Thus, an unintelligent sorter (the kind most word processing programs use) would sort the list as

```
142
23
5
```

Fortunately, however, Word can sort numerals as numbers, rather than as ASCII characters.

A second problem is that upper- and lowercase letters are normally separated in the sorting sequence; all words that start with uppercase letters are sorted before all words that start with lowercase letters. This list, for example,

```
Touch
tons
black
Victim
foolish
```

would be sorted as

```
Touch
Victim
black
foolish
tons
```

Most of the time you will want your lists sorted in alphabetical order, regardless of case. Word lets you specify this preference.

A third, minor, problem is that not all punctuation comes before all numerals in the ASCII system. Some characters, such as the equal sign, fall between the numerals and the letters; others, such as the caret, fall between the upper- and lowercase letters; and some, such as the vertical bar, follow the lowercase letters. In general, avoid sorting lists that include punctuation as the first character.

Figure 18-1 shows the ASCII sorting sequence.

LESSON 89: SORTING TEXT

The most frequent use for Word's sorter is sorting lists that are formatted as individual paragraphs. Usually, you will want to sort based on entire lines and you will want to sort text.

The Utilities Sort command is easy to use. First, select the range of paragraphs you want to sort (Word will only sort paragraphs, not lines separated by NEWLINE). For this example use the following list:

```
Touch
tons
black
Victim
foolish
```

space
! " # $ % & ' ( ) * +, – . /
0 1 2 3 4 5 6 7 8 9
: ; < = > ? @
A B C D E F G H I J K L M N O P Q R S T U V W X Y Z
[\ ] ^ – '
a b c d e f g h i j k l m n o p q r s t u v w x y z
{ ¦ } ~

FIGURE 18-1. The ASCII sorting sequence

Now, give the Utilities Sort command:

```
                       Sort
 Sort Order
  (•) Ascending        ( ) Descending

 Key Type
  (•) Alphanumeric  ( ) Numeric

  [ ] Sort Column Only
  [ ] Case Sensitive

                        < OK >  <Cancel>
```

In the "Key Type" option, Alphanumeric is already chosen. Execute the command, and Word sorts your selected list.

```
black
foolish
tons
Touch
Victim
```

The other options are also easy to use. The "Sort Order" option tells Word whether you want to sort from A to Z (Ascending) or from Z to A (Descending). If you choose Descending, your list looks like this:

```
Victim
Touch
tons
foolish
black
```

Selecting the "Case Sensitive" option indicates that Word should separate lower- and uppercase letters; you usually do not want this. If you select it, the output will be:

```
Touch
Victim
black
foolish
tons
```

The "Sort Column Only" option is described later in this chapter.

In addition to sorting lists, you can sort text that runs many lines; Word simply sorts full paragraphs in this case.

LESSON 90: SORTING NUMBERS

You can also sort numbers in their correct sequence. When you give the Utilities Sort command, choose Numeric for the "Key Type" option. For example, the following list,

```
509
22.7
448
100
1000
17
```

would be sorted as

```
17
22.7
100
448
509
1000.
```

You can, of course, sort numbers in either ascending or descending order.

Word will even let you sort numeric lists with certain punctuation marks. The following characters can appear anywhere in the numbers to be sorted:

$ % – , ( ) .

LESSON 91: SORTING IN TABLES

So far, you have only learned how to sort based on the first character in a paragraph. While this is usually what you want, there are some circumstances where you might want to sort a table by a column other than the first one. For instance, you may want to sort the following table on the far right column:

Terrence	88	Regular	88.00
Connors	150	Senior	125.00
Long	130	Regular	130.00
Yee	50	New	67.50

Word lets you sort a table by any column if you select just that column. To do this, use the column selection methods discussed in Chapter 8. After selecting the last column, give the Utilities Sort command and be sure that the Sort Column Only option is not selected. When you execute the command, the table is sorted on the selected column as shown here:

Terrence	88	Regular	67.50
Connors	150	Senior	88.00
Long	130	Regular	125.00
Yee	50	New	130.00

note The Sort Column Only option is rarely used. If you want to sort a column and have the rest of the table remain unchanged, select the option. However, because this changes the values in your table, it is only marginally useful.

REVIEW

1. *Numeric and alphanumeric*
   Describe the difference between numeric and alphanumeric sorting.

2. *Case option*
   Describe the use of the Case Sensitive option in sorting.

chapter 19

RETRIEVING DOCUMENTS

Lesson 92: Filling Summary Sheets
Lesson 93: Searching for Documents

You have probably noticed that the names of the files used in this book are somewhat descriptive of their contents. The name "SUMFUN.DOC," for example, was used for a summary funding proposal. However, MS-DOS file-naming conventions limit how much you can indicate in a file name. If you have more than a few dozen files (as you are sure to after using Word for a few weeks), it is hard to remember what each file contains. When you have hundreds of files, opening and closing each one to find a particular file is really time-consuming.

Since Word is designed for use in business, where efficiency is a primary concern, Microsoft has devised a method of scanning rapidly through a large number of files. Each Word file has a *summary sheet* where you can list information that will be helpful when you search. For example, to search for a letter, you might include the recipient, the subject, and a few keywords about the contents. Word automatically stores the dates when the letter was created and last updated, so you can also use those in your search.

When you search, Word scans the summary sheets of all the documents on the disks and directories that you specify. You can devise very specific searches (such as one for a file written after January 15, 1989 that lists the keywords "timing" and "starter") or general searches (such as one for all letters to a certain person). This flexibility is very convenient when you are working with a large number of files.

You can also have Word search for specific text in the files. For instance, you can locate every letter in which you mentioned "new manufacturing." Note, however, that searching for text in a file is slower than searching for words listed in the summary sheet, expecially if you have long documents.

To fill in or search summary sheets, use the File File Management command. Note that this command works only on Word documents, and not on the other files on your system. Also, you can create summary sheets only for files saved with Word's formatting (not for text-only files).

LESSON 92: FILLING SUMMARY SHEETS

Up to now, when Word has prompted you to fill in a summary sheet, you have simply pressed the ESC key and skipped over the sheet (or you may have guessed about how to fill them out). Now, you will start to fill in the summary sheets. First, issue the File File Management command. Your screen will look similar to this:

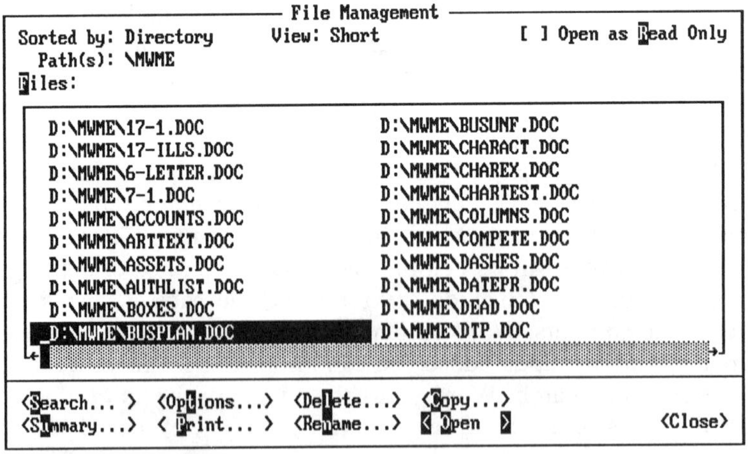

This screen lists all the Word files in the current directory. In the next lesson you will learn how to have other directories and disks included in this list.

Once you have a group of files listed on the screen (even if it is the default list), you can select files from that group by highlighting each file name and pressing SPACEBAR. An asterisk is put next to each selected file. To select all the files at once, press CTRL-SPACEBAR; to unselect all the files, press CTRL-SPACEBAR again.

Select the SAMPLE1 file. Choose the Summary button. Word presents you with the same summary information prompt you saw when you first saved the file.

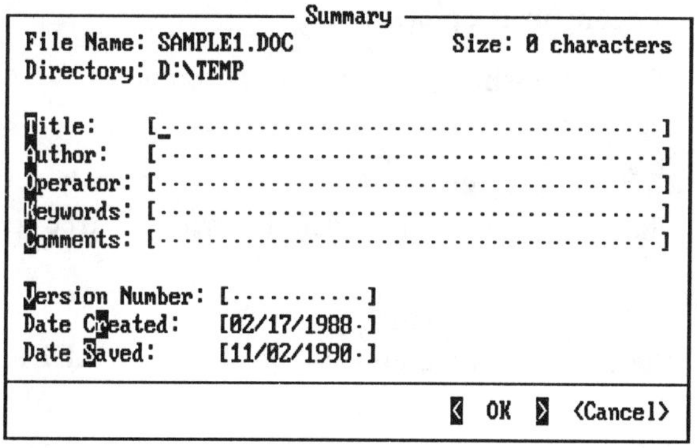

The fields are:

Title — A title for the document, which can be up to 40 characters long, such as "Request for information on new parts" or "Second notice on overdue accounts."

Author — The name of the person who wrote the document. It can also have up to 40 characters. It is good to use both your first and last names since the person searching the summary sheets may not know both.

Operator — The name of the person who keyed in the document, also up to 40 characters.

Keywords — Words or phrases that are likely to be searched for, up to 80 characters long. Examples are "accounts payable," "urgent," "third notice," and "final."

Comments — General comments, up to 256 characters. Note that information entered in this field is not searched by the File File Management Search option. Generally, this field is reserved for notes to anyone who is updating the summary sheet (such as information about updating the Version Number field).

Version Number — A number or letter that indicates which revision of the document this is, up to 10 characters. This is useful for documents that are updated frequently. Word does not change this field, but you can do it yourself when the document is updated.

Date Created — The date when the file was first created. Word fills this in for you, although you can change it.

Date Saved — The date when the file was most recently revised. Word fills this in for you as well, but you are free to change it.

You might use the following field entries for the SAMPLE1 file:

```
                          Summary
File Name: SAMPLE1.DOC                    Size: 0 characters
Directory: D:\TEMP

Title:    [Letter to Richford about products········]
Author:   [Thom Mead································]
Operator: [·········································]
Keywords: [letter fourth quarter DC50 loan··········]
Comments: [·········································]

Version Number: [··········]
Date Created:   [02/17/1988·]
Date Saved:     [11/02/1990·]

                                      < OK >  <Cancel>
```

The SUMFUN file might have these entries:

```
                              Summary
File Name: SUMFUN.DOC                    Size: 3880 characters
Directory: D:\MWME

Title:    [Summary funding proposal·················]
Author:   [Thom Mead······························]
Operator: [·······································]
Keywords: [summary funding proposal bank excerpts···]
Comments: [·······································]

Version Number: [···········]
Date Created:   [10/16/1987·]
Date Saved:     [10/11/1988·]

                                     < OK >  <Cancel>
```

LESSON 93: SEARCHING FOR DOCUMENTS

The File File Management command also lets you search for documents. The list of files it displays is actually the result of an initial search, during which the program locates all the Word files in the current directory, regardless of what they or their summary sheets contain.

For a more specific search, click the "Search" button:

```
                                 Search
Search Paths: [\MWME_········································]
                                                  D:\MWME
Author:    [·································]
Operator:  [·································]  Directories:
Keywords:  [·································]
Text:      [·································]   ..
Date Saved:    [························]        INSERTS
Date Created:  [························]        SCREENS
                                                 [-A-]
[ ] Match Case   [ ] Selected Files Only

                                            < OK >  <Cancel>
```

Author, Operator, Keywords, Date Created, and Date Saved are the fields from the summary sheet. "Text" is text to be searched for within the documents. You can tell Word to match or ignore differences in case during the search.

"Search Paths" is the list of disks and directories that Word is to scan for the files. Notice that it contains one entry, namely the current directory. You can type in new paths, using commas to separate them. The names you would type are those of MS-DOS directories, such as **\LETTERS** or **D:\THOM\LETTERS**. You can also enter the names of files and use wildcards (* or ?) to specify particular groups of files in the directories. If you fill in the path and no other fields, executing the command finds all the Word files in directories you listed. The list is remembered, even when you leave Word. Thus, if you have a long list of directories, you don't need to type it in each time. Here is an example of Search Paths:

```
                              Search
Search Paths: [\MWME,\NATGEN,C:\,C:\MEADPERS_...................]
                                               D:\MWME
Author:    [.................................]
Operator:  [.................................]  Directories:
Keywords:  [.................................]
Text:      [.................................]   ..
Date Saved:    [........................]        INSERTS
Date Created:  [........................]        SCREENS
                                                 [-A-]
[ ] Match Case    [ ] Selected Files Only

                                            < OK >  <Cancel>
```

Once you have established the Search Paths, using the other fields is easy. For instance, to find every file with the keyword "prosecute" in it, enter **prosecute** in the Keywords field and execute the command:

```
                              Search
Search Paths: [\MWME.............................................]
                                               D:\MWME
Author:    [.................................]
Operator:  [.................................]  Directories:
Keywords:  [prosecute_.......................]
Text:      [.................................]   ..
Date Saved:    [........................]        INSERTS
Date Created:  [........................]        SCREENS
                                                 [-A-]
[ ] Match Case    [ ] Selected Files Only

                                            < OK >  <Cancel>
```

If you fill in more than one field, Word finds only files that match the entries in *all* the filled fields. For example, the following set of entries

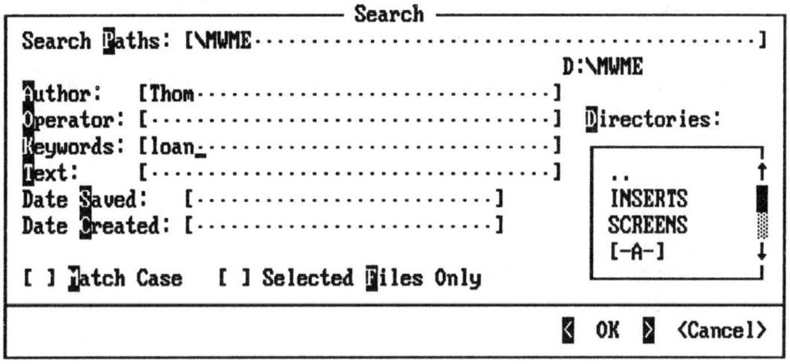

would find only documents whose Author field contains "Thom" and whose Keywords field contains "loan" in the same summary sheet.

You can also use special characters to be more specific. If you want to enter two words in a field, you can use special characters to indicate whether Word should find the file if both words are found or if either word is found. The special characters are

,	If the field contains either the first or second word
&	If the field contains both the first and second word (you can use a single space instead of the &)
~	If the field does not contain the following word
<	If the date field has a date before the one given
>	If the date field has a date after the one given

Thus, if you want to find all files written by Thom before 8/18/90, enter these fields:

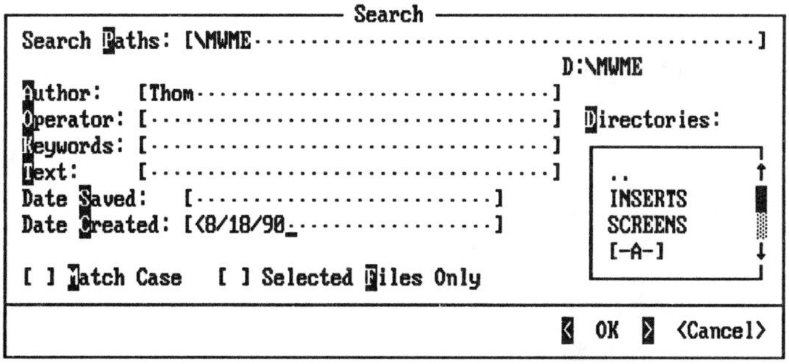

Remember that you can also enter text in the document Text field. However, be warned: although Word uses special methods for fast searching, this can be very slow if there are many files or large files. Thus, it is important to put as many useful keywords in the summary sheet as possible.

After you have selected files either by hand or with the Search dialog, there are many things you can do with them. The buttons at the bottom of the dialog act like their associated Word commands.

```
<Search... > <Options...> <Delete...> <Copy...>
<Summary...> < Print... > <Rename...> < Open >          <Close>
```

You can delete the files, copy them to another part of the disk or a different disk, fill in their summary sheets, print them, rename them, or simply open them in Word.

The "Options" button lets you specify how the files should be listed in the File File Management dialog:

```
┌───────────────── Options ─────────────────┐
│ ┌ Sort Files By ───┐                      │
│ │ (•) Directory    │  ┌ View Files ┐      │
│ │ ( ) Author       │  │ (•) Short  │      │
│ │ ( ) Operator     │  │ ( ) Long   │      │
│ │ ( ) Date Saved   │  │ ( ) Full   │      │
│ │ ( ) Date Created │  └────────────┘      │
│ │ ( ) Size         │                      │
│ └──────────────────┘                      │
│                                           │
│ [X] Update List After Copy or Rename      │
├───────────────────────────────────────────┤
│                    < OK > <Cancel>        │
└───────────────────────────────────────────┘
```

You can sort the file names in any order. The Long choice shows the Author and Title fields of each file, and the Full choice shows the entire summary sheet as you move from file to file.

REVIEW

1. *Summary sheet*
   What additional keywords might you use for the SAMPLE1 letter?
2. *Search command*
   How would you search for a document that had been updated after 2/2/88 and was about fluids?

chapter 20

MACROS

Lesson 94: Introduction to Macros
Lesson 95: Creating Macros
Lesson 96: Testing and Editing Macros
Lesson 97: Macro Instructions

LESSON 94: INTRODUCTION TO MACROS

You have probably noticed that many procedures require multiple commands in Word. For example, to briefly look at the hidden text in a document, you must give the View Preferences command once to display the text and again to hide it. You may repeat this sequence many times during a session with Word. Another multistep procedure you might perform frequently is saving the selected text to a different file.

Word gives you the ability to record a sequence of steps, save it in the glossary, and then invoke the entire sequence with a single keystroke. These recorded sequences are called *macros* (the term comes from early computer jargon). Many macros, such as those just mentioned, are of general interest to Word users. However, you can also design special macros to meet your particular needs.

Macros can save you an incredible amount of time. A macro can be any sequence of Word commands, so you can make complex macros that perform dozens of steps. It is likely that most of your macros will perform only a few steps; but using one or two keystrokes (usually CTRL and one other key) to replace even five or ten steps will significantly increase your productivity.

Macros not only save steps, they make your work more accurate. Imagine a long document in which all names are in last-name-first format (such as "Mead, Thom"). If you wanted to change the format to first-name-first ("Thom Mead"), you would take these steps:

1. Select the beginning of the last name.
2. Jump to the end of the last name.
3. Delete the comma and the trailing space.
4. Select the first name and cut it to the scrap.
5. Go back to the beginning of the last name.
6. Insert the first name and a space.

If there were hundreds of names to change, you'd surely make errors as you repeated these steps again and again. If you used a macro, however, the steps would happen faster, and you could be certain that they were always performed accurately.

Macros are somewhat like glossaries, but instead of simply inserting a word or phrase, a macro executes a series of steps. As previously mentioned, Word stores macros in glossary files. You can think of macros as glossaries that do work.

Macros always start their work at the cursor or selection. Thus, if you have a macro that works with selected text, Word acts on the text that is selected when you call the macro, not on the text that was selected when you created it.

Note that macros can record only keystrokes, not mouse movements and clicks. For example, you cannot record the movement of the mouse to the selection bar. You must use the keyboard equivalents of mouse commands when you create your macros. Of course, using macros does not prevent you from using the mouse at the same time.

Here is what you must do to use a macro:

- *Create the macro.* Do this by telling Word that you are recording a macro, then issuing commands that you want the macro to contain.
- *Save the macro in a glossary file.* Macros are automatically stored in the current glossary file under the name you give them.

- *Test the macro.* It is a good idea to test a macro once to see if you stored the correct sequence of steps. You can also view the macro to check it.

- *Edit the macro.* If you have made a mistake or if you want to improve a macro, you can easily edit. When you are finished editing the macro, you can store it in the glossary again.

Microsoft provides numerous macros with Word. Many of these are quite useful, and all are good examples of what macros can do. They are stored in the MACRO.GLY file. To use the macros, give the Macro Edit command, load them into your current glossary, then save them. The actions that the various macros perform are described in the Word manual.

As you read this chapter, keep in mind that the most useful macros are those that you think of yourself. Now you can refine your documents in ways that might have required too much work before because you can design a macro to do the tiresome, repetitive parts of the job. Whenever you find yourself performing a task more than once or twice, think about whether you can turn it into a macro.

LESSON 95: CREATING MACROS

Once you have decided what steps you want in your macro, it is easy to create it. A good example of a macro that saves a few keystrokes is one that shows or hides hidden text in the current window. As you saw in Chapter 13, to show or hide hidden text, you must give the View Preferences command and switch the setting to show hidden text.

To begin recording your macro, give the Macro Record command. When you are recording a macro, you cannot perform any actions with the mouse: you must use the keyboard. When you give the Macro Record command, you are prompted:

```
Record Macro
Macro Name:
[................................]

Macro Keys:
[.....................]

              < OK >  <Cancel>
```

Give the macro a name, **SwitchHidden**. Move to the "Macro Keys" option and press CTRL-Z. Then select the "OK" button. Word tells you that you are recording a macro by putting MR in the bottom line. Like glossary names, macro names can have up to 31 characters and cannot contain spaces. However, you can include periods (.), underscores (_), and hyphens (-).

Now enter the keystrokes for the macro. Press ALT-V, then E to bring up the View Preferences dialog:

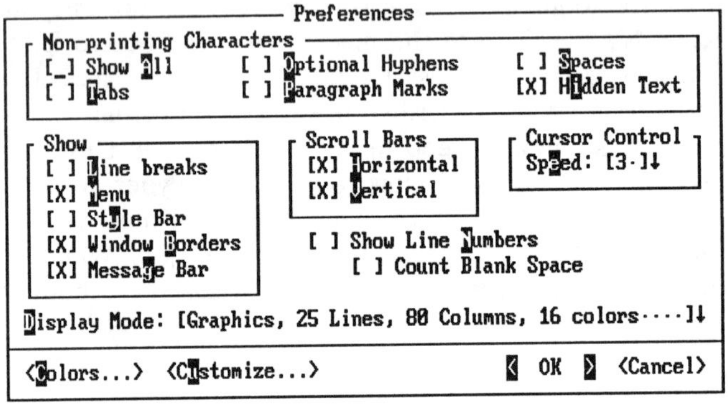

Press the TAB key five times to move the selection to the "Hidden Text" option:

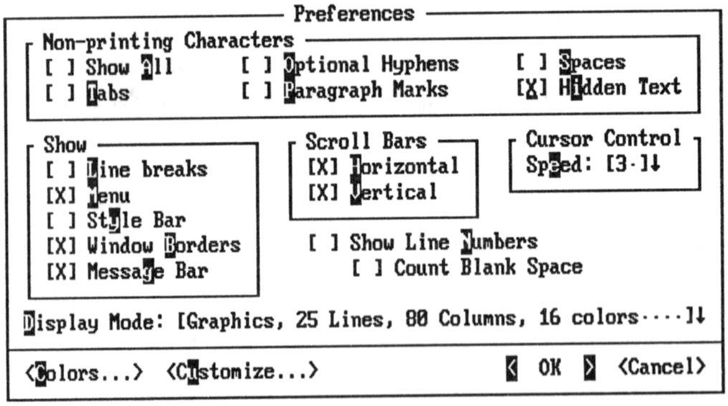

Press the SPACEBAR to switch the setting:

```
------------------------------ Preferences ------------------------------
 Non-printing Characters
 [ ] Show All        [ ] Optional Hyphens      [ ] Spaces
 [ ] Tabs            [ ] Paragraph Marks       [_] Hidden Text

 Show                    Scroll Bars           Cursor Control
 [ ] Line breaks         [X] Horizontal        Speed: [3·]↓
 [X] Menu                [X] Vertical
 [ ] Style Bar
 [X] Window Borders      [ ] Show Line Numbers
 [X] Message Bar            [ ] Count Blank Space

 Display Mode: [Graphics, 25 Lines, 80 Columns, 16 colors····]↓

 <Colors...> <Customize...>                      < OK >  <Cancel>
```

Now press ENTER to execute the command. To finish the macro, press ALT-M to pull down the Macro menu. Since "Stop Recorder" is highlighted, press ENTER.

To see how to use this macro, select the word "Vice" in the first paragraph and make it hidden.

```
January 11, 1990

Chris Richford, Vice President
Manufacturer's Bank of the Northeast
1000 First Avenue
Millerton, CT  06492
```

Press CTRL-Z. The hidden text now disappears. Experiment with this macro by pressing CTRL-Z a few times.

A slightly more complex macro is one that saves selected text in another file. This can be useful if you are selecting parts of a large document for another person's use.

To record the macro,

1. Give the Macro Record command to start recording the macro.
2. Name the macro **Save.selection** and designate CTRL-A as its CTRL-key equivalent. Click "OK."
3. Press ALT-E ALT-C to copy the selected text into the scrap.
4. Press ALT-F ALT-N ENTER to start a new file.
5. Press ALT-E ALT-P to paste the scrap in the new file.

To use this macro, select the text you want to save and press CTRL-A. Be sure to save the new file with the File Save As command. Note that this requires far less effort than performing all the steps one by one.

LESSON 96: TESTING AND EDITING MACROS

To test a macro, you can simply use it to perform its task. If it works, fine. If not, you can have Word execute the macro one step at a time so you can examine what Word does at each stage of the process. To cause a macro to execute in individual steps, select the "Steps" option in the Macro Run command. Word displays "ST" at the bottom of the screen.

```
Pg1 Co21          {}          <F1=Help>                    ST Microsoft Word
Edit document or press Alt to choose commands
```

When you execute a macro in step mode, Word stops after each step and waits for you to press any key. Thus, when you execute the SwitchHidden macro, Word first pauses after pulling down the View menu, and so on.

Editing macros is surprisingly easy. You can insert the text that makes up a macro into a document or an empty window, then edit the macro's text as you would any other text. When you are finished editing, give the Macro Edit command. You should see a dialog like this:

```
---------------------------- Edit Macro ----------------------------
 Macro Name:                                 Macro Keys:
 [tovga_.........................]           [.....................]
 Macros:
  DoClose <ctrl W>                  SwitchHidden <ctrl Z>
  DoColor <ctrl C>                  toherc
  DoNew <ctrl N>                    tovga
  DoOpen <ctrl O>
  FormatParagraph <ctrl M>
 tovga:                          Macro (Glossary) File: NORMAL.GLY
  <alt-V>e<alt-D><down-3><enter>

 <Define> < Delete >  <Open Glossary...>
 < Edit > <Clear All> <Save Glossary...>  <Merge...>       <Close>
```

Select the name of the macro you are replacing in the list, then click the "Define" button.

For example, assume that you want to alter the SwitchHidden macro so that it shows or hides the ruler as well as the hidden text. Start with an empty window. Give the Macro Edit command. Select the SwitchHidden macro from the list and click the "Edit" button to insert the text in the empty window:

```
<alt V><alt E><tab 5><space><enter>♦
```

Notice how Word encloses all the nonalphabetic keys in angle brackets. Thus, ENTER becomes "<enter>" and so on.

To add the ruler toggle, add **<alt v> <alt r>** as text, which is Word's way of saying "Press the ALT-V key, then press the ALT-R key."

Select all this text and give the Macro Edit command. Select the Switch-Hidden macro name from the list and click the "Define" button. Select the "OK" button in the replacement dialog.

LESSON 97: MACRO INSTRUCTIONS

Word has macro instructions that are similar to the merge instructions you learned about in Chapter 12. Macro instructions give you a great deal of flexibility when you create a macro. You'll find in Table 20-1 a list of the macro instructions.

Word's macro instructions give you advanced programming capabilities. If you have programmed in BASIC or another language, you will find Word's macros easy and powerful. These macro instructions, which are well beyond the scope of an introductory book like this, can help you to automate major tasks that you perform with Word.

Instructions can be incorporated into macros through the editing procedure described in the last lesson. All macro instructions appear enclosed in chevrons. For example, to add a comment to the beginning of the SwitchHidden macro, you might enter

```
«COMMENT makes text hidden and shows the ruler»
<alt V><alt E><tab 5><space><enter><alt v><alt r>♦
```

The Word manual provides details about the intricacies of the macro instructions. You will find many uses for them as you become proficient with macros.

Instruction	Use
ASK	Causes Word to prompt you to fill in variable
COMMENT	Puts a comment that is not executed in the macro
IF . . . ENDIF or IF . . . ELSE . . . ENDIF	Conditionally performs steps if a condition is met
MESSAGE	Puts a message on the screen in the message bar
PAUSE	Allows you to enter text or change a selection. Press ENTER to resume the macro.
QUIT	Ends execution of the macro
REPEAT...ENDREPEAT	Causes the commands between the instructions to be repeated
SET	Sets the contents of a variable
WHILE . . . ENDWHILE	Repeats while a condition is true

TABLE 20-1. Macro Instructions

REVIEW

1. *Creating macros*
   How would you create a macro that shows tabs?
2. *Editing macros*
   How would you edit a macro to include an additional ENTER at the end of the macro?
3. *Macro instructions*
   What macro instruction would you use to put a message on the screen?

chapter 21

LINKING DOCUMENTS

Lesson 98: Linking Spreadsheets
Lesson 99: Linking Pictures

Word lets you add information from a spreadsheet or a graphics program to your Word documents. Before this feature was added to Word, you could not include graphics in your documents at all. To include a part of a spreadsheet, you had to save that part as a text file and then merge it into your document.

When you add information from a spreadsheet or graphics file, Word keeps track of the file's name, so you can continue to update the file outside of Word and, with a simple command, have Word check the file for the current figures.

Note that you can specify an area of cells instead of an entire spreadsheet in Word. If you are using Multiplan, Excel, or Lotus 1-2-3, you can specify the range to be included by name instead of by cell references. For instance, assume you have a Lotus 1-2-3 spreadsheet that contains sales figures. When you write your monthly report in Word, you can refer to the range of the 1-2-3 spreadsheet that contains the current sales figures. You can then continue to update the spreadsheet using 1-2-3, and the latest figures will appear in your Word document when you print it.

LESSON 98: LINKING SPREADSHEETS

To link a spreadsheet, you must know the name of the spreadsheet file and the range or name of the spreadsheet cells you want to include in your Word document. The file name can include a path to the file. Word stores this information in your document so that you can update the information easily.

For the following example, assume that you have a Lotus 1-2-3 spreadsheet called C:\THOM\P&L.WK1 and that you want to view an area called "Current." Put the cursor at the point where you want the spreadsheet to appear. Add a new paragraph to the SAMPLE1 file:

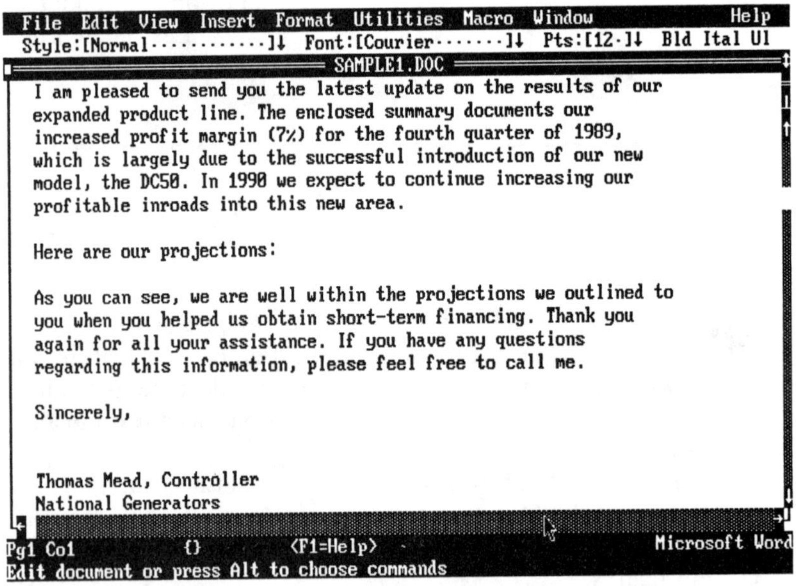
File Edit View Insert Format Utilities Macro Window Help
Style:[Normal············]↓ Font:[Courier·······]↓ Pts:[12·]↓ Bld Ital Ul
SAMPLE1.DOC

I am pleased to send you the latest update on the results of our expanded product line. The enclosed summary documents our increased profit margin (7%) for the fourth quarter of 1989, which is largely due to the successful introduction of our new model, the DC50. In 1990 we expect to continue increasing our profitable inroads into this new area.

Here are our projections:

As you can see, we are well within the projections we outlined to you when you helped us obtain short-term financing. Thank you again for all your assistance. If you have any questions regarding this information, please feel free to call me.

Sincerely,

Thomas Mead, Controller
National Generators

Pg1 Co1 {} <F1=Help> Microsoft Word
Edit document or press Alt to choose commands

Be sure the cursor is at the beginning of the line after the new line. Give the Insert File command. Word will prompt you like this:

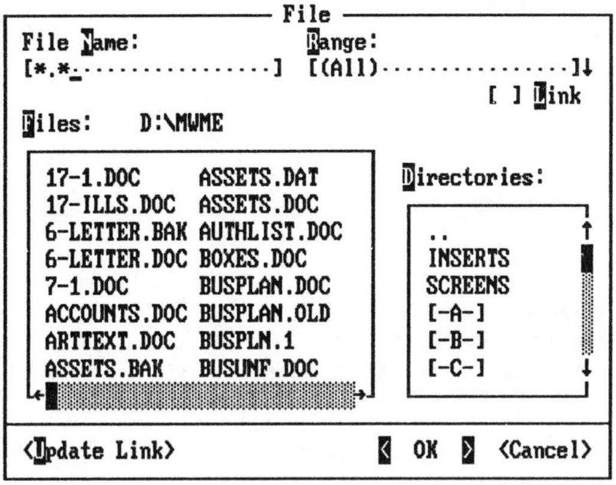

Enter the file name, then the range of cells. If the range you want to include is not named, you can indicate the range just as you do in the spreadsheet program. See the program manual for information on naming cell ranges.

When you give the Insert File command and select the "OK" button, Word reads that range and puts it in your document as shown on the next page.

```
which is largely due to the successful introduction of our new
model, the DC50. In 1990 we expect to continue increasing our
profitable inroads into this new area.

Here are our projections:
Sales      $19,030,000
Costs      $14,843,000
Profits    $4,187,000

As you can see, we are well within the projections we outlined to
you when you helped us obtain short-term financing. Thank you
again for all your assistance. If you have any questions
regarding this information, please feel free to call me.
```

Word also puts special information such as the selection range in hidden text.

```
which is largely due to the successful introduction of our new
model, the DC50. In 1990 we expect to continue increasing our
profitable inroads into this new area.

Here are our projections:
.L.C:\THOM\P&L.WK1,Current
Sales     $19,030,000
Costs     $14,843,000
Profits   $4,187,000
.L.

As you can see, we are well within the projections we outlined to
you when you helped us obtain short-term financing. Thank you
again for all your assistance. If you have any questions
regarding this information, please feel free to call me.
```

Also note that the entire chart, including the hidden text, is a single paragraph. Word ends each line with a NEWLINE character so that you can move the chart simply by selecting the paragraph.

If you change the spreadsheet and want the changes reflected in your Word document, select the paragraph, give the Insert File command, and click the "Update Link" button. This updates the paragraph with revisions from the specified spreadsheet. If you have many linked spreadsheets in your document, select the entire document, give the Insert File command, and click "Update Link." Word prompts you for each spreadsheet to be updated.

When Word updates a spreadsheet, it brings in the new data. If you have given paragraph formatting commands (such as setting tab stops) before updating, that formatting will be retained. However, character formatting that you have entered in the paragraph will be lost.

LESSON 99: LINKING PICTURES

You can use the Insert Picture command to insert graphics from a wide variety of sources. This command works very much like the Insert File command. Instead of inserting the graphic itself into your document, Word only inserts a pointer to that graphic. Word also stores the dimensions and alignment of the graphic.

You can include graphics in the following formats:

- Capture files created by the CAPTURE program that comes with Word.

- HPGL files. HPGL is a plotter format generated by most programs that work with pen plotters.

- Lotus-compatible picture (.PIC) files.
- Microsoft Windows Clipboard files.
- PageView picture files.
- PC Paintbrush-compatible (.PCX) files.
- PostScript files.
- TIFF files, which are produced by many image-scanning programs.

When you give the Insert Picture command, you see this:

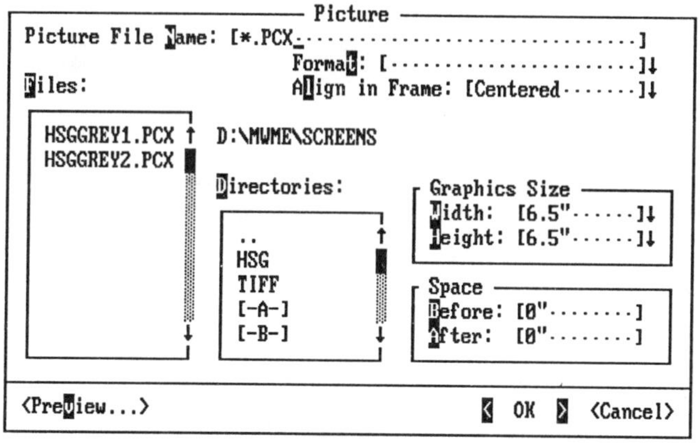

Fill in the file name. If Word can determine the format from the name and extension, it will fill in the file format field. If not, enter the format yourself or click the "Format" pull-down list to get the list of valid formats. Word also tries to determine the width and heighth of the graphic, but you can change those values in the dialog as well.

Graphics are not shown in gallery or layout mode, only in page view mode. Viewing (or pictures) often slows Word down, so you may want to use this sparingly in graphics documents that contain many pictures.

Like the Insert File command, Insert Picture stores the label for the graphic in hidden text. To move a graphic, simply move the paragraph containing the label text.

REVIEW

1. *Spreadsheets*
   How do you update all the spreadsheets linked in a file?

2. *Pictures*
   How do you view a picture before printing out your document?

chapter 22

REVISION MARKS

Lesson 100: Using Redlining for Revisions
Lesson 101: Saving Revised Documents

LESSON 100: USING REDLINING FOR REVISIONS

When you change a document and save the changes, the previous version of the document is replaced by the new one. This is usually what you want when you edit documents. Sometimes, however, you may want to see the changes you are making in your document while you are working on it and have them take effect later. Word's revision marks (called *redlining*) can be used for this purpose.

Redlining is commonly used in law offices for making changes to standard forms and contracts. It shows clearly what text is added and what text is deleted from a document. For example, look at the SAMPLE1 letter.

```
January 11, 1990

Chris Richford, Vice President
Manufacturer's Bank of the Northeast
1000 First Avenue
Millerton, CT  06492

Dear Ms. Richford:

I am pleased to send you the latest update on the results of our
expanded product line. The enclosed summary documents our
increased profit margin (7%) for the fourth quarter of 1989,
which is largely due to the successful introduction of our new
model, the DC50. In 1990 we expect to continue increasing our
profitable inroads into this new area.
```

With the Utilities Revision Marks feature turned on, if you change "pleased" to "happy," the screen might show this:

January 11, 1990

Chris Richford, Vice President
Manufacturer's Bank of the Northeast
1000 First Avenue
Millerton, CT 06492

Dear Ms. Richford:

I am ~~pleased~~ <u>happy t</u>o send you the latest update on the results of our expanded product line. The enclosed summary documents our increased profit margin (7%) for the fourth quarter of 1989, which is largely due to the successful introduction of our new model, the DC50. In 1990 we expect to continue increasing our profitable inroads into this new area.

Word's default is to show new or inserted text as underlines and deleted text as struck-through. As you edit, Word keeps marking your inserted and deleted text in this fashion. Of course, at some point you want to remove the underlining and delete the struck-through text so that you can print the document and start fresh with no marks. The next lesson will show you how to do this.

To turn the revision marks on, give the Utilities Revision Marks command. Word prompts you this way:

```
Mark Revisions
[_] Mark Revisions            Mark New Text with
Revision Bars                 ( ) Nothing          ( ) Bold
(•) None      ( ) Left        (•) Underline        ( ) Uppercase
( ) Right     ( ) Outside     ( ) Double Underline

<Search>  <Accept Revisions>  <Undo Revisions>          < OK >  <Cancel>
```

Select "Mark Revisions." When you are editing with revision marks on, Word displays RM on the bottom line.

To see how editing with revision marks is different, start editing the SAMPLE1 letter. Select "pleased" and press the DEL key.

January 11, 1990

Chris Richford, Vice President
Manufacturer's Bank of the Northeast
1000 First Avenue
Millerton, CT 06492

Dear Ms. Richford:

I am ~~pleased~~ to send you the latest update on the results of our expanded product line. The enclosed summary documents our increased profit margin (7%) for the fourth quarter of 1989, which is largely due to the successful introduction of our new model, the DC50. In 1990 we expect to continue increasing our profitable inroads into this new area.

Now type **happy**.

January 11, 1990

Chris Richford, Vice President
Manufacturer's Bank of the Northeast
1000 First Avenue
Millerton, CT 06492

Dear Ms. Richford:

I am ~~pleased~~ happy to send you the latest update on the results of our expanded product line. The enclosed summary documents our increased profit margin (7%) for the fourth quarter of 1989, which is largely due to the successful introduction of our new model, the DC50. In 1990 we expect to continue increasing our profitable inroads into this new area.

Position the cursor after "send" and press the BACKSPACE key. Word beeps at you because you cannot backspace over original text in your document when Revision Marks is on. To delete text, you must use the DEL key or the Edit Cut command. (You can, however, backspace over new text, such as the "happy" that you just typed in.)

If you are editing a large document with a great deal of formatting, it is sometimes difficult to see where the revisions are. Word makes it easy for you to find revisions by adding a bar to the left or right side of the screen on any line with revisions. To see this, give the Utilities Revision Marks command again. Choose "Left" for the revision bar position. When you execute the command, you can see the revision bar.

January 11, 1990

Chris Richford, Vice President
Manufacturer's Bank of the Northeast
1000 First Avenue
Millerton, CT 06492

Dear Ms. Richford:

| I am ~~pleased~~ <u>happy t</u>o send you the latest update on the results of our expanded product line. The enclosed summary documents our increased profit margin (7%) for the fourth quarter of 1989, which is largely due to the successful introduction of our new model, the DC50. In 1990 we expect to continue increasing our profitable inroads into this new area.

Some people prefer the revision bars on the right side of the page; in this case, choose "Right" for the revision bar position. Choosing "Outside" causes Word to put the revision bars on the outside margins if you are using odd and even pages.

LESSON 101: SAVING REVISED DOCUMENTS

When you save a document with redlining turned on, the revisions are saved with the file. Thus, if you leave Word and then come back to edit the file again later, your revisions are still there. This gives you the opportunity to edit your document as much as you want before you decide whether or not to implement the revisions.

When you are ready to accept the revisions, select the revised text, give the Utilities Revision Marks command, and click on the "Accept Revisions" button. For example, to accept the revisions on the entire document, select the whole document before giving the command. You can give the command for small portions of the document as well. Word then removes the struck-through text that you have marked for deletion.

If you decide to undo some of your revisions, select those parts you want to retain, give the Utilities Revision Marks command, and click the "Undo Revisions" button. Again, you can do this for the entire document or a selected portion. Word deletes any text you have added since you started revising.

Using these two commands lets you change selected parts of documents. For example, assume that Valerie and Alex are working together on a report. After Valerie writes the report, she puts it on a disk and gives it to Alex. He turns Revision Marks on and edits the text. When he gives the disk back to Valerie, she can easily see what changes he has made. If she disagrees with any of the changes, she can select them, give the Utilities Revision Marks command, and click on the Undo Revisions button. She then selects the entire document, gives the Utilities Revision Marks command again, and clicks on the Accept Revisions button.

REVIEW

1. *Revising text*
   What command do you use to add revision marks to your text?

2. *Saving revisions*
   How do you apply your revisions in the saved text?

chapter 23

DESKTOP PUBLISHING WITH WORD

Lesson 102: The Beginning of Desktop Publishing
Lesson 103: Desktop Publishing Software
Lesson 104: Some Desktop Publishing Techniques

In the last few years, many businesses have become intensely interested in desktop publishing. Although Word is not a desktop publishing program, it has features that allow it to function as one.

In the early 1980s most people thought of computers primarily as machines for word processing. But the poor print quality of early printers made it obvious that a document was computer generated. To make things worse, even the fastest printers were slow and expensive.

By the mid-1980s there was more demand for word processors that produced professional-quality documents. Printer technology had improved, and word processors (such as Microsoft Word for the IBM PC and the Macintosh) were doing a better job. However, the output available to most people still had several problems:

- Even though letter-quality printers had become faster and less expensive, their output looked like that of a typewriter. People wanted output that looked typeset.
- Word processing programs were designed to produce fairly simple business reports and memos. They could not provide output suitable for newsletters and brochures.
- Although a few computers were becoming faster and more efficient, the most common computers were slow and could not run advanced word processing programs efficiently.

LESSON 102: THE BEGINNING OF DESKTOP PUBLISHING

In early 1985, Apple began to emphasize a new concept in computer use: desktop publishing. The goal of this new approach was quality output from microcomputers.

People want desktop publishing capabilities for many reasons. For small jobs, like four-page newsletters and fold-over brochures, typesetting is expensive and inconvenient. For larger jobs, such as important reports or advertisements, typesetting can hold things up, since small changes often cause long delays. The ability to produce such documents in-house promised greater freedom and fewer headaches.

Apple's new desktop publishing marketing strategy was based on two things: the Macintosh's ability to display accurate graphics on the screen quickly, and the Apple LaserWriter's high resolution. Without this combination, simple desktop publishing would not have been possible. To know what your document looks like before you print it, you need a good graphics display. To make the output resemble typesetting copy, you need a laser printer.

The Macintosh had already established itself as the computer of choice for many designers. Its high-resolution screen and easy-to-use software made it attractive to writers as well. Many of these people were already producing high-quality output by taking printed copy (or, if they were lucky, a diskette) to a typesetting shop.

With the LaserWriter, designers and writers who wanted fairly high-quality type could produce it themselves. Instead of a large machine that used smelly chemicals to produce type, the LaserWriter was a relatively small, clean machine that could sit on a desk. Apple coined the term "desktop publishing" because of this capability.

LESSON 103: DESKTOP PUBLISHING SOFTWARE

Soon after Apple announced their desktop publishing marketing push, many software companies announced desktop publishing products. Most of the early ones were *page layout* programs. Page layout programs, such as PageMaker from Aldus, enable you to set up your document page by page. As you enter text, you see all the page formatting including where lines are broken in columns.

Microsoft does not market Word as a desktop publishing program, but with the new version of Microsoft Word, you can perform many functions that are typical of desktop publishing programs. And Word is much better at standard word processing tasks (such as editing) than are desktop publishing programs. Some of Word's most useful features for desktop publishing are

- *Advanced use of PostScript printers such as the Apple LaserWriter* Like a few other word processing software packages, Word can produce good-looking documents on the LaserWriter. Beyond that, however, you can use Word to give LaserWriter commands that produce graphics and special text effects. To do this, you must link Word to files that contain LaserWriter commands as described in Chapter 21. You also need to know about *PostScript,* the language used internally by the LaserWriter.
- *Precise page layout* Unlike other word processing programs, Word lets you define exactly where each element of your document will appear on the page. Not only can you place headers and footers exactly where you want them, but you can specify the spacing between lines and between paragraphs. This lets you expand and contract paragraphs to fill space precisely. Word also gives you much greater freedom to move the page margins so that the text fits on the page in a pleasing manner.
- *Style sheets* The concept has been around for years, but most desktop publishing packages do not incorporate style sheets, although they are immensely useful. If you are putting together a long report with many levels of headings, Word's style sheets will automatically format like headings consistently. They also provide an easy way to transfer style conventions between documents.

- *Graphics* Word's ability to include graphics from a wide variety of programs makes it especially useful for desktop publishing. You can create pictures and logos with many different programs and insert them into your Word documents.
- *Absolute positioning* Being able to place text and graphics anywhere on the page and have the rest of the page's text flow around them gives Word the power of the best desktop publishing programs.

LESSON 104: SOME DESKTOP PUBLISHING TECHNIQUES

Although this book has covered most of Word's capabilities, you will discover many additional tricks as you use Word. This section shows you some special techniques that relate specifically to desktop publishing.

You can use Word to create business forms. This is a very useful desktop publishing feature because businesses use so many forms, and because their design changes so often. Although you can use drawing programs to create forms, rearranging them and adding sections in the middle is especially easy with Word.

If your forms have long fill-in boxes or square check boxes, you can create these using empty paragraphs and box borders. You can place the boxes on the same line as the text with side by side paragraph formatting. For example, to create this form, follow the steps:

Name	
Address	
City, State, Zip	
Occupation	

1. Enter the text (Name, Address, and so on) in separate paragraphs. Select all these paragraphs and set their right margins to two inches.
2. Create a blank paragraph, and give the Format Paragraph command. Set the left indent to 2.25 inches. Give the Format Borders command and select a Normal (single) box border.

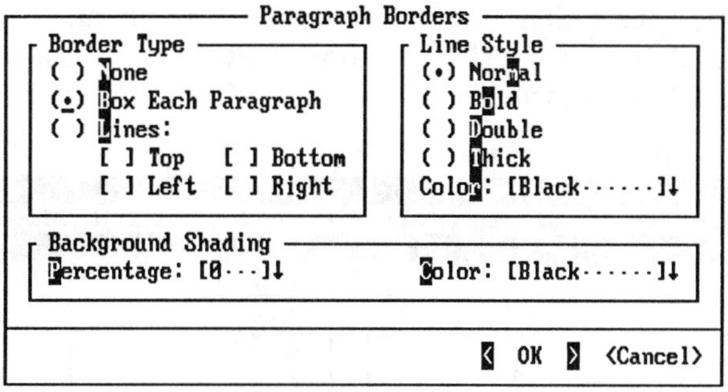

3. Copy this paragraph to the scrap and insert it between the text paragraphs.

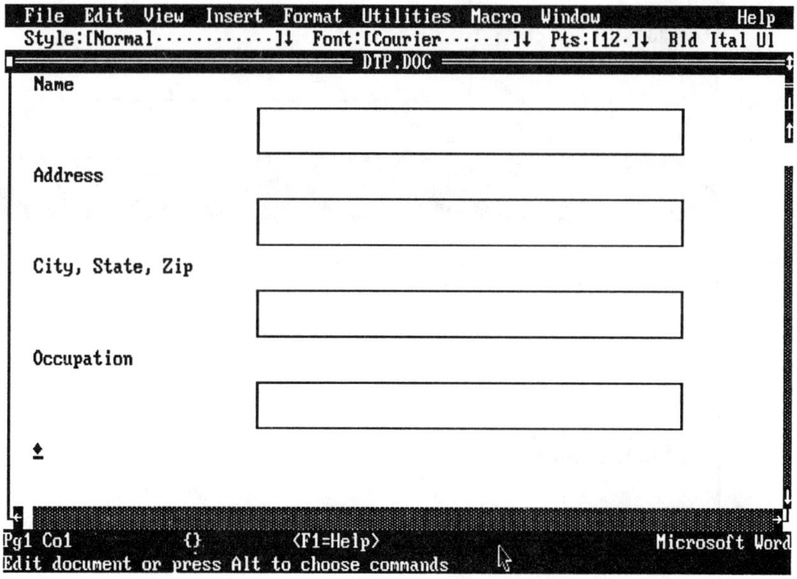

4. Select all the paragraphs, give the Format Paragraph command, select "Side by Side," and select 12 points for line spacing. You can view the result by printing out the form.

Some forms require grids; this is likely if you want a blank to be filled with a specific number of characters or with separate letters. To create a grid for the preceding illustration, select the box paragraph and give the Format Tabs command before copying the box. Place evenly spaced vertical tabs along the box. Place the vertical bars every 3/10 of an inch:

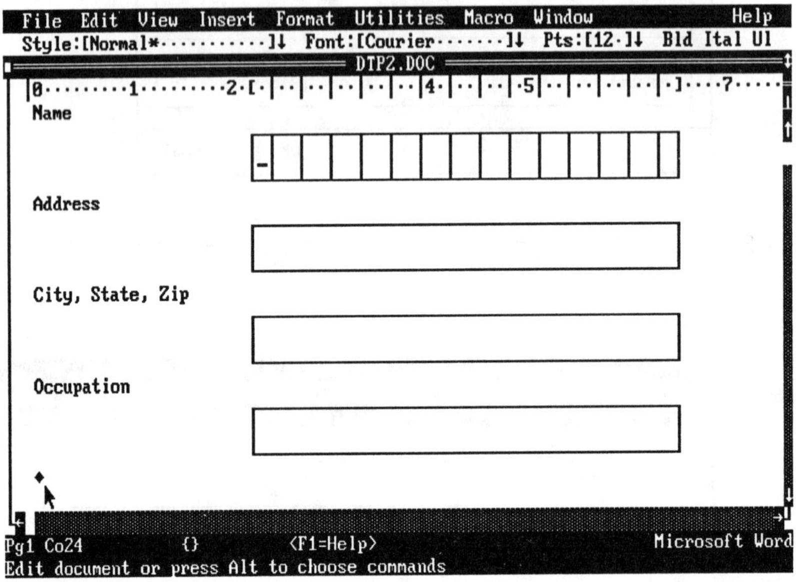

Finally, copy the box formatting to the other lines.

REVIEW

1. *Desktop publishing*
   List some of Word's desktop publishing features.

2. *Forms*
   How do you make a fill-in box appear next to its associated text?

part V

APPENDIXES

Editing Command Summary
Formatting Keystrokes Summary
Mouse Keyclicks Summary
Word Menus
Preparing the Word Program
Using Other Programs That Work with Word
Altering Printer Drivers
Answers to the Review Questions

appendix A

EDITING COMMAND SUMMARY

The tables in this appendix summarize the editing commands covered in Part I of this book. You can use them as a quick reference guide when you are entering or editing text.

Table A-1 shows the keys that you use when entering text with Word. Tables A-2 and A-3 list the ways you can select text with the mouse and from the keyboard. Table A-4 describes how to move through your text with the mouse and keyboard.

Key	Meaning
ENTER	End paragraph
SHIFT-ENTER	NEWLINE; end line but continue paragraph
CTRL-ENTER	End page
TAB	Go to next tab stop
HYPHEN	Normal hyphen
CTRL-SHIFT-HYPHEN	Nonbreaking hyphen; Word will never split a line here
CTRL-HYPHEN	Optional hyphen; Word will split a line here only to avoid wrapping a whole word to next line
CTRL-SPACEBAR	Nonbreaking space

TABLE A-1. Text Entry Keys

Where Pointing	Button	Selection
Character	Left	Character
Character	Right	Word
Character	Both	Sentence
Selection bar	Left	Line
Selection bar	Right	Paragraph
Selection bar	Both	Entire document

TABLE A-2. Selecting Text with the Mouse

Key	Selection
F8, twice	Word left
ALT-F6	Word right
ALT-F8	Sentence right
ALT-F10	Paragraph right
F8	Extend selection (toggle)

TABLE A-3. Selecting Text with the Keyboard

Key	Where Moved
←	Previous letter
→	Next letter
↑	Previous line
↓	Next line
CTRL-←	Beginning of previous word
CTRL-→	Beginning of next word
CTRL-↑	Beginning of previous paragraph
CTRL-↓	Beginning of next paragraph
HOME	Beginning of current line
END	End of current line
CTRL-HOME	Beginning of file
CTRL-END	End of file
PGUP	Previous window length
PGDN	Next window length
CTRL-PGUP	First character of first line of window
CTRL-PGDN	First character of last line of window
SCROLL LOCK	Line-by-line scrolling (toggle)

TABLE A-4. Moving Through Text with the Keyboard

appendix B

FORMATTING KEYSTROKES SUMMARY

The tables in this appendix summarize the formatting keystrokes covered in Part II of this book. You can use these as a quick reference guide when you are entering or reformatting text with Word. The character and paragraph formatting commands are covered in Table B-1 and Table B-2, respectively.

Characteristic	CTRL Key
Bold	CTRL-B
Italic	CTRL-I
Underline	CTRL-U
Small caps	CTRL-K
Double underline	CTRL-D
Superscript	CTRL-PLUS
Subscript	CTRL-MINUS
Normal	CTRL-SPACEBAR
Font name	CTRL-F
Font size	CTRL-P
Hidden	CTRL-H

TABLE B-1. Character Format Keystrokes

Characteristic	CTRL Key
Alignment	CTRL-L, CTRL-C, CTRL-R, CTRL-J
Left indent	CTRL-M, CTRL-N
First line	CTRL-F, CTRL-T
Left and right indent	CTRL-Q
Line spacing	CTRL-1, CTRL-2
Blank line above	CTRL-O
Normal	CTRL-X

TABLE B-2. Paragraph Format Keystrokes

appendix C

MOUSE KEYCLICKS SUMMARY

Pointing with the Mouse
Using the Buttons

The purpose of the mouse is to make interacting with software easier. However, its use is not foolproof, and it can be intimidating to people who are accustomed to using a keyboard. Fortunately, Word uses the mouse in a very consistent fashion, and there are only a few rules to learn about it.

When you first use the mouse, you may find it hard to aim the pointer exactly. You may select some text or execute a command that you didn't mean to. However, you will probably find that learning to use the mouse is much like learning to use a car with a standard transmission: at first it may seem clumsy, but soon it will be second nature.

Word does not require you to use the mouse, but you will find that editing with the mouse is often much easier than editing with the keyboard alone. Mice have become much more popular in the past few years and far more programs now support them.

POINTING WITH THE MOUSE

One reason that using a mouse is attractive to many people is that you can point at something without anything happening. You do not need to worry about accidentally pointing at the wrong thing, since only pressing the buttons causes an action; pointing never does.

The mouse stays the same shape (an arrow pointing up to the left) in almost all parts of the screen. The only time it changes is when you point in the selection bar, the area at the left of the text. There, it points up and to the right.

USING THE BUTTONS

When you are pointing at an area of the screen and want to cause an action, you have three choices: the left button, the right button, or both buttons. Fortunately, pressing either or both buttons produces consistent results in most situations, so after a while you can safely guess which button(s) to use in case you forget.

For most actions, you use the left button. In fact, unless you saw something in this book or the Word manual that says that you should use the right button for a particular action, always use the left mouse button.

Occasionally, you will have to double-click the left mouse button. This means that you have to click it twice fairly quickly. Double-clicking is sometimes awkward for beginners, who tend to wait too long between the first and second click.

appendix D

WORD MENUS

The following lists all of the commands in each menu in Word. Many commands have dialogs associated with them, and they are shown under those commands.

File Menu

File New

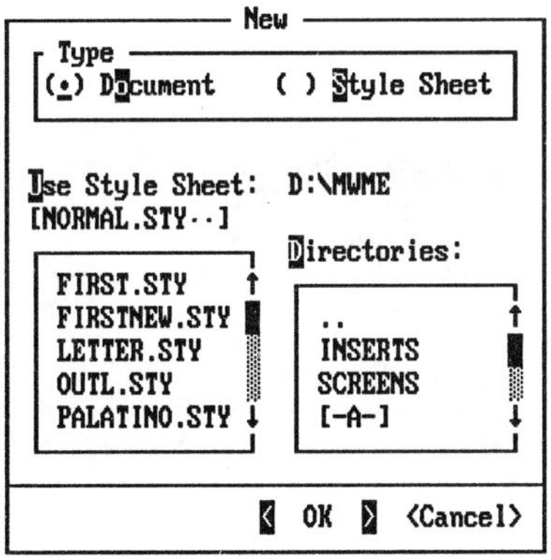

File Open

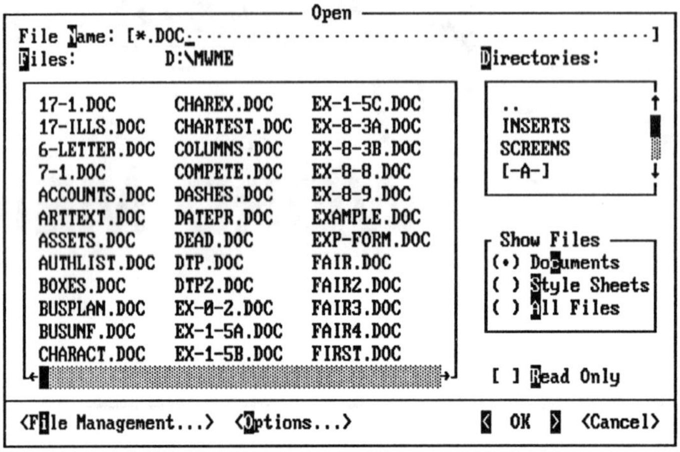

File Close
File Close All
File Save
File Save As

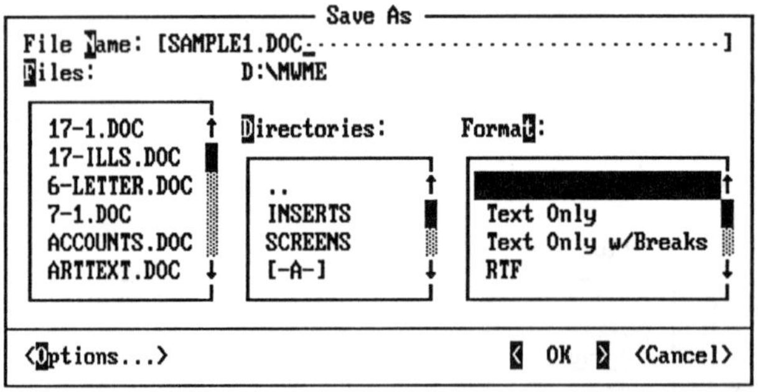

File Save All
File File Management

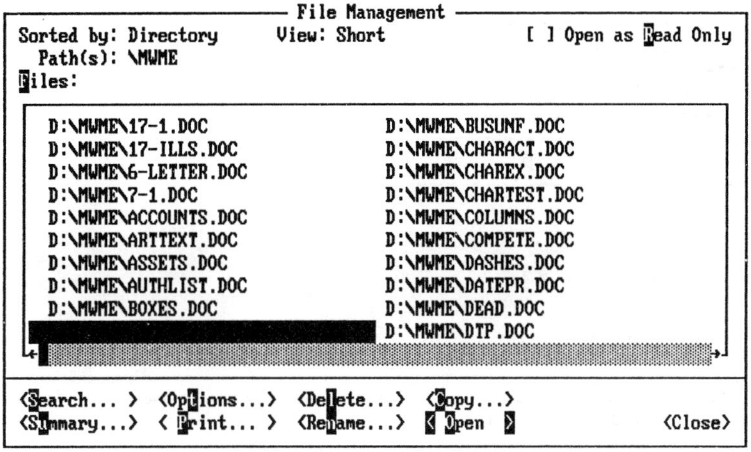

File Print

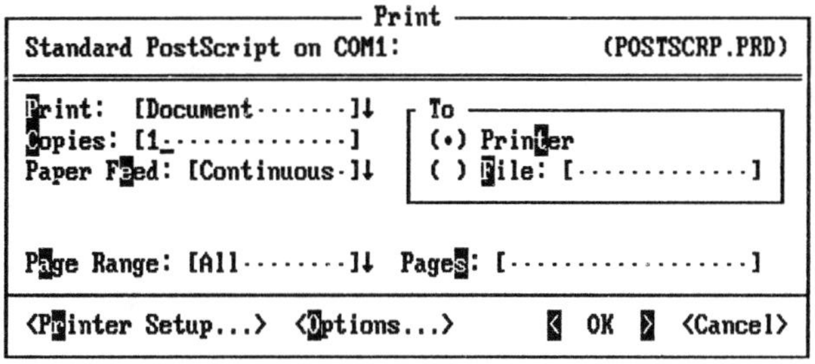

File Print Preview
File Print Merge

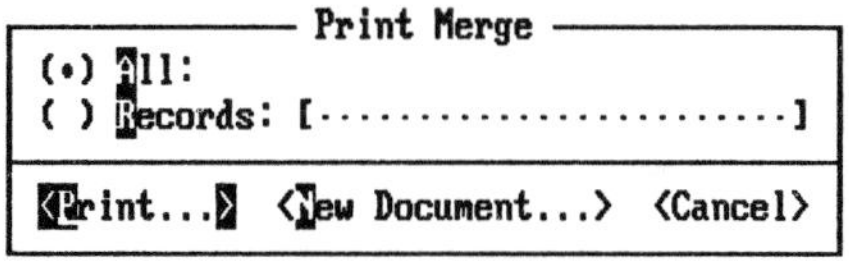

File Print Queue

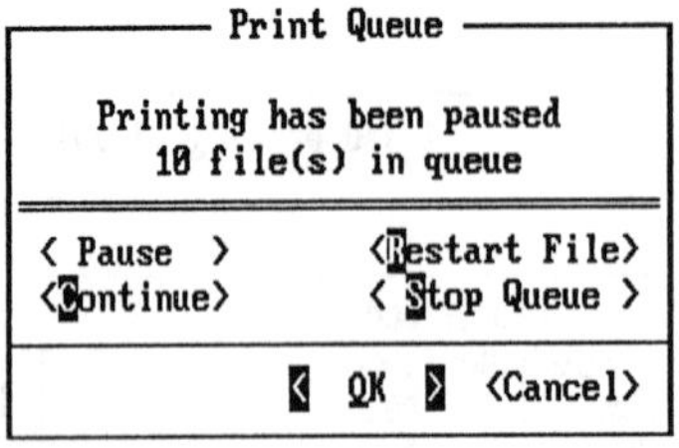

File Printer Setup

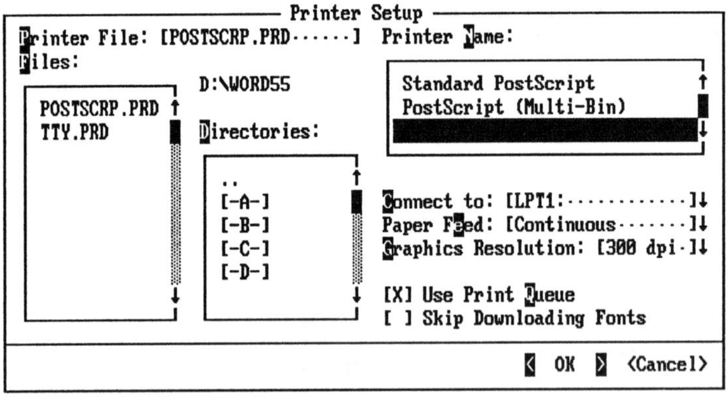

File DOS Commands

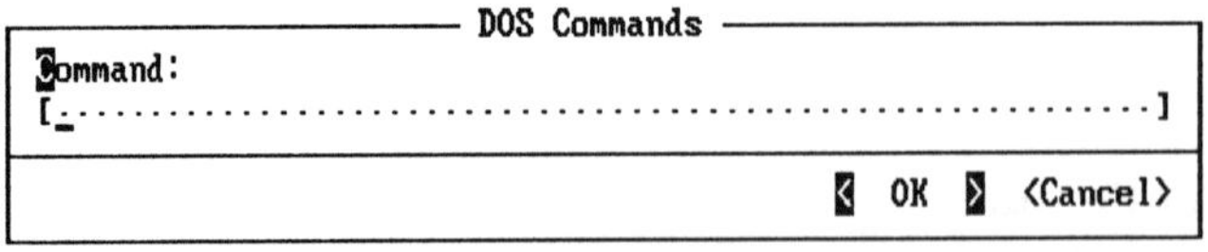

File Exit Word

Edit Menu

Edit Undo
Edit Repeat
Edit Cut
Edit Copy
Edit Paste
Edit Search

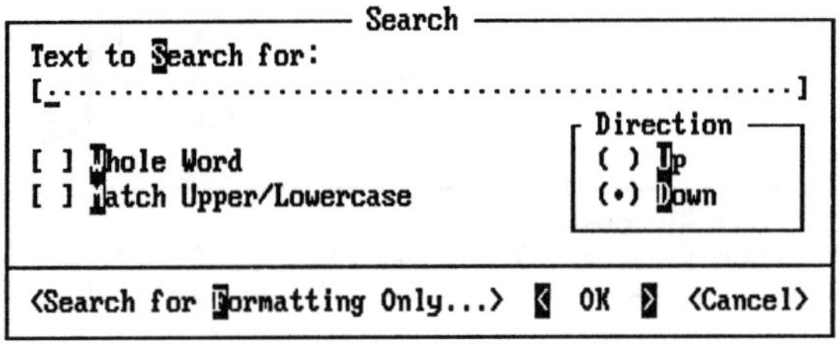

Edit Replace

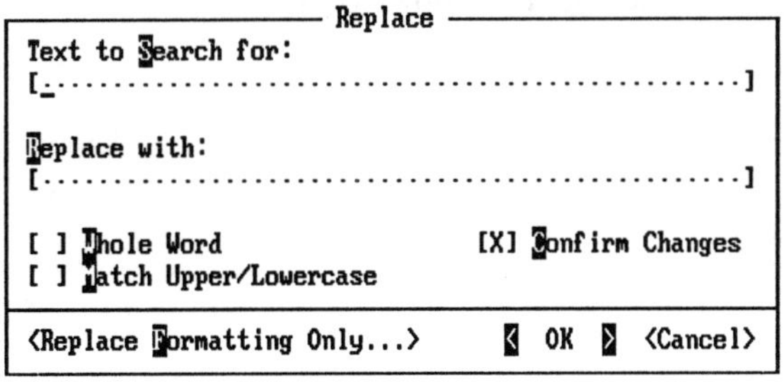

Edit Go To

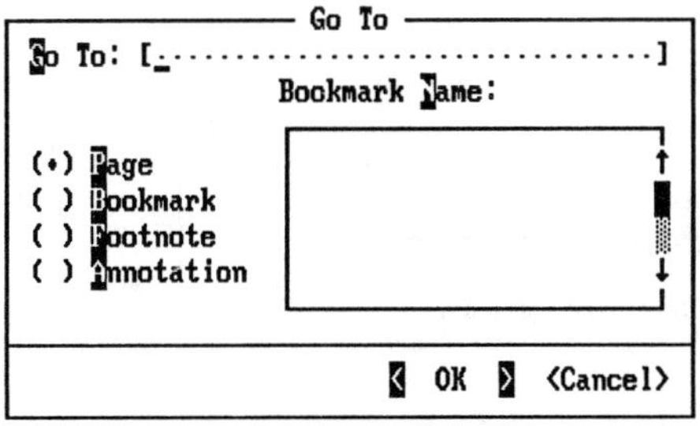

Edit Glossary

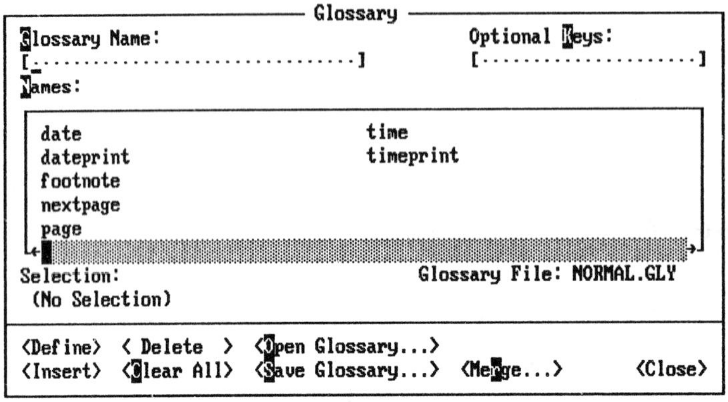

Edit Rename Style (style sheet windows only)

View Menu

View Outline
View Layout
View Ribbon
View Ruler
View Status Bar
View Footnotes/Annotations
View Preferences

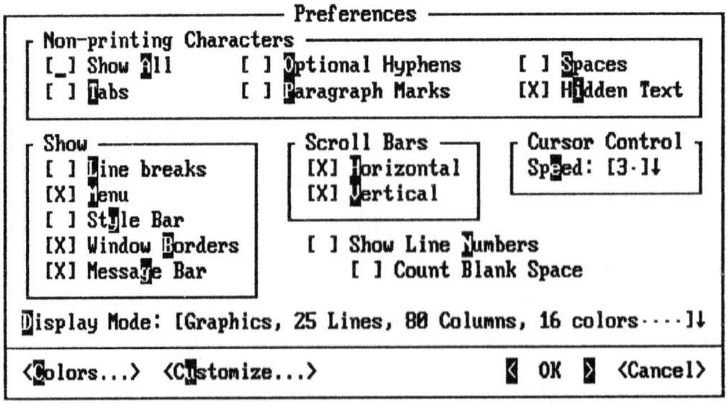

Insert Menu

Insert Break

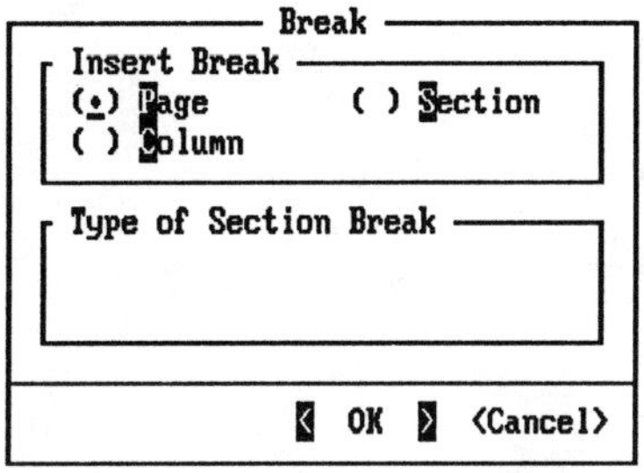

Insert Footnote

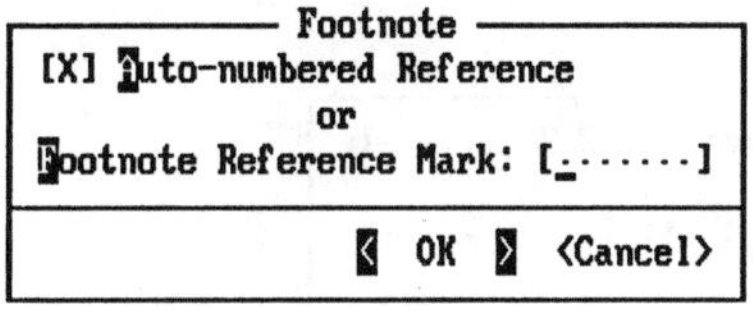

Insert File

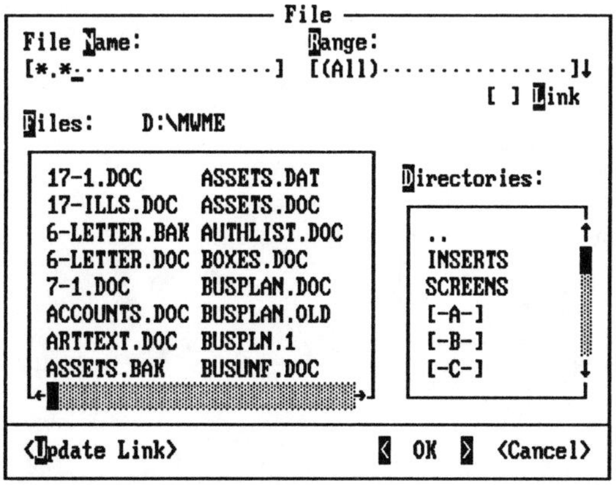

Insert Bookmark

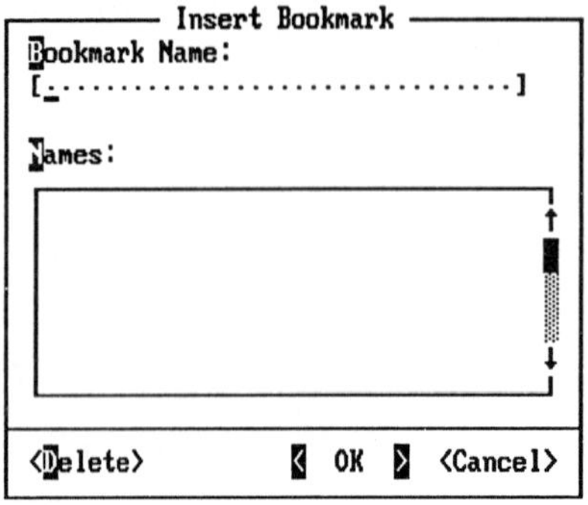

Insert Page Numbers

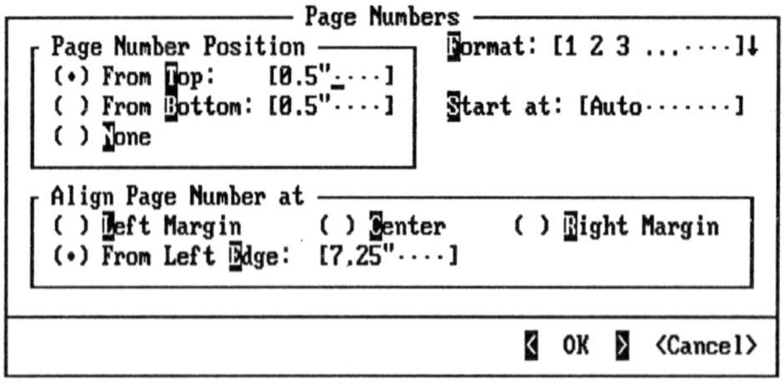

Insert Annotation

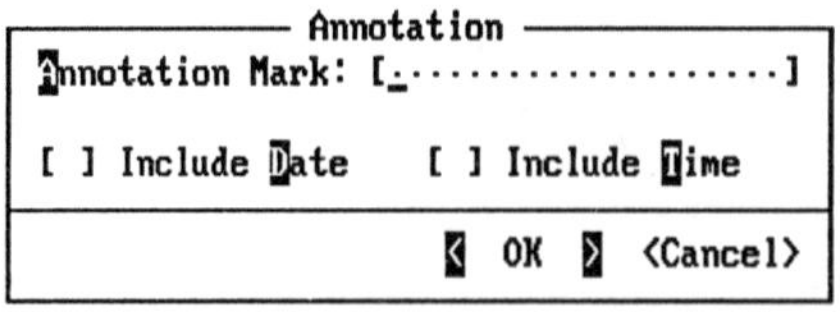

Insert Picture

```
Picture
Picture File Name: [*.PCX_.................................]
                    Format: [.........................]↓
Files:              Align in Frame: [Centered.......]↓

HSGGREY1.PCX ↑    D:\MWME\SCREENS
HSGGREY2.PCX
                  Directories:        Graphics Size
                                      Width:  [6.5"......]↓
                   ..            ↑    Height: [6.5"......]↓
                   HSG
                   TIFF               Space
                   [-A-]              Before: [0"........]
                   [-B-]         ↓    After:  [0"........]
             ↓

<Preview...>                               < OK >  <Cancel>
```

Insert Index

```
Index
Separate Page Numbers from Entry by: [^t_..]

Indent Each Level
(•) By: [0.2".....]          [X] Capitalize Main
( ) Use Style Sheet              Entries

                              < OK >  <Cancel>
```

Insert Table of Contents

```
Table of Contents
Create Table of Contents from
( ) Outline                          (•) Codes: [C.]

Page Numbers                         Indent Each Level
[X] Show Page Numbers                (•) By: [0.4".....]
Separate by: [^t...]                 ( ) Use Style Sheet

                                   < OK >  <Cancel>
```

Insert New Style (style sheet windows only)

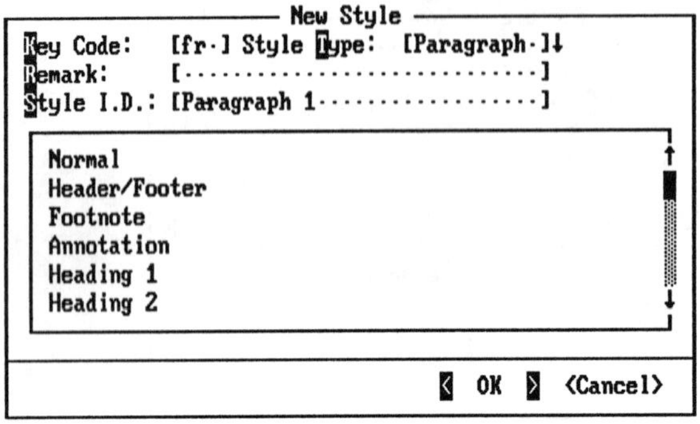

Insert Style Sheet (style sheet windows only)

Format Menu

Format Character

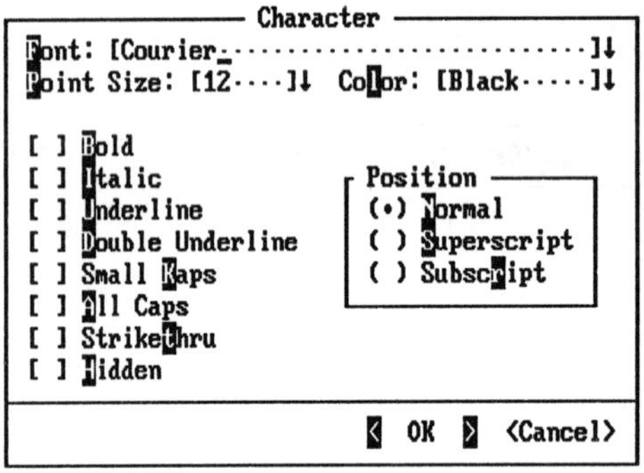

Format Paragraph

```
                          Paragraph
 Alignment
 (•) Left     ( ) Center     ( ) Right     ( ) Justified

 Indents                          Spacing
 From Left:   [0"·······]         Before:  [0 li······]
 First Line:  [0"·······]         After:   [0 li······]
 From Right:  [0"·······]         Line:    [1 li······]↓

 Keep Paragraph
 [ ] Together                     [ ] Side by Side
 [ ] With Next

<Tabs...> <Borders...> <Position...> < OK > <Cancel>
```

Format Section

```
                        Section
 Columns                        Place Footnotes
 Number:  [1_·······]           (•) Same Page
 Spacing: [0.5"·····]           ( ) End of Section

 Line Numbers
 [X] Add Line Numbers            Restart at
                                 (•) New Page
 From Text: [0.4"·····]          ( ) New Section
 Count By:  [1········]          ( ) Continuous

Section Start: [New Page···]↓

<Margins...> <Page Numbers...> < OK > <Cancel>
```

Format Margins

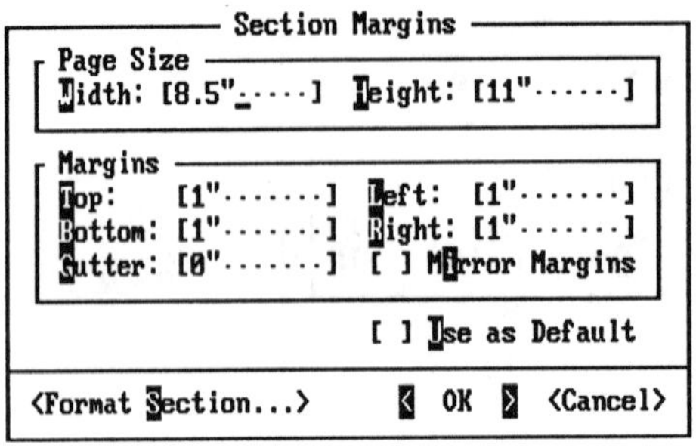

Format Tabs

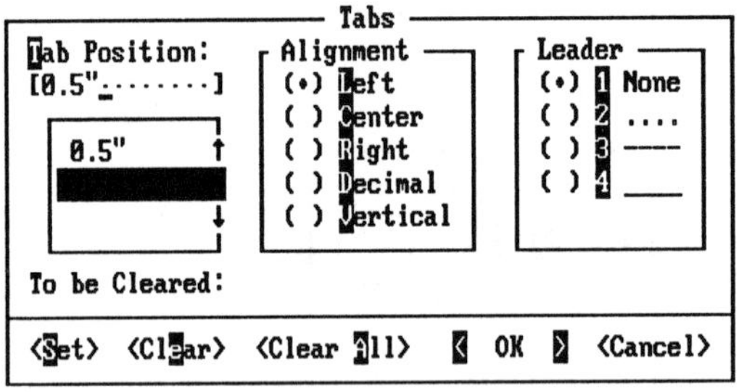

Format Borders

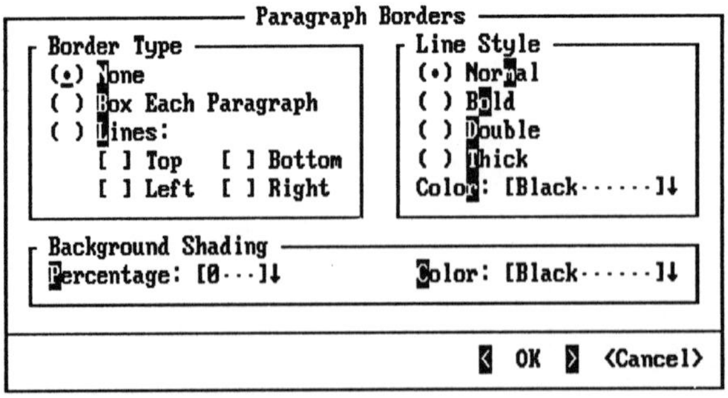

Format Position

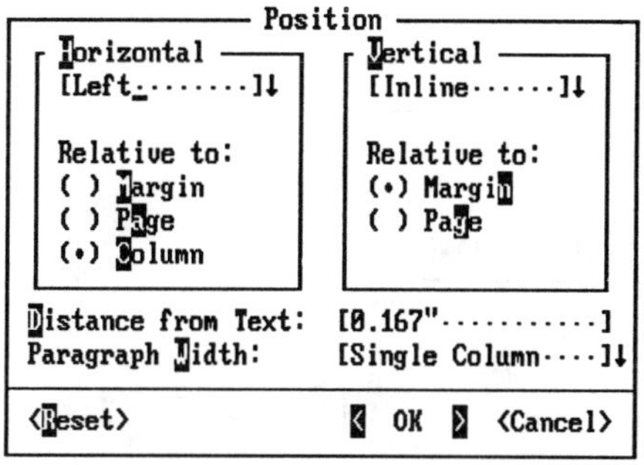

Format Header/Footer

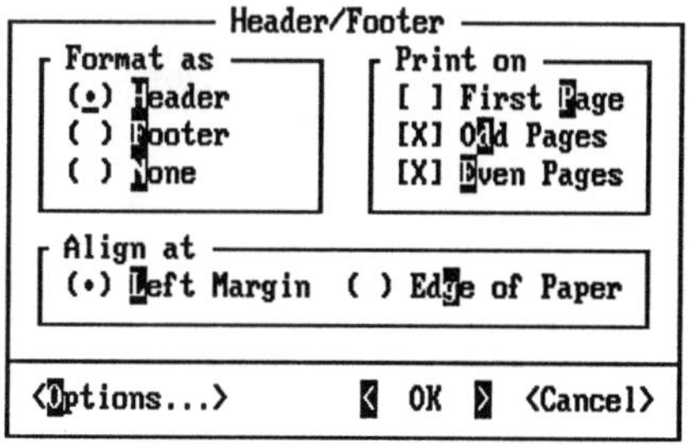

Format Apply Style

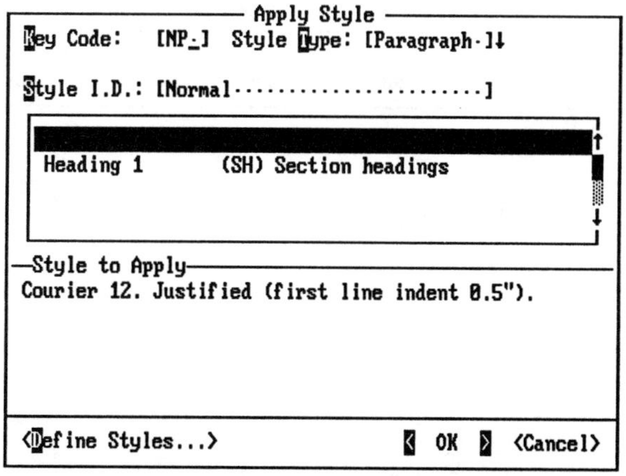

Format Record Style
Format Define Styles
Format Attach Style Sheet

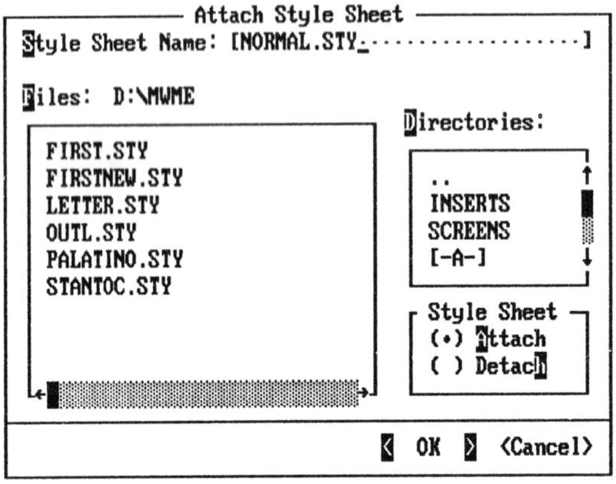

Utilities Menu

Utilities Spelling

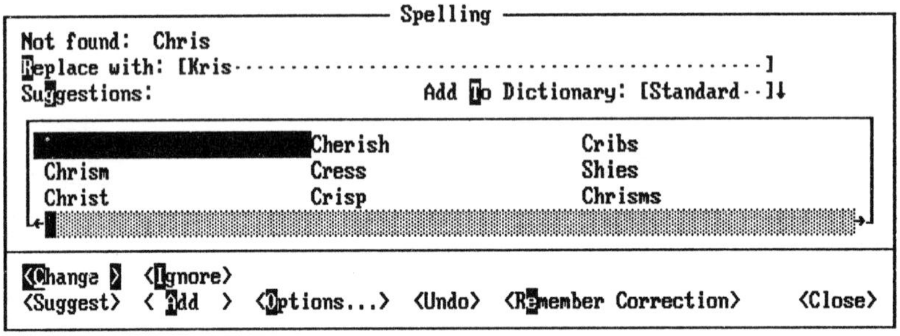

Utilities Thesaurus

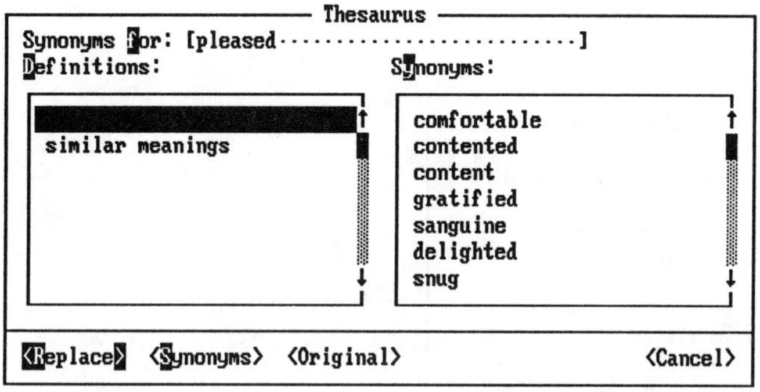

Utilities Hyphenate

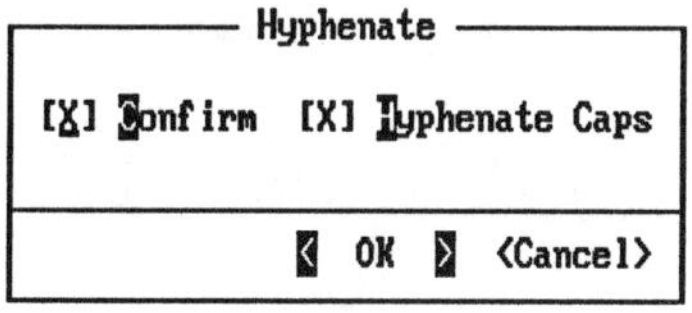

Utilities Renumber

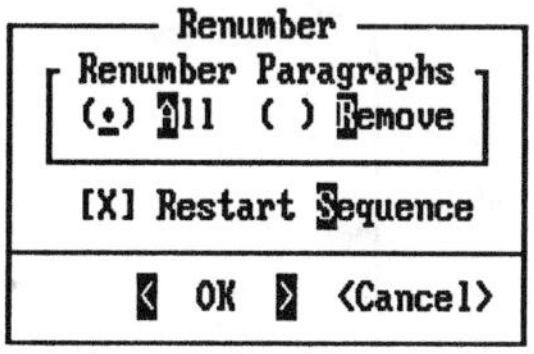

Utilities Revision Marks
Utilities Word Count
Utilities Line Draw
Utilities Sort

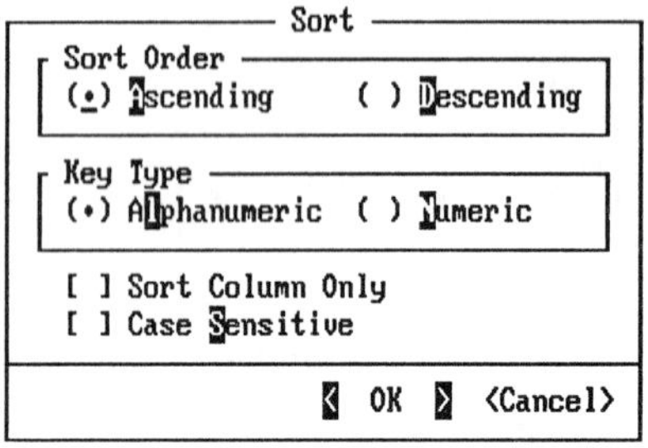

Utilities Calculate
Utilities Repaginate Now

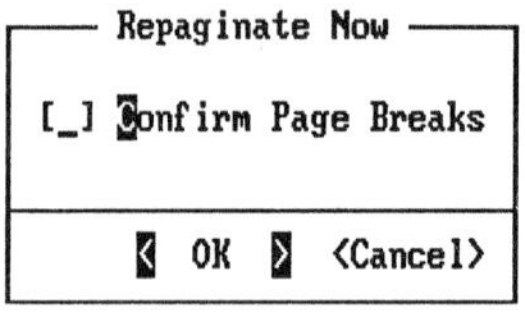

Utilities Customize

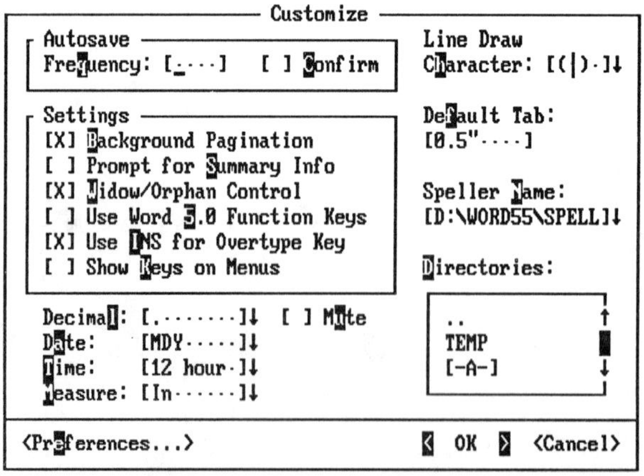

Macro Menu

Macro Record

```
Record Macro
Macro Name:
[································]

Macro Keys:
[····················]

          < OK > <Cancel>
```

Macro Run

```
Run Macro
Macro Name:
[_································]  [ ] Step

  DoColor <ctrl C>
  DoNew <ctrl N>
  DoOpen <ctrl O>
  FormatParagraph <ctrl M>
  SwitchHidden <ctrl Z>

<Macro Edit...>          < OK > <Cancel>
```

Macro Edit

```
Edit Macro
Macro Name:                                 Macro Keys:
[tovga_··························]          [·····················]
Macros:

  DoClose <ctrl W>              SwitchHidden <ctrl Z>
  DoColor <ctrl C>              toherc
  DoNew <ctrl N>
  DoOpen <ctrl O>
  FormatParagraph <ctrl M>

tovga:                        Macro (Glossary) File: NORMAL.GLY
 <alt·V>e<alt·D><down·3><enter>

<Define> < Delete  > <Open Glossary...>
< Edit > <Clear All> <Save Glossary...>  <Merge...>      <Close>
```

Window Menu

Window New Window
Window Arrange All
Window Maximize
Window Restore
Window Move
Window Size
Window Split
Window Close

Help Menu

Help Index
Help Keyboard
Help Word 5.0 to 5.5
Help Learning Word
Help Using Help
Help About

appendix E

PREPARING THE WORD PROGRAM

Setting Up Your Computer
Installing a Mouse
Using Other Mice
Preparing Word's Distribution Disks
Arranging Your Workspace

Although Word is easy to use, it is not always easy to set up on your computer. The Microsoft Word reference manual only briefly describes how to set up Word; this appendix gives you more detail and will help you decide how to use Word with nonstandard PC configurations.

Since this book assumes that you have used MS-DOS commands, some of the discussion in this appendix may use commands or concepts you are not familiar with. See your MS-DOS manual for more information.

SETTING UP YOUR COMPUTER

Before you install Word, it is important to set up your computer so that Word will work well with it. This will let you get the most out of Word on your system. It is also important to set the computer up for comfort, especially if you will be using it a great deal.

Word expects that your computer is an IBM PC, an IBM PC XT, an IBM PC AT, an IBM PS/2, or compatible. Since there is no absolute definition of PC compatibility, you should check with your computer's dealer or manufacturer to see whether Word has been tested on the configuration of the computer you own.

Word can work with a minimum of two floppy disks, but its performance is greatly improved by a hard disk or a RAM disk. Since Word reads information from the disk quite often, a faster disk improves the speed at which Word can find data on the disk.

INSTALLING A MOUSE

Word does not require that you use a mouse, but it works much better with one. The Microsoft Mouse is relatively inexpensive, and it is probably worthwhile for anyone using Word more than an hour a day. However, some people find the mouse cumbersome to use or hard to master. On the positive side, the Microsoft Mouse can also be used with a variety of other programs, even if they were not originally designed to be used with a mouse.

USING OTHER MICE

Instead of the Microsoft Mouse, you can use a PC Mouse from Mouse Systems (2336-H Walsh Avenue, Santa Clara, California 95051) if you wish. Since the PC Mouse uses an optical pad and scanner instead of a rolling ball, there are fewer moving parts to fail. Like the Microsoft Mouse, you can use the PC Mouse and its software with many other applications programs.

If you use the PC Mouse, be sure to use the Mouse Systems software instead of the Microsoft MOUSE.COM or MOUSE.SYS software to tell MS-DOS that you are using a mouse. There are many other mice available for the IBM PC; however, some of them will not work with Word. Before buying one of these mice, be sure to ask the dealer (or manufacturer) if it will work with Word.

PREPARING WORD'S DISTRIBUTION DISKS

Version 5.5 of Word comes on disks that are not copy protected, so making copies of your master disks is now very easy. Earlier versions of Word came on copy-protected disks that could not be copied with standard DOS commands.

You should copy each of your Word disks before using any of them. You can copy the disks with either the COPY or the DISKCOPY command in MS-DOS. After you have made a backup of each disk, store the master copies in a safe place, preferably away from your computer. If your copies are ever damaged, destroyed, or stolen, you can make new copies from the masters.

If you are running Word from a hard disk, use the SETUP program to copy all of the needed files to an appropriate subdirectory. Note that you do not need all of the files; in fact you will need very few.

ARRANGING YOUR WORKSPACE

Although the physical setup of your PC is not usually considered part of the installation of Word, it is nonetheless important. Two major aspects of your computer setup affect your use of Word: the placement of the mouse and your view of the screen.

Having the mouse directly next to your hand makes it easier to find and use. To place the mouse in this position, you have to place the keyboard about nine inches from the edge of the desk. Some people prefer to have the keyboard closer to the edge of the desk, with the mouse to the left or right of the keyboard; however, this takes up more lateral room on your desk.

The angle at which you view the screen is more important in Word than in many other programs, since Word uses the left and right edges of the text

FIGURE E-1. IBM PC with main box sideways and monitor angled

window to display information. Most users find that staring straight into the screen causes tension and stress, but that viewing the screen from a slight angle is better. Figure E-1 shows an example of an IBM PC setup that takes up little space on a desk and gives you a view of the screen at a comfortable angle as well as enough room for the mouse in front of the keyboard.

appendix F

USING OTHER PROGRAMS THAT WORK WITH WORD

Using Other Text Programs

Since Word works with text and text files, many other MS-DOS programs that read or write text files can be used with Word. However, it is important to remember that these programs sometimes only work with *unformatted* Word files. That is, most programs cannot read your Word files unless you specify "Text Only" in the Save As command.

Saving files without formatting means you lose all of Word's formatting when you read the file again. Thus, it is likely that you will not want to use many of the available programs if they force you to lose the capability to format your text. You can surmount this problem by saving two copies of the file (one formatted, the other unformatted) with different file names. However, if the applications program changes the unformatted file (such as a spelling checker correcting mistakes), your formatted file will not contain the changes.

You can still use Word to edit text files created with other programs and to include these files with your formatted Word documents. For instance, most spreadsheet programs allow you to save their results in a text file that can then be read by Word and included with Word documents.

There are hundreds of programs available for the IBM PC that can either work with formatted Word files or produce files that you can read and edit with Word. Even more programs can work with unformatted Word files, but they are not listed here because you will probably not produce many documents without formatting.

If you want to find out more about the software described here or about other programs that work with Word, you should read software reviews in computer magazines. Many such magazines specialize in the IBM PC, including *PC World* and *PC Magazine.*

USING OTHER TEXT PROGRAMS

Many of the currently available text programs that work with other word processing software will probably be updated to work with Word in the future. For example, Reference Software offers an excellent package called Grammatik IV that is available for Word files. Grammatik IV analyzes what you have written and makes suggestions about how to improve your text. It also finds common grammatical mistakes and incorrect punctuation.

If you need to keep your documents secure from intruders, there are many programs that will scramble the contents so only you can read them. This process is called *encryption.* Data security is becoming an important issue as people do more of their writing on computer, since it is easy to steal information from a computer by taking its disks.

Many people feel ill at ease about writing, so there are a number of companies that sell standard form letters on disk. Although the quality of these letters is variable, they are sometimes good starting points for your own writing.

If you use many other programs on your PC, you may want to convert your files to and from Word's document format. There are many good conversion programs, and almost all will convert Word files for you.

Editor's Choice Software publishes a catalog of products that work with Word. They can be reached at (800) 641-1116.

appendix G

ALTERING PRINTER DRIVERS

Running MAKEPRD
Using Character Translations
Using the Printer Control Sequence

This appendix is of interest to you only if you want to change the printer drivers in Word and you have some background in printer technology. Fewer than 5 percent of this book's readers will probably want to change printer drivers. Most people find that their printer drivers work fine for them or that the method for changing them involves so much arcane jargon that it just isn't worth it.

The appendixes of the Microsoft Word reference manual contain a detailed description of the internals of the printer drivers. Setting up a driver is nearly impossible unless you are intimately familiar with a printer's escape codes. However, Microsoft includes a utility that allows you to dump the contents of a printer driver into a text file, modify the text file, and create a new printer driver.

The conversion program, MAKEPRD, is on your Thesaurus Disk. It is documented in the *Printer Information* manual. You can, if you wish, construct your own printer driver by using the utility; this is a fairly major task, and you get little help from the documentation.

The following discussion shows you two ways to modify an existing printer driver.

- You can change the character translation table (CTT) so that your printer emulates the IBM PC screen characters more accurately.
- You can also modify the printer control-sequence descriptions (PCDs) to include escape sequences for various printing features (such as italics) or to change the printer initialization string to set the printer up in high-quality printing mode.

This discussion will not explain how to change or add fonts, since this subject is well beyond the capabilities of most people and is covered in depth in the Microsoft documentation.

The process for changing a printer driver is

1. Run MAKEPRD on an existing driver to make a text copy of the contents.
2. Edit the text copy.
3. Convert the new text copy into a new printer driver with MAKEPRD again.

RUNNING MAKEPRD

The MAKEPRD program unfortunately does not adhere to Microsoft's standards for user-friendliness; however, for the limited purposes described earlier it works all right. Copy the MAKEPRD program and the driver you want to modify to a blank disk, and give the MAKEPRD command after the prompt:

C>MAKEPRD

The program first prompts

PRD Editor 2.00 of October 27, 1988
Name of PRD file:

Enter the name of the driver you are modifying, including the **.PRD** extension, and press ENTER. The program now prompts

Name of Text file:

Enter the name of the text file you want to create. You should use a distinct extension like .TXT or .DAT so that you do not overwrite your driver. The program then prompts

Select PRD to Text (Press **T**)
or Text to PRD conversion (Press **P**):

Type **T** to tell Word that you are converting from a PRD to a text file. Word reads the input file (this may take a long time), creates the output file, and says

Conversion Complete

Throughout this appendix the OKI92 driver, for the Okidata 92 series of printers, is used as an example. The conversion would look like this:

C>**MAKEPRD**
PRD Editor 2.00 of October 27, 1988
Name of PRD file: **OKI92.PRD**
Name of Text file: **OKI92.TXT**
Select PRD to Text conversion (Press T)
or Text to PRD conversion (Press P): **T**

Conversion Complete

When you are finished altering the text file, run the MAKEPRD program again and give the new file names (or the same ones if you want to overwrite them), but change the answer to the last question to "P."

The text file produced by MAKEPRD is quite long. It contains all of the information covered in the Microsoft Word reference manual although in a somewhat cryptic manner. Since this section only explains how to change the character translation table and the printer control sequence descriptions, you can ignore most of the beginning of the file.

USING CHARACTER TRANSLATIONS

The printer driver contains a table of character translations. You can translate any ASCII character into any other character or into a two-character sequence with overstriking. Note, however, that overstriking only works on printers that can backspace; Microsoft may eliminate this restriction in the future and accommodate printers that can return the carriage to the beginning of the line and overstrike.

There are many uses for this table. If your printer has graphics symbols that are similar to the IBM PC's symbols but that are kept in different ASCII locations, you can use this table to have the printer print the codes you see on the screen. Since many of the PC's codes are for foreign characters that can be approximated by overstriking, you can correlate two characters for each of the graphics characters. For example, the PC's ASCII 133, à, can be formed by overstriking an "a" (ASCII 97) with a grave accent (ASCII 96).

You can also use the table to approximate some of the PC's other graphics and math symbols (ASCII 176-254). For example, the plus-or-minus sign (ASCII 241), ±, can be made with a plus sign (ASCII 43) and an underscore (ASCII 95).

The table holding the conversions is near the end of the text file and begins with the characters "{TO." The table included in the OKI92 file is shown in Figure G-1. Note that the file contains both spaces and TAB characters.

The format of this table is fairly easy to understand. The first line is a header for the MAKEPRD program. The second line contains the first and

```
{TØ
cCSD:1 chFirst:128 chLast:175
 128:67 44        129:117 34       130:101 39       131:97 94
 132:97 34        133:97 96        134:97 Ø         135:99 44
 136:101 94       137:101 34       138:101 96       139:105 34
 140:105 94       141:105 96       142:65 34        143:65 Ø
 144:69 39        145:97 Ø         146:65 Ø         147:111 94
 148:111 34       149:111 96       150:117 94       151:117 96
 152:121 34       153:79 34        154:85 34        155:99 47
 156:35 Ø         157:89 61        158:80 Ø         159:102 Ø
 160:97 39        161:105 39       162:111 39       163:117 39
 164:110 126      165:78 126       166:97 95        167:111 95
 168:168 Ø        169:169 Ø        170:170 Ø        171:171 Ø
 172:172 Ø        173:173 Ø        174:60 61        175:62 61

}T
```

FIGURE G-1. Conversion table for OKI92

last characters in the list. If you add character translations that are outside of the current range listed, you must change the two numbers and include translations for every character in the range.

Each entry consists of the ASCII code to be translated, the first character to translate to, and the second character (for overstriking). For example, the first entry listed is "128:67 44." This means that when Word sees an ASCII 128, it should print an ASCII 67 and overstrike it with an ASCII 44. If you don't want an overstrike, set the second character to 0 (as in the entry for ASCII 134). If you want to print the actual character, you must still include an entry, such as the entry for ASCII 168.

Many of the character tables in the drivers do not include characters past ASCII 175. You may want to add your own, especially if your printer has graphics characters in it. Table G-1 lists some suggested overstrike pairs for ASCII 176 through 244.

USING THE PRINTER CONTROL SEQUENCE

The last section of the text file is the table of characters that Word uses to invoke various printing options, like boldface or subscript. These are likely to be set correctly for your printer unless you are using one of the TTY devices.

The printer control section for OKI92 is shown in Figure G-2. The location indicated by "byte:" is the entry in the PCD table. You should refer to the table of PCDs in the Microsoft Word reference manual for this information. Although some of the entries are obscure, you will probably understand most of them.

The format of the table is fairly clear: the byte number, the mod, magic, value (if any), and the sequence of characters. You'll notice that the characters are representations of the actual characters sent, not the characters themselves. For instance, the string for byte 0 represents a CTRL-X and is a caret (^) followed by a capital "X." The string for byte 8 represents an Escape followed by a capital "F" and is a caret (^) followed by a left square bracket ([) and then a capital "F."

If you know the escape sequences for attributes like boldface or underline, you can change the values for these attributes in order to get at least some of the driver correct for your printer. If nothing else, this usually speeds up printing a bit.

However, you can do other interesting things, like changing the printer setup string. This is very useful, for instance, on the Okidata 92, because you

Character	IBM PC Character 1	Character 2
176	35	45
177	35	43
178	35	42
179	124	0
196	45	0
197	43	0
205	61	0
219	77	87
225	66	0
229	111	39
231	84	0
232	79	73
233	79	45
237	79	47
240	61	95
241	43	95
242	62	95
243	60	95
244	45	58

TABLE G-1. Suggested Additions to the Character Translation Table

can send the sequence "Escape 1" to automatically put the printer in a correspondence-quality mode. Since the initialization string is the string in byte 0, you can change

byte:0 mod:0 "**^X**"

to

byte:0 mod:0 "**^X^[1**"

```
{P
byte:0 mod:0 "^X"
byte:4 mod:0
byte:8 mod:2 magic:0 value:99 "^[F"
byte:14 mod:0
byte:18 mod:0 magic:0 value:127 "^[%9"
byte:24 mod:0
byte:28 mod:0 magic:0 value:0
byte:34 mod:0
byte:38 mod:0
byte:42 mod:0
byte:46 mod:0
byte:50 mod:0
byte:54 mod:0
byte:58 mod:0
byte:62 mod:0
byte:66 mod:0
byte:128 mod:0 "^[T"
byte:132 mod:0 "^[I"
byte:136 mod:4
byte:140 mod:0
byte:144 mod:0 magic:0 value:0 "^[C"
byte:150 mod:0 "^[D"
byte:154 mod:2 magic:0 value:0
byte:160 mod:0
byte:164 mod:2 magic:0 value:0 "^[C"
byte:170 mod:0 "^[D"
byte:174 mod:0 magic:0 value:0 "^[J"
byte:180 mod:0 "^[L"
byte:184 mod:0 magic:0 value:0 "^[L"
byte:190 mod:0 "^[J"

}P
E
```

FIGURE G-2. Printer control section for OKI92

You will want to save this to a different driver (since this feature slows the printer down significantly) and name the driver "OKI92COR."

Similarly, if your printer uses italics, you could change the information for bytes 136 and 140 to send the correct escape sequence. If you download characters to the printer or have alternate character sets available, you can change these character sets to use them.

Changing fonts is much trickier. You need to know a great deal about the fonts. If you follow the tables in the Microsoft Word reference manual, you should be able to add fonts that can be called from the driver.

appendix H

ANSWERS TO THE REVIEW QUESTIONS

GETTING STARTED

1. Include the file name after the WORD command:

   C>WORD B:TIMECLCK

   To open the last file you edited, use the /L option:

   C>WORD /L

2. With the mouse, point to the "b" in "below," hold down the left button, then move the pointer to the "t" in "limit." With the keyboard, move to the "b" in "below," hold down the SHIFT key, then press the → key until it is selected.
3. With the mouse, point at any letter in the sentence and press both buttons. With the keyboard, use ALT-F8 to move the selection indicator to the sentence. Then press the DEL key.
4. Use the SHIFT-ENTER combination to make a new line without ending the paragraph. In a business letter you would probably use NEWLINE in the opening and closing addresses.

CHAPTER 1

1. You see a list of possible file names in the File Open dialog. To load ORDER.DOC with the mouse:

   - Point at File in the menu bar and press the left button.
   - While holding down the button, drag down to Open and release the button.
   - Scroll in the list until you find the ORDER file. Select it and click the "OK" button.

   With the keyboard:

   - Press ALT-F then ALT-O.
   - Press TAB, then the ↓ key, to move the highlight bar to ORDER.DOC.
   - Press the ENTER key.

2. With the mouse pointing at text, the left button selects the letter, the right button selects the word, and both buttons select the sentence. With the mouse pointing in the selection bar, the left button selects the line, the right button selects the paragraph, and both buttons select the entire document. You can also drag the mouse while holding down either button to make a selection of variable length.

   You can extend the selection by holding down the SHIFT key and moving the selection. You can press the F8 key repeatedly to select larger areas of text.

3. To get to the top of the document, point at the thumb, press the left button, drag the box to the top of the scroll bar, and release the mouse button. To get to the bottom, point at the thumb, press the left button, drag the box to the bottom of the scroll bar, and release the mouse button. To get to the middle, point at the thumb, press the left button, drag the box to the middle of the scroll bar, and release the mouse button.

4. Only *b* and *c* can be undone, since the Undo command only reverses an editing change, not a change in the position of the selection indicator.

5. Before giving the File Print command, save your file, and be sure that your printer is turned on, has paper in it, and is connected to your PC.

CHAPTER 2

1. The scrap is shown near the lower left corner of the screen in the curly braces. The Edit Cut and Edit Copy commands are the only commands that put text into the scrap.
2. Select the first three words, including the comma and the space after the comma. Delete the selection, move the selection indicator to the "h" in "she," press the BACKSPACE key, and then type a capital **S**. Now move the selection indicator to the period and paste the text from the scrap. Use the BACKSPACE key to remove the space and comma, and then move to the "v" in "Over"; remove the "O" and type a space and a lowercase **o**.
3. Make a line of ten dashes, select them, and use the Edit Copy command to put them in the scrap. Press the ENTER key and give the Edit Paste command; then press the BACKSPACE key. Press the ENTER key again, press the BACKSPACE key twice, and continue until the design is complete.

CHAPTER 3

1. Use the Edit Search command and change direction to Up; type the text and choose "OK"; then give the Edit Search command again. Use the Edit Search command with the phrase, but change the "Match Upper/Lowercase" choice so that it will look specifically for the capital letter "F."
2. Be sure to unselect the "Match . . . Case" option to allow for the possibility that the words "Buy out" appear at the beginning of a sentence. This will ensure that the word "Takeover" will be capitalized.
3. You may have included nonrequired hyphens in the word since it is long. Try searching with various combinations of nonrequired hyphens.

CHAPTER 4

1. With the mouse, point at the split icon, hold down the left mouse button, and drag down to the desired position. With the keyboard, give the Window Split command, press the ↓ key to the desired position, then press ENTER.
2. *a* and *d*
3. If you were writing a report that compared the information in two other reports, you would use one window for the new text and a window for each of the reports being compared.

CHAPTER 5

1. The Insert File command does not change the scrap, and you can use it with very large files that might cause Word to run out of memory if you had used the Edit Copy command.

2. You cannot load files from another word processor if the file has special codes, and you cannot load programs or data bases that are stored in binary format.

CHAPTER 6

1. The easiest way to differentiate similar names is to add a letter to one.

    a. mw, mwi ("i" for italics)

    b. tnyt, nyt ("t" for "The")

    c. aicer, aeder (use the word ending)

2. By giving the Edit Glossary command.

3. By naming it NORMAL.GLY.

CHAPTER 7

1. a. Section

    b. Paragraph

    c. Character

2. a. Underlining or italics

    b. Boldface, underlining, or all caps

    c. Superscript

3. Select the word, then press CTRL-B, then press CTRL-U, and then press CTRL-SPACEBAR.

4. Be sure that your printer can print graphics characters; otherwise, unpredictable results may occur.

5. Select the characters you want to copy the format from, point at the characters with the mouse, hold down the CTRL-SHIFT keys, and press the left mouse button.

6. Use the Edit Search command, click "Search for Formatting Only," click "Character," then select the "Italic" and "Underline" check boxes.

CHAPTER 8

1. *b, d,* and *e*

2. a. Block rectangular, 1.2 inches from the left margin, no first-line indentation.

   b. Narrow, centered text.

   c. Outdented paragraph with first line against the left margin, ragged right margin.

3. Separate the first line from the rest with a paragraph mark (not a NEWLINE). Select both paragraphs and format them with a 1.5-inch indent from each margin. Center the first line and justify the rest of the text.

4. Triple spacing is useful if you are going to edit the text on paper and you expect to be adding a lot of text, or if someone else may be adding numerous comments.

5. Twelve lines. Justifying simply adds spaces to each line in a left-aligned paragraph to make the right margin even; it never changes the overall line length.

6. No, since this is done automatically by Word. Only use the Together option if you want to be sure that the paragraph is not broken at all.

7. a. Decimal

   b. Left, center, or right

   c. Right or decimal

8. The tab is decimal-aligned with a dot leader character.

9. Use the Format Border command to add a box around the paragraph. Then use the Format Tabs command to add vertical tabs at 2 inches and 4 inches.

10. The Format Position command with the Horizontal Centered and Vertical Centered options selected.

CHAPTER 9

1. *a* and *d*
2. If you will be printing on paper with letterhead, you will want to leave room for the letterhead at the top (and, of course, an address at the bottom if your letterhead has one).
3. Give the Format Section command and set the number of columns to 2 and "Spacing" to .5 inches. Use left-aligned formatting, and use nonrequired hyphens when possible. Also, you may want to put footnotes at the end of the text instead of at the bottom of the page.
4. Enter (**page page**, press F3, ENTER), select the text, give the Format Paragraph command, choose center alignment, and then give the Format Header/Footer command.
5. It ends the current page and starts a new page.
6. The footnotes option of the Format Section command.
7. You can either use CTRL-ENTER or create a new section.

CHAPTER 10

1. Style sheets allow you to format consistently and to easily make global changes to the format of a document.
2. The key code, style type, style I.D., and remark. The new style could have character formatting (bold) and paragraph formatting (centered, two lines after). The key code could be "TI," the style type, "Paragraph," and the style I.D., "Heading1."
3. Give the Format Define Styles command. Use the Insert New Style to create new styles. Save this sheet with the File Save As command, then select the document window again. Use the File Open command to load your document, then give the Format Attach Style Sheet command to attach the new style sheet to the document.
4. You can enter the styles directly either by pressing the CTRL-SHIFT key and the two-letter key code from the "Style" option on the ruler, or by copying the style with the mouse.

CHAPTER 11

1. TTY, TTYBS, or one that is equivalent to your printer.
2. You need to give the MODE command to MS-DOS.

3. With the File option in the File Print command.
4. With the File Print Queue command.
5. With the "Paper Feed" choice of the File Print command.

CHAPTER 12

1. You make a main document with merge commands and field names and make a datafile with a header of the field names followed by data records. You then use the File Print Merge command.
2. CTRL-[and CTRL-]
3. a. «IF policy-type=home»«ELSE»We also have a home policy... «ENDIF»

   b. «IF policy-type=car» We have new car plans...«ENDIF»
4. You must put quotation marks around any fields containing commas.
5. a. INCLUDE

   b. ASK

   c. IF

CHAPTER 13

1. a. View Preferences

   b. Utilities Customize

   c. View Preferences

   d. View Preferences

   e. Utilities Customize

CHAPTER 14

1. Outline edit mode only lets you select full paragraphs or headings, and the cursor control keys function differently.
2. With the SHIFT-F2 key.

3. PLUS and MINUS.
4. With the Utilities Renumber command.

CHAPTER 15

1. Precede the entry with **.c.** or use a "Heading" style.
2. If an entry contains either a colon or a semicolon, the entire entry must be in quotes. If the entry contains a quote, that quote must be preceded by an additional quote.
3. You can format the table of contents in the same way you format normal text. If you want Word to format it for you, use a style sheet.
4. Precede figures with hidden text **.f.** (or any other letter other than "c" or "i"). Give the Insert Table of Contents command, and indicate the letter for the table.
5. Precede the entry with **.i.**.
6. Word will either follow your capitalization exactly or it will capitalize the first letter of a level-1 entry.

CHAPTER 16

1. Annotation can be used to leave notes for yourself or for other people.
2. Give the Edit Go to command and choose "Bookmark."
3. Page numbers, paragraph numbers, footnote numbers, and series.

CHAPTER 17

1. If a word does not appear in Word's dictionary, in the user dictionary, or in the document dictionary, Word reports it as misspelled.
2. Use - (HYPHEN) for a normal hyphen, CTRL-SHIFT-HYPHEN for a nonbreaking hyphen, and CTRL-HYPHEN for an optional hyphen.
3. Select the word, then give the Utilities Thesaurus command. Highlight the desired synonym and press ENTER or click "Replace."

CHAPTER 18

1. Numeric sorting follows the rules of math while alphanumeric sorting follows the ASCII sequence.

2. If you do not select the case option, Word sorts in strict ASCII order. If you select it, Word ignores the case of letters, mixing upper- and lowercase words.

CHAPTER 19

1. Richford, 1990, and projections.
2. Specify >**2/2/88** for Date Saved and **fluids** for Keywords.

CHAPTER 20

1. Give the Macro Record command. Name the macro and press ENTER. Press ALT-V ALT-E TAB SPACEBAR ENTER ALT-M ENTER.
2. Give the Macro Edit command, choose the macro from the list, and click the Edit button to put the macro text in your window. Input **<enter>** at the end of the text, select it all, and give the Macro Edit command. Choose the macro from the list, click the Define button, then press ENTER.
3. The MESSAGE instruction.

CHAPTER 21

1. Select the entire file, give the Insert File command, and click "Update Link."
2. With the File Print Preview command.

CHAPTER 22

1. Utilities Revision Marks.
2. Select the text in which you want to apply the revisions, give the Utilities Revision Marks command, and click "Accept Revisions."

CHAPTER 23

1. Advanced LaserWriter capabilities, graphics and text, precise page layout, and style sheets.
2. Use side by side paragraph formatting.

INDEX

?, 50
1-2-3, 271

A

Absolutely positioned paragraphs, 119
Alignment, 105
ALT key
  commands, 11
  graphics characters, 90
ALT-F10, 30
ALT-F6, 30
ALT-F8, 30
Annotations, 232
Apple, 284
Arrow keys, 12
ASCII characters, 247
ASCII format, 69
ASK instruction, 183
ASSETS file, 186
Author, 255
Automatic pagination, 142
Autosave, 192

B

Background pagination, 192
BACKSPACE key, 8, 14, 39
Beep, 193
Binding, 130

Boldface, 86
Bookmarks, 233
Borders, 118
Boxes, 118
Business uses, *xx*

C

Cancel button, 14
CAPTURE program, 274
Caret characters, 50
Center tabs, 109
Center-aligned paragraphs, 105
Centimeters, 193
CHARACT file, 85
Character size, 88
Check boxes, 13
Chevrons, 176
Clipboard, 76, 275
Collapsing headings, 198, 204
Colors, 191
Columns, 112, 133, 251
Command buttons, 13
Commands
 dialogs, 12
 giving, 6
 introduction, 2
 keyboard, 11
 mouse, 10
Comments, 256
Conditional insertion, 182
Copies to be printed, 170
Copying character formatting, 93
Copying paragraph formatting, 107
Copying text, 40
Cross-references, 234
CTRL-[, 176
CTRL-], 176
CTRL key, 11, 74, 89, 104
CTRL-END, 24, 27
CTRL-ENTER, 141
CTRL-HOME, 24, 27
CTRL-PGDN, 27
CTRL-PGUP, 27
Cursor control keys, 2

Cursor speed, 191
Customizing Word, 189

D

DATA instruction, 177
Datafile, 175
Date created and saved, 256
Date format, 193
Date glossary entry, 76
Decimal character, 193
Decimal tabs, 109
DEL key, 14
Desktop publishing, 283
Dialogs, 12, 299
Dictionaries, 238
Direct formatting, 81
Display mode, 191
Document dictionary, 239
Document view, 198
Double-spacing, 103
DOUBPRT.STY file, 160
Drop-down lists, 13

E

Edit Copy command, 57, 67
Edit Cut command, 10, 38, 57
Edit Glossary command, 72
Edit Go to command, 142, 144, 232, 233
Edit Paste command, 39, 57, 67
Edit Replace command, 48
Edit Search command, 46, 95, 121
Edit Undo command, 11, 31, 38
Editing, 1, 21, 291
End-of-file mark, 6, 8
ENTER key, 22, 82
    dialogs, 14
    paragraphs, 15
ESC key, 14
Even and odd pages, 126
Excel, 271
Eyestrain, 191

F

F1 key, 16
F3 key, 73, 234
F8 key, 11, 31
Fields, 175
File File Management command, 254, 257
File New command, 40, 200
File Open command, 23, 68
File Print command, 32, 156, 169
File Print Merge command, 179
File Print Preview command, 131
File Printer Setup command, 12, 32, 168
File Save As command, 22, 155
Files
    linking, 271
    opening, 23
    retrieving, 253
    saving, 22
    searching for, 257
First line indenting, 99
FIRST.STY file, 155
Fonts, 88
Footers, 135, 137
Footnote glossary entry, 76
Footnotes, 143, 232, 235
Foreign characters, 90
Form letters
    conditional insertion, 182
    DATA instruction, 177
    datafile, 175
    fields, 176
    general, 175
    header, 177
    main document, 175
    merge instructions, 179
    printing, 179
    record, 175
Format Apply Style command, 159
Format Attach Style Sheet command, 155
Format Borders command, 118
Format Character command, 85, 154, 216
Format Define Styles command, 150
Format Header/Footer command, 138
Format Margins command, 127

Format menu, 84
Format Paragraph command, 99, 154
Format Position command, 119
Format Section command, 125, 154, 228
Format Tabs command, 108
Formatting, 1
  characters, 82, 85, 296
  columns, 112
  copying character formats, 93
  copying paragraph formats, 107
  CTRL key, 89, 296
  direct, 81
  general, 81
  paragraphs, 82, 97, 296
  searching character formats, 95, 121
  sections, 82, 125
  style sheets, 147
  tabs, 108
  units, 82
Function keys, 2

G

Galley view, 131
Generalized Markup Language, 147
Getting started, 1
Global replacement, 49
Glossaries
  additional uses, 77
  assigning CTRL keys, 74
  creating, 71
  cross-references, 234
  files, 75
  general, 71
  inserting entries, 72
  macros, 264
  merging, 75
  removing entries, 75
  special entries, 76
  storing, 75
GLY files, 75
GML, 147
Graphics characters, 90
Gutter, 130

H

Hanging indent, 101
Headers, 135, 137
Help, 15
Hidden text, 89, 190, 216, 220, 273
HPGL files, 274
Hyphenation, 241

I

IF instruction, 182
Inches, 193
INCLUDE instruction, 186
Indenting, 2, 99
Indexes
    general, 226
    generating, 227
    marking entries, 226
    see references, 226
Initial screen, 5
INS key, 192
Insert Annotation command, 232
Insert Bookmark command, 233
Insert Break command, 126, 142
Insert File command, 68, 272
Insert Footnote command, 143
Insert Index command, 227
Insert New Style command, 150
Insert Page Numbers command, 136
Insert Picture command, 274
Insert Style Sheet command, 155
Insert Table of Contents command, 222
Insertion mark, 6, 8
Installing Word, 3
International characters, 90
Introduction, *xv*
Italics, 86

J

Justification, 3, 105

K

Keeps, 3, 105
Key code, 151
Keywords, 255

L

LaserWriter, 284
Lawyers, 144
Leader characters, 111
Learning Word disk, 16
Leaving Word, 16
Left tabs, 109
Left-aligned paragraphs, 105
Line breaks, 190
Line draw character, 192
Line numbers, 144, 191
Line spacing, 102
Linking
  pictures, 274
  spreadsheets, 272
List boxes, 13
Lotus 1-2-3, 271

M

Macro Edit command, 268
MACRO.GLY file, 265
Macro Record command, 265
Macro Stop Recorder command, 267
Macros
  creating, 265
  editing, 268
  general, 263
  instructions, 269
  steps, 264
  testing, 268
Mail merge, 175
MAKEPRD program, 323
Margins, 127
Maximizing windows, 63
Measurements, 193
Menu bar, 190

Menus, 6, 299
Merge instructions, 179
Merging data, 175
Merging non-Word files, 68
Merging text files, 67
Message area, 7
Message bar, 38, 191
MODE command, 168
Mouse
  buttons, 30, 42, 298
  installing, 318
  moving in text, 25
  pointer, 5
  selecting, 8
  using, 6, 297
Moving text, 38
Moving windows, 61
Multi-column text, 133, 228
Multiple windows, 58
Mute option, 193

N

NEWLINE, 15, 102, 106, 274
NEXT instruction, 186
Non-printing characters, 190
Nonbreaking hyphen, 242
NORMAL.GLY file, 75, 150
Normal hyphen, 242
NORMAL.STY file, 155
Notes, 232
Number of lines, 191
Numbering an outline, 210
Numbering pleadings, 144
NUMLOCK key, 90

O

Odd and even pages, 126
OK button, 14
Operator, 255
Option boxes, 13
Optional hyphens, 190, 242
Orphans, 107, 192
Outdent, 101

Outlining
body text, 200
collapsing headings, 198, 204
creating, 200
CTRL keys, 202
document view, 198
general, 197
numbering, 210
outline edit mode, 199, 203
outline view, 198
rearranging, 208
text edit mode, 199, 203
Overtyping, 23, 192

P

Page glossary entry, 76
Page layout, 125
Page margins, 127
Page numbers, 135, 235
Page size, 127
PageView, 275
Panes, 53
Paper feed, 169
Paragraphs
absolutely positioned, 119
alignment, 105
boxes and borders, 118
general, 15
indenting, 99
keeps, 105
line spacing, 102
placement, 119
side by side, 114
viewing marks, 190
Parallel printer, 168
PATTERNS file, 40
PAYLET1 file, 177
PAYLET2 file, 182
PC Paintbrush, 275
PCX files, 275
PIC files, 275
Pictures, 274
Pleadings, 144
Plotter files, 274
Points, 193

PostScript files, 275
PRD files, 33, 165
Print preview, 131
Printer drivers, 33, 165, 323
Printing
    character formatting, 88
    choosing a driver, 167
    copies, 170
    fonts, 88
    form letters, 179
    general, 32, 165
    options, 168
    pages, 171
    paper feed, 169
    queue, 169, 171
    setting up printers, 168
    to a file, 172

Q

Queue, 169, 171
Quitting, 16

R

Rearranging an outline, 208
Records, 175
Redlining, 277
Reference mark, 143
Remarks, 153
Repagination, 142, 192
Replacing
    case matching, 49
    general, 48
    global or confirmed changes, 49
    special characters, 49
    whole word, 49
REPORT1 file, 59
Resizing windows, 61
Retrieving documents, 253
Review answers, 331
Revision marks, 277
Ribbon, 87, 158
Right margin indenting, 99
Right tabs, 109

Right-aligned paragraphs, 105
RS-232 printer, 168
Ruler
 marks, 101
 setting tabs, 110
 showing, 98

S

SAMPLE1 file (saving), 22
Saving files, 22
Scrap, 38
Scroll bar, 25
SCROLL LOCK, 27
Scrolling, 2
Searching
 case matching, 47
 character formats, 95
 direction, 47
 general, 46
 introduction, 2
 paragraph formats, 121
 special characters, 49
 whole word, 47
Section formatting, 125
Section mark, 126
See references, 226
Selecting
 F8 key, 11, 31
 introduction, 2
 keyboard, 30, 293
 mouse, 8, 27, 292
Selection bar, 29
Serial printer, 168
Series, 235
SET instruction, 183
Setting up Word, 3
SHIFT-ENTER, 15, 102
Side by side paragraphs, 114, 286
Sorting
 columns in tables, 251
 general, 247
 method, 249
 numbers, 248, 251
 uppercase letters, 248
Special characters, 49

Speed copying and moving, 42
Speed of cursor, 191
Spelling
checking, 239
dictionaries, 238
dictionary name, 193
general, 238
Splitting windows, 54
Spreadsheets, 272
Standard dictionary, 238
Starting Word, 4
Step mode, 268
Strikethrough, 278
STY files, 149
Style bar, 157, 191
Style I.D., 152
Style remarks, 153
Style sheets
attaching, 155
creating, 149
editing, 155
general, 83, 147
merging, 155
new styles, 150
printing, 156
saving, 155
tables of contents, 219
using, 156
Style type, 152
Subscripts, 88
Summary information, 192
Summary sheets, 253
Superscripts, 88
Synonyms, 244

T

TAB key, 100
Tab width, 193
Tables of contents
advanced uses, 225
figure lists, 225
general, 217
generating, 222
heading styles, 219
hidden text, 220
specifying entries, 219

Tabs
    general, 108, 190
    leader characters, 111
    setting, 110
    vertical, 117
Text
    copying, 40, 42
    entering, 14, 21
    formatting, 81
    graphics, 90
    hidden, 89, 216, 220
    inserting, 23
    merging, 67
    moving, 38, 42
    moving around, 23, 25, 293
    multi-column, 133, 228
    overtyping, 23
    printing, 32, 165
    replacing, 48
    searching, 46
    selecting with keyboard, 30, 293
    selecting with mouse, 27, 292
    size, 88
    sorting, 249
    special keys, 292
Text boxes, 13
Thesaurus, 244
Thumb, 25
TIFF files, 275
Time format, 193
Time glossary entry, 76
Title, 255
Toggle, 23
Triple-spacing, 103
TTY driver, 167
TTY.PRD file, 33

U

Underlining, 86
Undoing editing and formatting, 31
Updating links, 274
User dictionary, 239
Utilities Customize command, 107, 142, 191
Utilities Hyphenate command, 243
Utilities Line Draw command, 192

Utilities Renumber command, 211, 234
Utilities Repaginate Now command, 142
Utilities Revision Marks command, 278
Utilities Sort command, 249
Utilities Spelling command, 239
Utilities Thesaurus command, 244

V

Version number, 256
Versions of Word, *xvii, xix-xx*
Vertical tabs, 117
Vertical windows, 64
View Layout command, 131
View Outline command, 199
View Preferences command, 157, 190, 217
View Ribbon command, 87
View Ruler command, 98

W

Widows, 107, 192
Window borders, 191
Window Maximize command, 64
Window Move command, 62
Window Size command, 62
Window Split command, 55
Windows
  definition, 25
  general, 53
  maximizing, 63
  moving, 61
  multiple, 40, 58
  panes, 53
  resizing, 61
  splitting, 54
  vertical, 64
Windows Clipboard, 76, 275
Word
  help, 15
  installation and setup, 3
  leaving, 16
  preparation for, 317
  starting, 4
Wordwrap, 15, 242
Wrapping lines, 15

The manuscript for this book was prepared and submitted to Osborne **McGraw-Hill** in electronic form. The acquisitions editor for this project was Elizabeth Fisher and the technical reviewer was Michael Katz.

Text design by Judy Wohlfrom, using Times Roman for text body and Univers for display.

Cover art by Bay Graphics Design, Inc. Color separation and cover supplier, Phoenix Color Corporation. Screens produced with HotShot Graphics, from Symsoft, Inc. Book printed and bound by R.R. Donnelley & Sons Company, Crawfordsville, Indiana.

Command Summary

Text Entry Keys

Key	Meaning
ENTER	End paragraph
SHIFT-ENTER	NEWLINE; end line but continue paragraph
CTRL-ENTER	End page
TAB	Go to next tab stop
HYPHEN	Normal hyphen
CTRL-SHIFT-HYPHEN	Nonbreaking hyphen; Word will never split a line here
CTRL-HYPHEN	Optional hyphen; Word will split a line here only to avoid wrapping a whole word to the next line
CTRL-SPACEBAR	Nonbreaking space

Selecting Text with the Keyboard

Key	Selection
F8, twice	Word left
ALT-F6	Word right
ALT-F8	Sentence right
ALT-F10	Paragraph right
F8	Extend selection (toggle)

Moving Through Text with the Keyboard

Key	Where Moved
←	Previous letter
→	Next letter
↑	Previous line
↓	Next line
CTRL-←	Beginning of previous word
CTRL-→	Beginning of next word
CTRL-↑	Beginning of previous paragraph
CTRL-↓	Beginning of next paragraph
HOME	Beginning of current line
END	End of current line
CTRL-HOME	Beginning of file
CTRL-END	End of file
PGUP	Previous window length
PGDN	Next window length
CTRL-PGUP	First character of first line of window
CTRL-PGDN	First character of last line of window
SCROLL LOCK	Line-by-line scrolling (toggle)

©1991 Osborne McGraw-Hill

Character Format Keystrokes

Characteristic	CTRL-Key
Bold	CTRL-B
Italic	CTRL-I
Underline	CTRL-U
Small caps	CTRL-K
Double underline	CTRL-D
Superscript	CTRL-PLUS
Subscript	CTRL-MINUS
Normal	CTRL-SPACEBAR
Font name	CTRL-F
Font size	CTRL-P
Hidden	CTRL-H

Paragraph Format Keystrokes

Characteristic	CTRL-Key
Alignment	CTRL-L, CTRL-C, CTRL-R, CTRL-J
Left indent	CTRL-M, CTRL-N
First line	CTRL-F, CTRL-T
Left and right indent	CTRL-Q
Line spacing	CTRL-1, CTRL-2
Blank line above	CTRL-O
Normal	CTRL-X